MAKING PICTORIAL PRINT

Media Literacy and Mass Culture in British Magazines, 1885–1918

Making Pictorial Print

Media Literacy and Mass Culture in British Magazines, 1885–1918

ALISON HEDLEY

UNIVERSITY OF TORONTO PRESS
Toronto Buffalo London

Toronto Buffalo London
utorontopress.com

ISBN 978-1-4875-0673-5 (cloth) ISBN 978-1-4875-3475-2 (EPUB)
ISBN 978-1-4875-3474-5 (PDF)

Studies in Book and Print Culture

Library and Archives Canada Cataloguing in Publication

Title: Making pictorial print : media literacy and mass culture in British magazines, 1885–1918 / Alison Hedley.
Names: Hedley, Alison, author.
Series: Studies in book and print culture.
Description: Series statement: Studies in book and print culture | Includes bibliographical references and index.
Identifiers: Canadiana (print) 20210290471 | Canadiana (ebook) 20210290595 | ISBN 9781487506735 (cloth) | ISBN 9781487534752 (EPUB) | ISBN 9781487534745 (PDF)
Subjects: LCSH: Illustrated periodicals – Great Britain – History – 19th century. | LCSH: Illustrated periodicals – Great Britain – History – 20th century. | LCSH: Mass media – Great Britain – History – 19th century. | LCSH: Mass media – Great Britain – History – 20th century. | LCSH: Popular culture – Great Britain – History – 19th century. | LCSH: Popular culture – Great Britain – History – 20th century.
Classification: LCC PN5124.I44 H43 2021 | DDC 052.0941–dc23

University of Toronto Press acknowledges the financial assistance to its publishing program of the Canada Council for the Arts and the Ontario Arts Council, an agency of the Government of Ontario.

Canada Council for the Arts
Conseil des Arts du Canada

Funded by the Government of Canada
Financé par le gouvernement du Canada
Canada

For Lorraine

Contents

Illustrations

Acknowledgments

Foremost, I wish to thank Lorraine Janzen Kooistra for mentorship and guidance at every stage of this book's development. I am grateful to Dennis Denisoff and Jan Hadlaw for contributing insights on early drafts, as well as to Tina Choi and James Mussell for input at crucial stages of the writing process. Thanks are also due to the editors and peer reviewers who assessed previous iterations of this work. Chapter 2 expands on an essay that appeared in the *Victorian Periodicals Review*; chapter 3 is based on an essay published in the *Journal of Victorian Culture*. I am grateful to Paul Fyfe for helping me think through the argument, and to Arun Jacob for always having a citation on hand to fill the gaps in my knowledge of all things digital. I wish to acknowledge Margaret Beetham, Julie Codell, Alexis Easley, and Tom Gretton for sharing scholarship in progress or difficult to obtain. Thanks go to Natalya Androsova and Ryerson Writing Support for holding space, and to Emily Murphy and Sean Conforti for giving writing companionship. I am grateful to everyone at the University of Toronto Press who has supported the publication process, including Mark Thompson, Leslie Howsam, and my anonymous readers.

I thankfully acknowledge that this work was supported by the Social Sciences and Humanities Council of Canada as well as the Liss Jeffrey Award for Research in New Media, through which Dr. Jeffrey's family and friends honour her legacy at Ryerson University. Conference travel related to this research was supported by the Yeates School of Graduate Studies, the Ryerson Faculty of Arts, Ryerson International, the Ryerson Communication and Culture program, the Research Society for Victorian Periodicals, and the North American Victorian Studies Association.

Thanks are also due to the many libraries and archives that facilitated my research and permitted me to reproduce print images: the

Archives and Collections at the Library of Birmingham; All Saints Library at Manchester Metropolitan University; Clara Thomas Archives and Special Collections at York University; John Rylands Library at the University of Manchester; Kodak Canada Corporate Archives and Heritage Collection at Ryerson Special Collections; Robarts Library at the University of Toronto; Marilyn and Charles Baillie Special Collections Centre at the Toronto Reference Library; and the Victoria and Albert Museum. I am grateful to Alison Skyrme at Ryerson Archives and Special Collections for consulting on the history of the hand camera. Three figures in chapter 3 appear courtesy of Ana Rita Morais, and two figures appear in chapter 4 courtesy of Fariha Shaikh.

Finally, I am tremendously grateful to my family and to John Greenwell for offering every kind of support throughout the years of research and writing that culminated in this book.

MAKING PICTORIAL PRINT

Media Literacy and Mass Culture in British Magazines, 1885–1918

Introduction

A History of Victorian Print Media Literacy and the Technological Imagination

The general tendency of modern development has been to bring many more levels of culture within the general context of literacy than was ever previously the case.

Raymond Williams, *Culture and Society* (1963)

Making Pictorial Print is about popular illustrated magazines in Britain at the turn of the nineteenth century. Using the concept of media literacy as a guide, its case studies reveal how an evolution of design aesthetics affected the terms of engagement that magazines presented to readers, creating opportunities for them to participate in and even contribute to popular culture actively, creatively, and critically. The immediate result was that popular illustrated periodicals maintained a central place in the media landscape at a time when mechanical communication technologies were rapidly displacing print. The increasing interactivity of magazine design also had farther-reaching consequences: the terms of engagement fostered by the magazines shaped the emerging mass culture of the twentieth century and continue to influence aspects of popular culture today. The evolution of pictorial magazines is instructive for media historiography: studying how it was understood by both critics and participants of Victorian popular culture will sharpen our historical perspective on a perennial debate about new media's effect on the masses.

The past two centuries have seen the media landscape of Britain, and of the West broadly, evolve at a remarkable pace. Produced in greater variety and on a larger scale than ever before, print media dominated popular culture by the end of the nineteenth century. Within mere decades new mechanical media such as the gramophone, film, and the radio ushered in a new media milieu, displacing print from its position at the centre of cultural life. In turn, mechanical media were displaced by digital technologies at the advent of the twenty-first century. Though this narrative might suggest a tidy line of succession, the evolution was far from linear for popular mass media – by which I mean, after Lisa Gitelman, the socially realized structures of communication that materially mediate popular culture on a large scale.[1] Every new media technology and the culture formed around it inherit traits of previous technologies and cultures. This is equally true of the debates about media in society provoked by technological change: criticism of new media consistently revitalizes assumptions and ideals of the past that are embedded in existing cultural practices, knowingly or (more often) unknowingly dragging these beliefs into the present and future.

This book investigates the contributions of a particular medium, the popular illustrated magazine, to the non-linear genealogy of British mass culture – the widely practised, non-specialized, cross-class cultural activities of British society – between the mid-1880s and the First World War.[2] Over the course of the nineteenth century, reading became, as Richard Altick puts it, "a popular addiction" in Britain,[3] and periodicals constituted one of the foremost platforms for this vice. Thanks to technological innovations in production and distribution, magazines and newspapers became Britain's first mass media, circulating on a scale of millions.[4] By the late nineteenth century, top weeklies such as the *Illustrated London News* (*ILN*) sold up to half a million copies per issue,[5] and popular monthlies such as *Pearson's Magazine* sold up to one million copies.[6] Technological innovations in production and distribution gave print media unprecedented reach; print readerships encompassed nearly the whole of society as Britain approached universal literacy for the first time.[7] Periodicals increasingly profited from advertisements, as well as selling price, an economic model that contributed to both increasing diversity and the consolidation of titles by early media barons.[8] Profitability also incentivized periodical producers to align mass print with industrial consumer capitalism. Assembling lively, up-to-the-minute subject matter from a spectrum of written and visual genres and reproduced using cutting-edge methods, periodicals were the lifeblood of late-Victorian mass culture.

Although it belonged to a class of media historically dominated by letterpress, the popular illustrated periodical was a major visual medium in an era of proliferating spectacle, and its visuality was key to its role in emerging mass culture.[9] As Jerome McGann observes, in the nineteenth century, "image and word began to discover new and significant bibliographical relations"; technological innovations in image reproduction signalled "a culture-wide effort for the technical means to raise the expressive power of the book through visual design."[10] Such efforts were not limited to books, however. The illustrated periodical, as print's most widely distributed form, occupied a uniquely powerful position in image-conscious British society. In an article written for the *Illustrated London News Jubilee Number* in 1892, illustrator Joseph Pennell declared that the artist had achieved the same importance as the author had in daily and weekly journalism.[11] A decade later, E.H. Lacon Watson further privileged journalism's pictorial aspect, declaring that "the journalistic eye is now of far greater importance than the journalistic pen."[12] Similarly, in 1899, Clement Shorter boasted that illustrated journalism could "no more be crushed out now than . . . Sir Henry Irving's picturesque stage or 'the three R's.'"[13] Such comments were typical in the late-Victorian pictorial press.

The transformative growth of illustrated journalism in the nineteenth century was underwritten by a number of major technological and infrastructural developments that also shaped the role of magazines in emerging mass culture. The British government's repeal of taxes on stamps, advertising, and paper between 1830 and 1861 invigorated the periodical market, enabling an expansion of newspaper and magazine titles, circulation, and pictorial content.[14] Between the 1840s and 1880s, wood-engravers adopted an industrial-style division of labour that enabled rapid, large-scale image reproduction.[15] In the 1870s the rotary press increased the pace of printing.[16] By the early 1880s, paper makers had perfected a process for using wood pulp to make bleached newspaper, thereby increasing the quantity and affordability of paper for periodical print.[17] Linotype, patented in 1886, sped up the typesetting process.[18]

The technological innovation that proved most significant to the modern illustrated press, and one that defines the aesthetics of this book's subject matter, was the rise of photomechanical image reproduction in the 1880s and 1890s. Photomechanical line-block and halftone processes enabled the reproduction of detailed images at an unprecedented speed and scale.[19] In the line-block process an artist's drawing is photographed, and the resulting negative is exposed on a plate; through a series of chemical interactions the plate is etched to reveal the line drawing in relief.[20] Each image is directly translated onto the relief block used for printing. [21] This process eliminated the intermediary role that engravers had played in wood-block image reproduction, the method that previously dominated the pictorial press. As the first mass-produced photomechanical images, line blocks remediated artists' drawings through industrial mechanization without compromising their hand-sketched appearance.[22]

The line-block process was accompanied in the illustrated press by its photomechanical sibling, the halftone process. In contrast to the line-block process, which reproduced linear, black-and-white images, the halftone process reproduced the nuanced tones of paintings and photographs in shades of grey.[23] In the halftone process the negative from a photograph or artwork is developed on an image block that is covered by a screen. This screen filters the tones of the image during development. Dark regions of the original work become larger and denser dots in the image, conveying a granulated facsimile in greyscale.[24]

Both line-block and halftone processes were adopted by popular pictorial magazines at the turn of the twentieth century. In the late 1880s, periodicals such as the *ILN* and the *Graphic* began including line-block images alongside wood engravings. The halftone process superseded wood-engraving in the 1890s as halftone screens became more readily available.[25] A major advantage of this process was its capacity to reproduce photographic images directly onto the periodical page. As periodical producers adopted halftone reproduction, the number of photograph-based graphics in the illustrated press increased dramatically.[26]

The new photomechanical processes resulted in a greater number and variety of images in popular illustrated magazines. As British print media became more pictorial, they also became more self-conscious of their multimodal aesthetics. Periodical producers – including authors, artists, engravers, editors, advertisers, and printers – used increasingly varied design techniques, compelling readers' attention to how the images, letterpress, page layout, organization, and material characteristics contributed to meaning. Through their diverse, innovative aesthetics, popular print media embodied the technological developments that propelled industrial modernity and shaped cultural sensibilities.

Given the cultural prominence of illustrated periodicals and the striking design techniques they implemented at the end of the century, this book begins by asking, How did the aesthetics of popular pictorial magazines shape reader engagement? What can these terms of engagement tell us about the role the magazines played in emerging mass culture? I investigate these questions using evidence from four popular periodicals between 1885 and 1918: the *Illustrated London News*, the *Graphic*, *Pearson's Magazine*, and the *Strand Magazine*.

Making Pictorial Print proceeds from the premise that the distinctive, production-based aesthetics of illustrated print media were essential to the way in which readers encountered these artefacts. The aesthetics told a story of production that readers interpreted alongside and in relation to the stories of culture and society depicted in a magazine's pages. Informed by this premise, case studies are guided by two conceptual tenets. The first is Victorian *print media literacy*: as this introduction elaborates, readers had the capacity to recognize and interpret the material traces of production that were part of a periodical's aesthetics. Print media literacy enabled readers to attend to how the physical characteristics of a print object attested to its production history, and how those characteristics shaped the object's representations of cultural knowledge – in other words, its mediation of popular culture. Readers used this literacy to situate a periodical in its real and imagined socio-technological contexts. This hermeneutic behaviour serves as the book's second foundational tenet: the *print technological imagination*, one of many interpretive practices informed by the mechanical innovations of the industrial age. The print technological imaginary functioned collectively and individually. While periodical producers used aesthetic strategies that fostered and engaged the imagination of whole readerships, evidence indicates that individual readers also exercised their imagination according to subjective priorities. As the case studies of the ensuing chapters show, print media literacy and the technological imagination contributed significantly to how readers interpreted periodical depictions of mass culture and their own roles in it.

Print Media Literacy in the Victorian Age

Throughout the Victorian era, print media literacy and the technological imagination were fostered by letterpress articles and images that the illustrated press produced to educate readers about its material production. Such content combined two trends characteristic of nineteenth-century print culture: the regular inclusion, in both general and specialized publications, of instructional journalism that reported on innovations in science and technology; and the use of recursive meta-commentary on the production of print. Periodicals were Victorian society's primary means to announce technological developments and frame how they would be understood by various audiences, including general readerships of all classes. Indeed, illustrated articles on technological and scientific processes were a mainstay of popular nineteenth-century journalism.[27] Such journalism was consistently instructional in tone, offering verbal and visual explanations that were detailed enough to convey general principles without requiring specialized knowledge of readers. This genre underscored the material and intellectual progress of the industrializing Western world, particularly

Britain. It also instructed readers on the material processes of newspaper and magazine production, showcasing how the press leveraged Britain's industrial innovations to circulate state-of-the-art communication media.

Journalism on periodical production was consistent with the reflexive, participatory character of Victorian print culture as a whole. Various nineteenth-century print genres and media, from novels to newspapers, showcased their own practices to influence readers' perception of the print industry and the craft of literature, as well as to encourage readers' sense of investment and belonging within print culture communities. For example, George Eliot devotes a long passage of the novel *Adam Bede* to defending her realist approach to depicting rural English life. Mary Elizabeth Braddon depicts two of the main characters of *Lady Audley's Secret* as devotees of sensation fiction, the genre of this novel.[28] Victorian newspaper correspondence columns often discoursed on the correspondence column itself, and periodical essayists regularly discussed the state of journalism.[29]

Such meta-commentary was not limited in scope to authorial and editorial labours: Victorian print extensively documented its own production, circulation, and consumption. The periodical press was a focus of much work in this vein. Books such as P.G. Hamerton's *The Graphic Arts* (1882) and Henry Blackburn's *The Art of Illustration* (1896), and journal articles such as Carl Hentschel's "Process Engraving" in the *Journal of the Society of the Arts* (1900), were written for print professionals, while Mason Jackson's *The Pictorial Press* (1885) and Gleeson White's *English Illustration: The Sixties* (1897) were written for a more general, if somewhat elite (upper-middle-class) audience. Less specialized publications also documented the production, circulation, and consumption of periodicals. The illustrated poem "The Post Office Van, Calling at the Office of the *Illustrated London News*," printed in 1845, presents an early pictorial example; Wilkie Collins's essay "The Unknown Public," published in *Household Words* in 1858, and Thomas Wright's responding article, "Concerning the Unknown Public," published in *Nineteenth Century* in 1883, offer two of the many instances of journalistic discourse seeking to characterize popular print and its patterns of consumption. As many Victorian scholars have pointed out, print culture's recursive commentary directed readers' attention to the contextual layers of production and reception that shaped publication. Readerships could boast at least a modicum of insider knowledge – and probably more – about what went on at the desks of writers and illustrators; the offices of editors and publishers; the studios of engravers; the shops of printers; and the libraries and stalls of vendors.

Articles instructing readers in the material aspects of print production contributed to not only readers' critical awareness of print culture as such, but also their literacy of specific media as physical objects. How print media literacy informed reader interpretation was unique to each print format, but I posit that it was essential to the reading of popular illustrated periodicals. Combining letterpress and illustrations on topics ranging from industrial print technologies to the history of journalism, pictorial magazines offered a rich education in media literacy to a popular audience dominated by the middle classes but including members of the working and upper classes. What is more, the periodicals functioned as multimodal instantiations of the print media knowledge they imparted. They embodied the industry's latest techniques in their layout, ornamentation, and illustration, drawing readers' attention to graphic design and medium materiality as outputs of industrial processes.

The *ILN*'s supplement to the Great Exhibition, printed in 1851, exemplifies how a periodical object signified as an industrial artefact. As Paul Fyfe relates, this supplement functioned as "a material souvenir of the mechanical processes on display" at the exhibition: the printing of illustrated journalism using the *ILN*'s own, customized Applegath press.[30] The penultimate page of the supplement is labelled as a product of that machine. Through its materiality, temporality, and visual veracity the supplemental souvenir advanced the exhibit's cultural work by telling a story about the industrial production history and the representational functions of modern illustrated journalism.[31]

As the Great Exhibition example suggests, literacy of Victorian periodical media involved situating print objects within their production history and recognizing how the unique material characteristics of print objects shaped their meaning. Through articles about periodical production and circulation the illustrated press drew readers' awareness to the ways in which the material history of a print object influenced their own encounter with it. In the language of modern-day media theory, periodical producers drew readers' attention to media affordances and mediation. The Victorians did not frame their engagement with print in these terms, but it is no coincidence that conceptions of media and mediation as such began to coalesce at the fin de siècle. As chapter 1 relates in more depth, these concepts evolve in response to public interest in the functions of different technologies and practices of cultural expression.

As I have suggested, the *ILN*'s Great Exhibition supplement was but one of many entertaining and educational pieces about illustrated journalism's production that encouraged a Victorian reader to appreciate the periodical in his or her hands as an artefact of progress. Such instructional articles could be found in both special publications such as the *ILN* Great Exhibition supplement and regular numbers of the illustrated press. "The Commercial History of a *Penny Magazine*," a series of monthly supplements published from August to December 1833, offers perhaps the earliest nineteenth-century example of illustrated journalism depicting its own production. The series appeared in the *Penny Magazine* (1832–45), a weekly periodical published by the Society for the Diffusion of Useful Knowledge. The educational thrust of the series is consistent with the *Penny Magazine*'s mandate of edifying self-instruction. The series' didactic tone and thematic conflation of industrialization and the rise of popular print also make it a quintessential example of self-reflexive pictorial journalism on journalism.

"The Commercial History of a *Penny Magazine*" documents every facet of journal production, from paper making to printing. Intricate descriptions and occasional illustrations invite readers to recreate mentally the process of printing the *Penny Magazine* at every step. The author (or authors; no name is given, and the narrative uses the editorial *We*) takes an enthusiastic amateur's point of view, describing in admiring tones machinery, labourers, and processes. For example, paper making is "as rapid as it is beautiful,"[32] and the compositor's redistribution of used type is "a remarkable example of the dexterity to be acquired by long practice."[33] Recounting visits to each of the mills and offices where facets of the *Penny Magazine*'s production took place, the narrative enables readers to imagine themselves along for the tour. However, it is the magazine itself, as an artefact of production, that makes the verbal and visual descriptions of the series most tangible, enabling readers to link imagined industrial settings with their own experiential reality. The *Penny Magazine* supplements prompted early nineteenth-century readers to engage with a periodical's material signs of production as well as its words and pictures, instructing them in print journalism's mediality.

Over the course of the nineteenth century, illustrated journalism continued to educate readers about its processes of production while commenting on changes in print culture and technology. Two years after it began publication in 1842, the *Illustrated London News*, the world's first serious pictorial weekly magazine,[34] produced a supplement series that familiarized readers with the material history of pictorial journalism in more detail. "Wood-Engraving: Its History and Practice" appeared in several instalments between 20 April and 6 July 1844. Unlike many periodical supplements, this series was included in the magazine's paginated numbers, meaning that it was available to all readers. William A. Chatto, co-author of *A Treatise on Wood Engraving, Historical and Practical*, provided the supplements' letterpress.[35]

In its structure and tone, the "Wood-Engraving" series resembles the *Penny Magazine* supplements, but Chatto's articles focus exclusively on image production. The series frequently includes state-of-the-art illustrations, as befitted the subject matter and the *ILN*'s reputation as an eminent pictorial weekly. Indeed, in many of the supplements a large, detailed engraving dominates the article, accompanied only by one or two columns of letterpress. The articles survey the history of wood engraving in the West, from ancient Egypt to modern Europe, particularly focusing on eighteenth- and nineteenth-century England. As the series transitions to nineteenth-century wood-engraving, Chatto intersperses more aesthetic and technical criticism, effectively grooming his readers as amateur historians of the art and craft of engraving. He also includes considerable technical detail about modern practices. The last instalment of the series, titled "The Practice of Wood-Engraving," includes information about this process, including the materials used, the roles of designers and engravers, and even diagrams of tools such as the leather sandbag on which the wood-block sits, and the lamp that concentrates light on the block (see figure 0.1).

Throughout the series Chatto emphasizes that wood-engraving possesses special expressive capabilities that artists are obliged to exploit to their fullest potential. Indeed, Chatto argues that unlike the "servile copies of copper-plate engravings," wood-engraving has "peculiar powers" to translate "subjects into its own graphic language, with a view to their being multiplied by means of the steam press."[36] Wood-engravings, as a form of relief printing, could be printed on the same steam-powered press as type could. Chatto's comment suggests that wood-engraved images had a unique relationship with the steam press, industrialization's foundational technology. As Peter Sinnema observes, Chatto's series "sanctifies" the *ILN* as both the "culmination of an ancient, increasingly refined art" and an emblem of modernity,[37] instructing readers to imagine wood-block images as the graphic language of modern industrial culture.

Wood-block engraving remained essential to illustrated journalism throughout most of the nineteenth century. Pictorial papers such as the *ILN* continued to boast about ongoing refinements to this ancient art as the press expanded its profitability and range of titles and audiences. From January to August 1879 the *ILN* published "Illustrated News: A Sketch of the Rise and Progress of Pictorial Journalism," a series by art editor Mason Jackson that educated readers in illustrated print production.[38] Like "Wood-Engraving," this series posits the *ILN* as the culmination of advances in journalism and print technology and includes in the last instalment a detailed account of contemporary engraving practices. By the late 1870s, decades of pictorial journalism had made the *ILN*'s

July 6, 1844.] SUPPLEMENT TO THE ILLUSTRATED LONDON NEWS. 425

HISTORY OF WOOD-ENGRAVING.

(Concluded from page 417.)

THE PRACTICE OF WOOD-ENGRAVING.

Box is the wood mostly used by modern wood-engravers; pear-tree, and other wood of a similar grain and fibre, being now only used in executing large cuts for posting-bills. In the time of Albert Durer, pear-tree appears to have been most generally employed. The original blocks of the "Triumphs of Maximilian," now preserved in the Imperial Library at Vienna, are all of pear-tree. In the time of Papillon, though box was preferred for small cuts requiring great delicacy in the execution, the wood of the apple, pear, and service tree, was still frequently employed. Papillon considered that the box brought from Turkey, though of larger size, was inferior in quality to that of Provence, Italy, and Spain. Next to box, Papillon preferred the wood of the service tree. In his time it appears to have been customary to engrave on the length-way, not on the cross section of the wood. The old wood-engravers, who chiefly used pear-tree and other wood of similar grain, appear to have used, for the purpose of cutting their outlines, a knife with a point slightly curved inwards, in the manner of what is termed a "Wharncliffe," the old "*jack-a-legs*," with a straight edge, is now nearly obsolete, both name and thing. This knife they held in the manner of a pen, and cut *towards* them, not *from* them, as is now the practice in using the graver. A figure of such a knife is frequently to be seen in old wood-cuts, together with that of a graver which was probably used in the execution of cross-hatchings.

Box, for the purposes of engraving, is sawn into slices, about three-quarters of an inch thick, which is the height of type, and the cross way of the wood. Sometimes, for the purpose of obtaining pieces of greater length, it is sawn obliquely. Such pieces, however, are not so good to engrave on as those of the same wood which are sawn directly across, in consequence of the obliquity of the grain impeding the equable action of the point of the tool; and rendering it extremely difficult to cut a clear line, in consequence of small portions tearing away at the sides. As the usual diameter of even the largest logs of box does not exceed five or six inches, it becomes necessary when a large block is wanted, to join several pieces together, and to do this properly, so that the joinings may not be perceptible in the impression, requires very great dexterity on the part of the person who prepares the block; indeed, the joining together of several pieces of box so as to form one large compact block of uniformly smooth and level surface, requires as much skill as the most delicate piece of cabinet-work. The largest block of this kind ever made or engraved, was the "View of London," presented in 1843, by the proprietors of the Illustrated London News to their subscribers.

The best box is that which is of a yellow colour, like gold, throughout the whole surface, displaying neither specks of white nor reddish-coloured rings. Such box being of a close grain, and uniformly dense and tenacious, allows of the lines being cut with the greatest clearness and precision, but is also the least liable to display unevenness at the surface, which is usually occasioned by inequality in the density of the several layers of the wood. Wood of a red colour usually wants tenacity, and cuts soft and short; and if it displays many distinct rings it is extremely liable to shrink irregularly, and to thus render it difficult to obtain a perfect impression. Wood containing whitish specks or streaks is apt to break away under the graver in such places. All kinds of box are subject to warp or turn up at the edges and become hollowed in the middle, but more especially such as have not been well seasoned. When a block has become slightly warped in the progress of engraving, it will generally return to a level on being kept for a day or two with its face downwards on a table or shelf. Sometimes, however, it can only be remedied by means of overlays in printing, to bring up the hollow parts of the surface.

Some artists, before they commence their drawing, are accustomed to whiten the smooth surface of the block with a slight wash of flake white and gum-water; others merely rub the surface with a little finely-powdered Bath brick, mixed with pure water, rubbing it off perfectly clean when dry. The latter seems to be the least objectionable mode of preparing the slippery surface of the block for drawing on with a black-lead pencil, the usual instrument with which drawings on wood are made. All the lines which appear in a wood-cut are generally drawn on the block by the designer or draftsman in pencil, with the exception of what are technically called "tints," indicative of the atmosphere and the sky, such tints being merely washed in with Indian ink. The most faithful wood-engraving of an artist's design is that in which the engraver has, without adding or diminishing, *worked out* a perfect fac simile; this, however, according to those who make drawings on wood, is but rarely effected, there being always some alterations or omissions made by the engravers, and invariably for the worse. Wood-engravers, however, deny the truth of the charge in its absolute extent; for, while they admit that a drawing is occasionally marred in their hands, they also insist that it is sometimes mended. They also further allege, in their own justification, that an artist who has but little knowledge of the practice of wood-engraving, and no idea whatever of adapting his drawing to the purposes of printing, will frequently produce a design, which, though it may appear very pretty on the block, may yet take more time and pains to engrave than it is worth; and prove, after all, but an indifferent wood-cut, which it may be very difficult to print well, even with the aid of overlays, by a hand-press, and utterly impossible to print decently at a steam-press. From the want of such knowledge in the designer, it frequently happens that wood-cuts, though carefully and elaborately engraved, yet appear very insipid when printed; and thus the engraver, who, closely adhering to the drawing, may have done for them all that his art could effect, is blamed for deficiencies which are entirely owing to the designer. For the production of a drawing that will print well and display the full power of wood-engraving, something more is required than the ability to make it on paper or on wood: to succeed—unless by chance—it is necessary that the designer should know how to manage his drawing, so that it may be capable of being properly printed; and he should always bear in mind that he is *working for the press.*

In the present day it is usual to have the subject completely drawn on the block, in all its details, and with the intended effect of light and shade; in the time of Papillon, however, it appears to have been customary with the French engravers to trace at first on the block merely the outlines of the subject from a finished drawing on paper, to which they referred for the details and the effect, as they proceeded with their work, just as a copperplate engraver refers to the drawing of his subject.

As the pencil-drawing on the block would be liable to become obliterated in the course of engraving, were it to remain quite exposed, it is customary for wood-engravers to cover all the block, except the part on which they may be actually employed, with a cap of paper, fitting close and tied tightly round the edges. As the drawing on the block is apt to be injured by the breath, a kind of screen or shade, formed of a piece of card-board or stiff paper, covering the nostrils and mouth, and secured by a string passing behind the ears, is frequently worn by wood-engravers, in damp or frosty weather, when employed on fine work. They also usually wear a shade, both to protect the eyes, and to more particularly confine the view to the work before them.

As all the lines in an engraved wood-block are in relief, their extremities, both at the edges and in the middle of the subject, are extremely liable to come off too heavy in printing, in consequence of the paper in such places being pressed not only on to, but, to a certain extent, down over them. In order to remedy this, when it is particularly desirable that certain parts should be lightly printed, and show the lines gradually declining till they become lost in the paper, the block is lowered in such places before the drawing is made on it; by which means the pressure of the platten or the cylinder on such places is reduced, and the desired lightness obtained. In vignette subjects, where the edges are required to be light, the lowering of the block in such places is extremely simple; lowering in the middle of the block, however, is not so easy an operation, and before it can be properly done, it is necessary to have the parts intended to be light sketched in as a guide to the operator. For lowering a block in this manner, a tool something like the burnisher of a copperplate engraver is used. Sometimes, also, the lines in such places are lowered by means of a fine file, after the cut has been engraved on a perfectly flat surface. Though "lowering" has been claimed as a *recent* invention, it was known to the old wood-engravers: Papillon has described his method of lowering by scraping down the lines after the block was engraved; and instances of lowering are frequent in Bewick's works.

When a block has been damaged, or badly engraved, in any part, the injury may be repaired, if not extending over a large surface. This is effected by drilling the part out, and inserting a plug, on the face of which the defective portion of the subject is re-drawn and engraved. Many instances of such repairs are perceptible in old wood-engravings, but in them the face of the plug is generally square. However well the repair may have been made, it is extremely difficult to prevent the trace of it appearing, to a scrutinising eye, like a white line round the plug, which is very liable to become loosened from the action of the press. Of a cut which has had a plug inserted it is generally advisable to take a cast, and to print from that, and not from the original block.

The tools which a wood-engraver employs to execute his work are extremely simple. They consist of gravers, to cut the lines defining the forms, and suggesting the idea of the varied tint and texture of his subject; and of chisels and gouges, to cut or scoop out the larger masses of wood where the subject has to appear white. The gravers are of two kinds—gravers simply so called, and "tint-tools." The

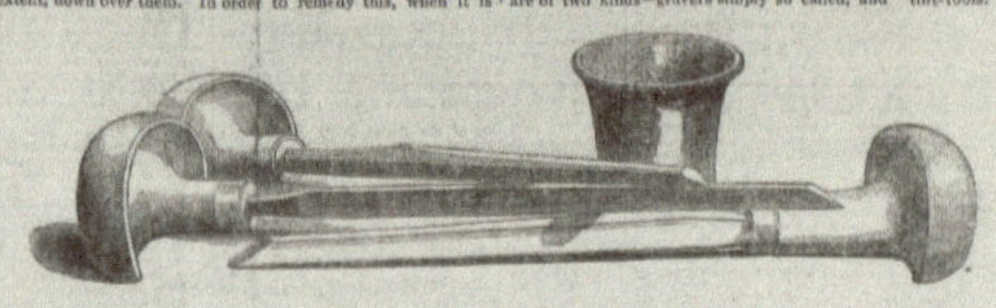

GRAVERS.

gravers-proper are used to cut the various lines, straight, crooked, curved, or crossing, which define the forms of the different objects, and indicate their character and texture; tint-tools, which are thinner in the blade, and more acutely angular at the point than gravers-proper, are used to cut the parallel lines which constitute what is technically termed a tint. In the use of these tools, in clearly cutting the more delicate portions of his subject, is displayed the engraver's skill; if in the adaptation of lines of all kinds to significantly convey as complete an idea of his subject as his art will allow, he displays both a knowledge of pictorial effect, and a power of representing it by the means of wood-engraving, he is justly entitled to the name of an artist.

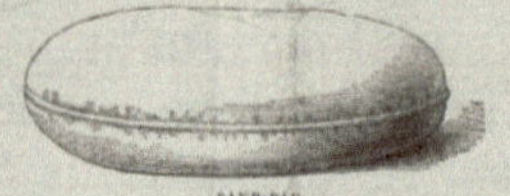

SAND-BAG.

Most wood-engravers, when at work, are accustomed to place the block on a leather sand-bag, which at once affords a firm rest, and allows of the block being turned with facility in any direction, by the left hand, while the right is employed in cutting a line. Some, however, place the block on a kind of frame, on which it is moveable by means of a pivot. Of the comparative merits of those two modes of resting the block it is not easy to decide, seeing that each is adopted by some of the best wood-engravers of the time. Those who have been accustomed to the one mode rarely abandon it for the other; to us, however, the sand-bag appears the most preferable, as being the simplest, and affording the greatest facility of turning the block, and suiting it, by the motion of the left hand, to the action of the graver.

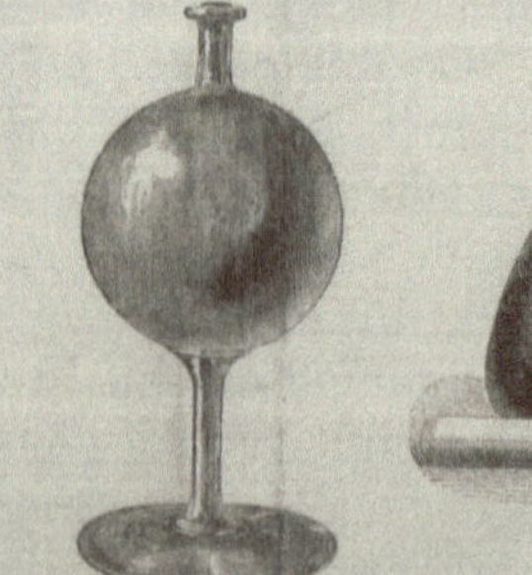

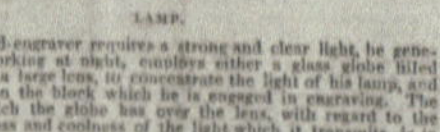

LAMP.

As the wood-engraver requires a strong and clear light, he generally, when working at night, employs either a glass globe filled with water, or a large lens, to concentrate the light of his lamp, and to cast it upon the block which he is engaged in engraving. The advantage which the globe has over the lens, with regard to the greater clearness and coolness of the light which it transmits, is in some degree counterbalanced by its greater liability to become broken, and the water become spilled over the table and among the blocks.

In taking a proof of his cut—which can only be done when the whole of the subject is engraved, otherwise the drawing would be effaced—the wood-engraver employs a small dauber to ink it, and a blunt-edged burnisher, to rub off the impression, which is usually taken on India paper, a piece of card being placed above to equalise the friction, and to prevent the lines being broken. Wood-engravers are frequently charged with heightening their proofs, by distributing a little more or less ink on certain parts of the block, and by burnishing such parts more or less, accordingly as they wish them to appear dark or light in the impression; thus giving to the cut an effect which it is impossible it should have when fairly printed. In consequence of this practice printers are not unfrequently blamed for not bringing up a cut equal to the engraver's proof, when, in fact, it is utterly impossible to obtain such an impression by means of a press, however careful the pressman may be in overlaying. The wood-engraver who employs great labour in the execution of a cut which cannot be properly printed, not only misemploys his time, but also deceives the person who employs him.

One of the great advantages which wood-engraving possesses over copper as a means of multiplying pictorial subjects, is the facility and cheapness with which its productions can be printed at the same time with letter-press. Wood-engravings are not to be estimated by a comparison with copper-plates; but are to be judged of by the power and significance with which they excite ideas in the mind, with reference to the means employed in their execution, and on a consideration of the thousands whose knowledge is thus extended, and whose pleasure is thus increased, compared with the hundreds who can afford to purchase copper-plate engravings. Though wood-engraving in connection with the press has already done much for the dissemination of both useful and entertaining knowledge, it has yet more to do. Artists of talent are not only every day becoming convinced of the advantages of wood-engraving as a means of communicating to the great body of the people a knowledge and a taste for works of art, but are also furnishing wood-engravers with new designs. The steam-press, a mighty engine, multiplies their joint productions by tens of thousands, almost with the rapidity of thought; and yet the demand increases with the supply, as if in those, for whose gratification they are intended, the "appetite increased with what it fed on."

For the purpose of showing how efficiently wood-engraving, in connection with the steam-press, can represent some of the higher creations of art and convey an idea of their most striking characteristics as displaying the sentiment or imagination of the original artist, the following subjects have been drawn and engraved, not as servile copies of copper-plate engravings, but with regard to the peculiar powers of wood-engraving to *translate*, if we may so speak, such subjects into its own graphic language, with a view to their being multiplied by means of the steam-press. How far the draftsman and the engraver have succeeded, we leave our readers to decide for themselves. The subjects are—1. "The Prophet Jeremiah," from an engraving after the original painting by Michael Angelo, among his frescoes in the Sistine Chapel, at Rome. 2. "Virgin and Child," after a

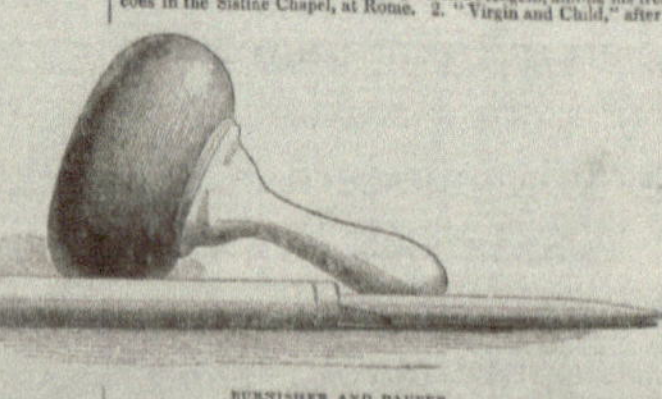

BURNISHER AND DAUBER.

drawing by Raffaelle. 3. A Cartoon by Raffaelle. It is to be observed that this subject is entirely executed by means of horizontal, parallel lines, intended to indicate its uniformity of colour as a chiaro-scuro. 4. "Garden Scene" from Watteau. 5. "Head of Captain Coram," the liberal promoter of the Foundling Hospital, after Hogarth. 6. "The Infant Hercules," after Sir Joshua Reynolds. 7. A portion of "The Death of the Children of Niobe," after Wollett's engraving form the painting by Wilson. The foliage, which, in the copper-plate, would cost the engraver much time and pains, is, in the wood-cut, executed with great facility. 8. "Imogene," after Westall.

For the proper execution of those cuts, the proprietors of the Illustrated London News have spared no expense; for their wish has been to present them to their subscribers and readers as the best specimens of wood-engravings of their kind and character that have ever been previously printed by means of a steam-press.

(The End.)

Figure 0.1. Wood-engraved illustration for "The Practice of Wood-Engraving" by William A. Chatto, *Illustrated London News*, 6 July 1844, 425.

field illustrators, termed "special artists," central to the publication's brand. Jackson draws on his experience as an *ILN* engraver and art editor to regale readers with exciting tales from the field, mentioning along the way other British journals such as the *Penny Magazine*, *Punch*, and the *Graphic*. Jackson calls this network an "English institution" and boasts that its yields are "the perfection of 'multiplying art' and a marvel of patient and persevering ingenuity."[39] Like the author of "The Commercial History of a *Penny Magazine*" and Chatto, Jackson invites the reader to share in this awe of modern print processes and culture, observing that "while the printing-machine has become the potent agent of human power and wisdom, it also fulfils the remarkable function of sending forth to the world a constant supply of 'illustrated news.'"[40]

Throughout the rest of the Victorian era, the *ILN* and other illustrated magazines continued interweaving a rhetoric of aesthetic sophistication and state-of-the-art technical accuracy to characterize the power of illustration. The pictorial press also continued to highlight the technological innovations essential to the representational power of illustrated print – most notably, its increasing use of photography. "A Description of the Offices of the *Strand Magazine*," published by the *Strand* in 1892, educates readers about print production in photographic detail (see figure 0.2). Over half of the article's thirteen pages are devoted to rich visual documentation in the form of engraved illustrations, identified as taken from photographs. "A Description" is also notable for its ethnographic approach to describing the production processes of illustrated journalism, taking readers through a series of scenes constituting a day in the life of the journal's offices. Characteristics range from the furnishings and interior decoration (editor George Newnes's "sanctum sanctorum" is "decorated in pale tints of salmon, green, and cream")[41] to the roles and behaviours of the people in each scene. Detailed letterpress descriptions accompany images of various production processes, such as stereotyping and electrotyping. The article thus interweaves visual and verbal details into a textured representation of the magazine's socio-technological production. In addition to offering a material history of the magazine object, it invites readers to energize their technological imagination with a visit to the *Strand*'s offices. There George Newnes had installed a permanent public gallery showcasing other material artefacts of print production. Open "every day, and all day," the gallery displayed original drawings and image-reproduction blocks for both the *Strand* and the *Million*, another of Newnes's illustrated magazines, to be viewed by "whomsoever may like to inspect them."[42]

These examples from the *Penny Magazine*, the *ILN*, and the *Strand* educated readers while stoking their interest in the making of the

STEREOTYPING ROOM.

a hand-press, a few of which machines are here to be observed, kept only for proof purposes. When all the matter is corrected in this form, and all the illustration-blocks prepared of their proper size and shape, the type and the blocks, if any, are "made up" into pages, being fixed in iron frames, called chases. All this is very quickly said, and seems very simple, but numbers of corrections and revises are made, and much labour, patience, and ingenuity expended in fixing the proper sizes of the illustrations, and fitting them to their proper places.

When at last the pages are "made up" and firmly screwed and wedged into their chases, the work is but begun. More proofs are taken and corrected, and the chases, with their contents, then go to the electrotyping department, at the top of the building. This workshop is the dirtiest and the most interesting in the place. The dirt cannot be helped—it is clean dirt, so to speak—and is simply graphite, or powdered black-lead, which, being an absolute essential to the process, gets everywhere.

But first let us suppose the made-up page

ELECTROTYPING ROOM.

Figure 0.2. Halftone illustration for "A Description of the Offices of the *Strand*," *Strand Magazine*, December 1892, 601.

very magazines they held in their hands. Appearing over decades of print innovation, the articles also instructed readers to attend to how the aesthetics of illustrated periodicals were shaped by their technological production. They also strove to reinforce readers' perception of illustrated periodicals as embodiments of modernity, offering readers various socio-technological contexts for recognizing how print media innovation was tied to industrialization.[43]

While articles in the press served as the most direct means of educating readers, print media literacy was informed by other cultural forms intended to edify and entertain. As suggested by Fyfe's study, the exhibition was among the most prominent of these forms. Just as articles about print production served as material testaments to that process, exhibitions that showcased text and image technologies physically situated print production within a network of other industrial products and processes. Exhibitions became a particularly informative venue for print media literacy as the press began incorporating photography-based illustration processes at the fin de siècle. As a forum for showcasing cultural and material innovation, the exhibition was a particularly effective venue for sharing photography, which combined fine art practices with the mechanical and chemical innovations of the age. Photography enthusiasts and wider publics alike learned about new photographic technologies and processes and admired their outputs through events such as the annual Exhibition of the Royal Photographic Society of Great Britain.[44]

The photography-based methods showcased by exhibitions were a driving force of a transformation in popular illustrated magazine design between approximately 1885 and 1910. Given that readers were equipped to interpret pictorial print objects as expressions of techne, as well as culture, it follows that their engagement with the magazines became more complex during these years. The images produced by the two image-reproduction processes driving this aesthetic transformation – photomechanical line-block and halftone engraving – are the principal subjects of this book. Both halftone and line-block images were sufficiently distinctive to be noticeable to readers who were accustomed to interpreting the material characteristics of print media. As I have already related, halftone images were characterized by their tonal shadings and distinctive granular pattern, and line-block images by their clean pen-and-ink appearance. Both the tonal granularity of halftone pictures and the stark, black-and-white look of line-block pictures attested to their status as mechanical reproductions. Line-block pictures bore some resemblance to wood-engraved images that were styled to evoke the simple lines of sketches through extensive relief work, but halftone pictures looked altogether different from the image types that had previously dominated the magazines.

I have demonstrated that throughout the nineteenth century, magazines could be interpreted by print media literate readers as modern, industrial artefacts. However, this was especially true of the late-Victorian periodicals populated with line-block and halftone images. These items derived a distinctive cultural value from their status as products of ever more mechanized, massive, and cutting-edge industrial manufacture. In a material sense, line-block and halftone images were more modern than wood engraving. The aesthetics of both line-block and halftone images attest to their reproduction by a method that did not require the manual labour of scooping out a relief block. By visibly reducing the intervention of the graver, photomechanical processes aligned with industrialization's inclination towards mechanizing and automating steps of production to improve efficiency and output volume.

Though I have yet to come across a popular magazine article detailing the photomechanical image-reproduction process, the history of published articles on print production indicates that readers would, at the very least, have been attentive to the physical characteristics of photomechanical images that distinguished them from wood-engravings and other established image types. Those popular magazine readers who were also familiar with elite publications on art and photography would have learned about photomechanical image reproduction as discussed and advertised in these venues. Additionally, a wide portion of popular readerships would have learned about photomechanical engraving through exhibitions such as that of the Royal Photographic Society of Great Britain, which documented this set of processes along with other methods for reproducing photographic images in print.[45] The ubiquity of exhibitions that educated the public about print and photographic processes is perhaps the strongest indicator that many readers would have possessed a general knowledge of what photomechanical processes entailed on a technical level.[46]

Print Media Literacy and the Technological Imagination at the Fin de Siècle

At the turn of the century, an additional context for readers' enhanced awareness of media materiality was the emergence of new communication technologies such as the gramophone, hand camera, and film. As Friedrich Kittler argues in his account of discourse networks circa 1900, the emergence of mechanical media facilitated a new concept of communication in which meaning was perceived as not inherent to a written or spoken word but the result of a process in which a reader's or user's senses engaged with the data inscribed on and stored in a specific media object.[47] New media mechanically parsed the steps of data inscription, storage, and transmission; they made mediation, as such, visible in a new way. In this regard they contributed to the modern formulations of media and mediation that John Guillory documented as emerging in the early twentieth century. As theorized by Matthew Kirschenbaum, they also contributed to the general public's capacity to recognize the physical characteristics of a media object that were commensurate with the processes of information inscription, storage, and transmission.[48]

That the mechanical media of the late nineteenth century engendered new conceptions of communication, media, and mediation is undeniable. This evolution of media thought, however, has a Victorian lineage that has often been overlooked by those who study it. As many scholars of historical print and literature have argued, awareness of the textual conditions that shape interpretation – mediation in a broader sense – has long been a feature of print culture.[49] I posit that, additionally, attention to the materiality of communication and media – mediation in a materially and technologically specific sense – was facilitated by the illustrated press, beginning several decades before the discursive shift that Kittler traces to 1900 and continuing into the twentieth century, although this engagement did not achieve the nuances of what Kirschenbaum describes as the forensic imagination. The illustrated journalism about journalism that was printed in the *Penny Magazine*, *ILN*, and *Strand* demonstrates that readers of the popular press had many opportunities throughout the Victorian era to hone a capacity to recognize how a periodical's material production shaped its aesthetic affordances and, in turn, mediated its contents. The magazines encouraged readers to interpret the aesthetic elements of print as technological signifiers as well as discursive components. In other words, they facilitated readers' critical and imaginative engagement with periodicals as media. Popular journalism also extended such strategies to include new media, educating readers about the technological features and mechanical functions of, for example, the hand camera and film, as well as reporting aspects of the culture forming around these technologies. In these and many other ways popular illustrated magazines prepared mass readerships for modern media systems.

Theoretical Framework: Periodical Media and Reader Engagement

This book participates in a growing body of periodical scholarship that intersects traditional book and print history methods with media studies, particularly media archaeology. Periodical studies have long explored the relationship between socio-cultural contexts, editorial content, and material form. Over the past two decades, processes of remediating archives digitally and engaging with periodicals in online environments have challenged prior notions of literacy and textual engagement. Concepts derived from media scholarship have galvanized new ways of theorizing how print facilitates meaning-making. In recent years, the use of media theory by Victorian-print scholars has also been informed by a materialist turn in the humanities.[50] Media archaeology offers a useful methodological tool-kit for scholarship at the junction of media theory, print history, and new materialism. Its foundational premise is that the media cultures of the present can be understood more fully by recovering their relationship to the media cultures of the past. This recovery involves identifying material characteristics inherited from past technologies and excavating the network of agents and physical conditions that shaped their creation and use.[51] Such an approach has been applied successfully by a number of print history scholars.[52]

To investigate how readers engaged with historical magazines, I began from a conception of texts as interpretive environments, following Jerome McGann; these environments offer a set of dynamic aesthetic and procedural conditions that afford a specific range of possibilities for making meaning.[53] Periodicals incorporate a variety of experience- or perception-based aesthetic modes, including the verbal, pictorial, spatial, and material; a reader's interpretive engagement with a magazine is conditioned by characteristics ranging from the visual display of letterpress and image content to the materiality of illustration and type, page layout, and other extra-textual factors. How readers decide to distribute their attention is just as important to the interpretive process as the aesthetic affordances on which their attention is bestowed; meaning is not determined wholly by reader or text but through their interaction.[54]

My analyses of case studies focus on the aesthetic affordances to which readers could attend in specific periodical environments. For most of these case studies, limited evidence of historical reader engagement impedes the reconstruction of how specific readers experienced periodicals. Rather than attempt such reconstructions, then, my analyses delineate the interpretive horizons made possible by each magazine, given its contexts and what McGann terms its "rules of engagement."[55] I address each periodical's contexts and form-specific organization in tandem with its aesthetics, first to explicate the techniques that periodicals used to invoke the technological imagination and to condition reader interpretation, and then to theorize the ways in which readers responded to those techniques.

To analyse the interaction between periodical producers and readers at the site of the periodical object, I draw on Michel de Certeau's theory of strategy, tactic, and poaching. De Certeau characterizes the dynamic between a modern society's dominant cultural representations and its individual citizens as the dialogical interaction of strategies and tactics.[56] Dominant representations of society, such as those expressed in popular illustrated periodicals, are strategies produced to shape citizens' interpretive agency and, in turn, their behaviour as participants in mass culture. Individuals can respond to those strategies with tactics that insinuate temporary, heterogeneous interpretations. In each of my case studies I locate the aesthetic strategies that illustrated periodical producers used to engage readers' technological imagination and to condition how they interpreted the periodical's representations of mass culture. I also identify tactics through which readers could exercise their imagination to formulate alternative interpretations of popular culture and assert agency as both consumers and producers of periodical content.

I developed the concept of the print technological imagination to theorize how readers related specific periodical practices and characteristics to the socio-technological contexts of print culture. This idea is indebted to Benedict Anderson's theory of imagined communities and to others who have taken up his work in specific media contexts. According to Anderson's theory, modern nationalism is the result of a social imaginary facilitated by two media, the newspaper and the novel.[57] As attested by the many adaptations of Anderson's account in cultural studies, literature, and media scholarship, the notion of a historically specific collective imaginary offers a useful heuristic for understanding how a public engages with specific media expressions and with mass media and culture *in toto*.

A number of these adaptations, such as Kirschenbaum's formulation of the forensic imagination, emphasize the technological dimensions of a public's collective imagination in a time of media change. In the domain of Victorian print culture specifically, scholars have employed multiple versions of the concept of the technological imagination to understand better the Victorians' relationship with their increasingly mechanized, industrial world.[58] Notable for the purposes of the present study is Gerry Beegan's use of such a concept to analyse how changing magazine aesthetics influenced the terms of engagement for late-Victorian mass culture. Beegan posits that the aesthetic traces of print image reproduction both reflected and contributed to the public's understanding of modernity, analysing the relationship between the late-Victorian socio-technological milieu and a social imaginary fostered by mass print.[59] Although my conclusions about this relationship depart somewhat from Beegan's,[60] his theoretical approach to and careful contextualizing of late-Victorian mass illustrated print have laid important groundwork for subsequent studies of illustrated print media history, including this one.

The concept of Victorian print media literacy similarly represents a synthesis of the theories and historical insights garnered by the aforementioned scholars. Theorizing reader engagement with illustrated magazines in terms of print media literacy enables me to trace a hermeneutic pattern running from nineteenth- through twentieth- and twenty-first-century media cultures, contributing to a more historicized understanding of contemporary media and the perennial debate about media change and its adverse effects. Seminal twentieth-century theorists of popular media and culture such as Max Horkheimer and Theodor Adorno argued that over the late nineteenth and early twentieth centuries consumers became passive cogs in the machinery of culture.[61] More recent media criticism has added complexity to this narrative, but histories of mass media and culture still tend to overlook the important role that new and existing print media played in the changing terms of popular-culture participation at the turn of the twentieth century.[62]

Using the concept of print media literacy as a methodological prism, this book investigates late-Victorian pictorial print to reveal changing dynamics between periodical producers and consumers. These dynamics affected how publics understood media and culture and their own agency as audiences. I incorporate additional concepts from social, media, and technology theorists as appropriate to situate each case study within both a specific moment of periodical history and a larger-scale history of media in popular culture. According to the narrative that builds in these cases, readers in the age of mechanized media continued to perceive production and consumption as interrelated processes for circulating cultural knowledge. Indeed, as I show, readers as both consumers and producers used their media literacy and technological imagination to engage with popular print and new media. This book thus contributes to media history and periodical studies in a few different ways. It presents research on periodical titles, genres, and techniques that have largely disappeared from view but that exemplify innovative and influential uses of the illustrated periodical. It highlights the importance of periodicals' material aesthetics and production history, particularly their image-reproduction processes, in reader engagement. Most significantly, it showcases how the concept of print media literacy can be used to characterize historical reader engagement and why such an approach is particularly productive for studying moments of media and technological change.

Overview of Primary Texts and Case Studies

This book's case studies have been selected from some of the most widely circulated periodicals of the late nineteenth and early twentieth centuries. The *ILN* and the *Graphic* are often characterized as newspapers, rather than magazines, because they focus on reporting current events instead of assorted subjects of interest, but their aesthetic similarity to the illustrated magazines of the period is such that I have classified them as magazines for the purposes of this book. The *ILN*, founded in 1842, and the *Graphic*, founded in 1869, enjoyed the widest circulation of Britain's pictorial news weeklies in the latter half of the Victorian era. Both periodicals were quick to incorporate print innovations and thus managed to dominate the market for illustrated weeklies well into the twentieth century, despite the growing number of competitors. *Pearson's* and the *Strand* emerged in the 1890s. Effectively utilizing New Journalism's formal variety and new image technology's spectacular affordances, *Pearson's* and the *Strand* became two of the most widely circulated turn-of-the-century illustrated monthlies.

Taken together, the *ILN*, the *Graphic*, *Pearson's*, and the *Strand* represent the general character and features of the era's popular pictorial journalism. These four magazines simultaneously contributed to and recorded key ideas, preoccupations, and discourses of late-Victorian popular culture, which was largely informed by and informing of the values of the middle classes but was increasingly treated as emblematic of British social life as a whole. While all four magazines had pictorial formats, the weekly *ILN* and *Graphic* were shaped by a journalistic focus on current events, whereas the monthly *Strand* and *Pearson's* engaged current events less directly, focusing instead on temporally durable entertainment genres that readers might return to in biannual, bound volumes. The longer publication cycles of the monthlies allowed for more sophisticated aesthetics, but pictorial news weeklies also used images in innovative ways to depict the most action-packed moments of each news cycle.

The *ILN*, the *Graphic*, *Pearson's*, and the *Strand* all boasted general audiences across gender and class, with the broad middle classes comprising their largest subsets of readers. It is important to note that my focus on mass culture here necessarily means that the book's scope is informed by the push and pull between the dominant orientation of Victorian culture and the diffuse perspectives of individuals. As depicted in general interest magazines, the widely practised, non-specialized, cross-class cultural activities of late-Victorian readers tended to place a middle-class, white, male, English subject at their centre. The case studies of chapters 1, 2, and 3, which focus chiefly on magazine contents developed by proprietors and advertisers, reflect this orientation. However, as engaged by historical individuals, mass culture encompassed a broader spectrum of subjectivity and, in turn, of consumption and production. The case studies of chapters 4 and 5, which investigate reader responses to the contents of illustrated magazines, illuminate some of this spectrum's range.

Relatedly, most of the major political and cultural issues that preoccupied fin-de-siècle British society, such as gender roles, class conflict, and New Imperialism, are addressed in this book only where they are essential contexts for understanding the interaction of periodical producers and consumers in specific case studies. Serial and short fiction, which were mainstays of popular Victorian periodicals and therefore constitute a main focus of Victorian print scholarship, receive little attention after the first chapter. The publication history of fiction in the news weeklies offers evidence of how pictorial journalism evolved to reposition itself in the late-Victorian media ecosystem, as I discuss in chapter 1. Although fiction remained a staple of the popular press throughout my period of study, however, it did not engage readers' print media literacy on the dynamic terms evident in the new (and newly multimodal) genres and features that make up this book's case studies in chapters 2 through 5.

Chapter 1 investigates the technological imagination's role in the rise of self-consciously multimodal representation in the *ILN* as this magazine transitioned from wood-engraved reproduction of images to photomechanical processes. These technologies had a profound impact on the visuality of the *ILN* and, consequently, on reader engagement. Between 1885 and 1907, this news weekly increasingly relied on images, which interacted with letterpress, page design, and material aesthetics to convey information. Drawing on the work of André Gaudreault and Phillippe Marion, who argue that "a medium is always born twice," I demonstrate that this transition from verbal to visual storytelling galvanized the birth of pictorial weeklies – and illustrated magazines more broadly – as new media in their own right.[63] Though the weekly's initial, integrating birth occurred in the 1840s, its second, constitutional birth at the turn of the twentieth century, propelled by changes in the technologies of image reproduction, endowed it with unique representational capacities. Through its second birth, the *ILN* transitioned to a more deliberately multimodal aesthetic to participate in the late-Victorian new media milieu. Other illustrated magazines similarly evolved into new media during this period, although the particulars of the shift were unique to each form. I profile the pictorial weekly's transition in the *ILN*'s changing text-to-image ratio, decreasing reliance on verbal apparatuses to aid pictorial interpretation, disappearance of illustrated fiction, and increase in image frequency and variety. Analysis of three examples – the *Coronation and Procession* number (1902), "Stories without Words" (1906), and "Fairy Stories by Photography" (1907) – demonstrates that the *ILN*'s second birth affected how readers engaged with the pictorial weekly. The magazine's increasingly multimodal aesthetics engaged their technological imagination to draw attention to mediation itself. By 1907 the pages of the *ILN* presented popular culture as mediated and its participants as media users.

Chapter 1 establishes that as a new medium, the late-Victorian illustrated periodical stimulated readers' awareness of magazines as mediating popular culture. Chapter 2 explicates how mediality and the technological imagination figured in the dynamic between periodical producers and readers. Analysing aesthetic developments in the advertising pages of the *ILN* and the *Graphic* between 1885 and 1906, I argue that readers' critical awareness of mediation influenced their perception of consumer culture. In the last years of the nineteenth century, advertising space infiltrated magazine contents, and advertisements became more sophisticated. I show how advertisers used aesthetic strategies, including hybridity and kitsch, to engage the technological imagination of their readers and to encourage them to conflate reading and consumption. Readers could also use their print media literacy and technological imagination to develop counter-interpretations. Using N. Katherine Hayles's theory of hyper-reading, I identify reading tactics that were made possible by the periodical environment, such as scanning, skimming, and juxtaposing.[64] Engaging the technological imagination within the context of print magazines, advertisements not only encouraged readers to conceive of themselves as consumers of mass culture but also presented the means for them to exert agency as curatorial and appropriative producers of that culture.

Chapter 3 addresses the political implications of the dynamic between producer strategies and reader tactics in illustrated magazines, focusing on the population journalism published in *Pearson's* between 1896 and 1902. This previously unrecognized periodical genre combined statistical narrative with lively data visualizations. Drawing on Michel Foucault's theory of biopolitics, I analyse the aesthetic strategies through which *Pearson's* population journalism prompted readers to conceptualize themselves and other popular-culture participants using a rubric of normalization.[65] Where periodical advertisements strategically conflated reading and consumption, population journalism strategically conflated popular culture and population politics. In the abstract data visualizations that *Pearson's* population journalism used between 1896 and 1898, the minimalist aesthetic encouraged individual readers to conceive of themselves as statistical units within a demarcated socio-biological population: the British nation. In contrast, the photorealistic data visualizations used between 1898 and 1902 remediated the individual body as a component of multimodal, mass print spectacle. I argue that the spectacular aesthetic strategies through which population journalism engaged the technological imagination also created space for readers' tactical agency and dissent, as evident in the 1899 article "Statistics Gone Mad."

Taking a selection of scrapbooks as a case study, chapter 4 examines archival evidence of how historical readers poached magazine contents by removing them from their material contexts to create itinerant, personal media. The scrapbook exemplifies the prevalent Victorian cultural practice of extracting and reassembling paper materials, such as magazine contents, cards, tickets, and photographs. Scrap-books instantiate the farthest extension of the hermeneutic process of simultaneous consumption and production first discussed in chapter 2. Just as importantly, scrapbooks offer material traces of how historical readers engaged with periodicals. Compilers remediated periodical content and adopted periodical design techniques in order to represent specific domains of cultural knowledge as they saw fit. Through this process scrapbook makers produced new knowledge about both those domains and print mediation itself. Readers drew on their print media literacy and technological imaginations to compile scrapbooks and, in so doing, enhance their understanding of and ability to intervene in popular print culture.

Readers responded to the strategies of periodical producers, not only with idiosyncratic and critical readings of magazine content, as discussed in chapters 2 and 3, and by creating personal media, as discussed in chapter 4, but also by contributing to mainstream periodicals. Chapter 5 examines how readers used their media literacy and technological imagination to produce their own periodical content for "Curiosities," a novelty journalism feature appearing in the *Strand* from 1896 to 1918. Readers appropriated the production of magazine material by assuming control of a new media technology, the hand camera. "Curiosities" became a participatory forum for the *Strand* community to share curated snapshots and commentary on the photographic process. I use Patrice Flichy's theory of technological integration to demonstrate that the dynamic interaction of periodical producers and readers helped shape snapshot photography's place in twentieth-century mass culture.[66] During its most innovative years "Curiosities" marked a high point in participatory journalism and the illustrated magazine's interaction with the new media milieu.

Chapters 1–5 delineate the influential position that late-Victorian popular illustrated periodicals occupied at the moment when mass non-print media began transforming the cultural landscape. The case studies from the *ILN, Graphic, Pearson's,* and *Strand* document how the illustrated press responded to Britain's increasingly visual and mass-mechanized popular culture with aesthetic strategies that invoked socio-technological authority and drew readers' attention to the spectacle of cultural mediation. Through these strategies, illustrated journalism repositioned itself within the new media milieu. The terms of engagement offered by popular magazine aesthetics also shaped the horizons for audience engagement with other mass media in the early twentieth century.

In the conclusion, I examine a latent theme of this book, the centuries-old debate about new media's effects on the masses, before gesturing to the vast Victorian inheritance of digital media that remains to be explored. The reception history of Victorian illustrated periodicals shows a pattern of ambivalence that has long structured how critics talk about media change. Many cultural critics, from the Victorian age to the present, have failed to assess new media on their own terms; as a result, these critics have been unable to appreciate the new aesthetic registers engendered by such media or recognize the dynamic terms of reader, audience, and user engagement that they afford. Seen through the lens of this book, the legacy of illustrated periodicals offers a corrective to this perennial narrative. Additionally, the politics of media engagement that I have outlined in this book's case studies are instructive because the digital media landscape retains many characteristics of its Victorian heritage. The dynamic terms of reader engagement across illustrated magazine formats, genres, and features left an enduring legacy, shaping how popular-culture participants have engaged with the media cultures of the twentieth and twenty-first centuries. Comparing past and present media literacies can enhance our understanding of how users interact with mass media today as well as how Victorian cultural practices and values continue to play a role in that interaction.

Chapter One

The *Illustrated London News*, Popular Illustrated Journalism, and the New Media Landscape, 1885–1907

> The illustration of books, and even more of magazines, may be said to have been born in our time, so far as variety and abundance are the signs of it; or [have] born, at any rate, the comprehensive, ingenious, sympathetic spirit in which we conceive and practice it.
>
> Henry James, *Picture and Text* (1893)

On 5 January 1907, readers opening the latest issue of the *Illustrated London News* encountered a pictorial transformation. Ornate, thematic headers now embellished the *ILN*'s most prominent regular features, including those that previously had included few pictures, such as local event briefs and science news. Perhaps the most striking aesthetic enhancements were those adorning the *ILN*'s editorial essay, "Our Note Book," which had held no pictorial appeal before (figure 1.1). Drawn by Amédée Forestier, a frequent contributor to the *ILN*, the header for this feature depicts an early modern scene in which a lively crowd socializes. Against this backdrop, a central figure sits upon a monumental bench, carved in a vaguely classical style. The quill and sheets in this young man's hands indicate that writing is his trade. His body language, as he leans back to observe the crowd over his shoulder, implies that he writes from life; his amused facial expression suggests that the tone of his creative output is playful or sardonic.

This theme, the mirthful documentation of society, resonates with the subject matter of "Our Note Book," written at the time by the witty author and critic G.K. Chesterton.[1] In the editorial essay appearing below the header, Chesterton remarks with mock awe on the feature's new look: "I perceive with astonishment, mingled with gratitude (and terror, which is the very soul of gratitude), a beautiful picture erected upon the top of this article. Such decoration is all to the good." He then

BY G. K. CHESTERTON.

I PERCEIVE with astonishment, mingled with gratitude (and terror, which is the very soul of gratitude) a beautiful picture erected upon the top of this article. Such decoration is all to the good; and if the Editor chooses to print all my words in different colours I, for one, shall consider them vastly improved. Still, you may dwell for a moment on the composition of this admirable design. In the foreground (you will observe) I am myself seated, clad in that close and clinging fifteenth-century costume which best sets off my elegant but too ethereal figure. I am engaged (somewhat ostentatiously) in dipping a quill pen in ink; and I seem to be wearing (in case of accidents) another quill pen in my hat. A long procession of the most important human types pass behind me, for none of them have the courage to pass in front of me. The two busts or terminal figures which decorate the seat are portraits of the Editor and his trusty lieutenant.

I mentioned last week that the doctors have now discovered that Christmas pudding is an exquisitely hygienic and harmless food. That is typical of all the developments of scientific thought in our day. Many prophets and righteous men, many thinkers and idealists, have wasted their lives in running after scientific truth. Never run after scientific truth. Stand where you are, and in a few years scientific truth will run after you. Continue to eat pork, and sooner or later the doctors will say that pork is the only food that is perfectly digestible. Continue to drink port, and sooner or later a Man will arise in medical circles who will prove that port is the only certain safeguard against gout. The specialist may have told you to take your children to the seaside. But if you are only long enough in packing he will very likely have discovered that sea air is poison before you start. The best authorities may have told you (if your chest is weak) to make your bed in your back garden for a year. They may be telling you to grow your tulips in your bedroom the next year. In fact, I did definitely see in a medical article the other day that the fresh-air cure ought to be given up, as fresh air was not so good a thing as had been supposed. The truth of the matter is, I suppose, that what a medical theorist has to do is almost exactly the same as what a social or historical theorist has to do: he has to strike an average between an enormous number of effects produced by one thing, all of them different effects, some of them contradictory effects. It is as difficult (I expect) to say whether the effect of sherry is good or bad as to say whether the effect of Napoleon was good or bad. Among these ordinary human things there is no such thing as the simple poison and the simple antidote. Napoleon was not a poison; he was a dangerous stimulant. Wellington was not an antidote; he was a very dangerous substitute.

Certainly, if science has its startling changes, so has history. I have recently come across a case of reversal which (though individuals, of course, have often advanced it) is in ordinary popular assumption quite as sensational as the change touching Christmas pudding. First, I learnt that plum pudding was wholesome. Now I learn that King Richard III. was wholesome. I do not know whether any of the readers of this controversialists, who has made a particular study of historical mysteries. But in so far as a man having only the common culture of the middle-class omnivorous reader can be said to be convinced on a point of history, I confess that I am convinced by Sir Clements Markham's argument and theory. What his theory is I have already indicated: it is simply the complete justification of Richard III. The wicked Richard Crookback, whom I have known from childhood, gradually disintegrates and disappears before my eyes. He was not wicked; he was not even a Crookback, it seems, to any particular extent. One feels as if the only other discovery left would be that his name was not Richard.

Photo. Elliott and Fry.

THE LATE PRINCIPAL RAINY, D.D.,
Greatest Scottish Ecclesiastical Statesman.

(SEE "PERSONAL NOTES AND NEWS.")

It is as well to insist, to begin with, on what may be called the journalistic quality in the story; its sensationalism or practical novelty for the existing public. Sir Clements Markham holds that Richard III. did not murder the Princes in the Tower, but that Henry VII. did. This is full of exactly that abrupt and staggering substitution or reversal which is the very essence of the success of a detective story. By this, to the popular historical eye, Henry VII. stands in history as the crowned avenger of a crime that he really committed himself. Now, apart from the elements of fact, we may dwell upon this interesting element of fiction; for this change is artistically credible, as is the climax of a good detective tale. Nothing is more false than the phrase that romance, even detective romance, ends

his reputation from the very first; the thing has been done excellently in Gaboriau's "Widow Lerouge." Similarly, the scoundrel who is to be exculpated must be slightly fascinating, even as a scoundrel. We must love him a little as the Beast before he turns into the Prince.

It is interesting to note that these romantic conditions are exactly fulfilled in the case of Henry VII. and Richard III. Henry VII. may have been the champion of justice; but even his friends admit that he had that particular vice that goes least with any disinterested championship—avarice. Richard III. may have been a mean, cold-blooded person. But even his foes admitted that he had that quality which goes least with mere meanness: a flamboyant and high-speaking courage on the field of battle, that ecstasy of war in which bright words and bright swords go together. It is at least significant, I think, that even the Tudor tradition has left all the prose with Henry and all the poetry with Richard. It is significant that even those who make Richard wrong make him attractive; that even those who make Henry right make him unattractive. Here is the first hint of something that may be a broken and defaced tradition, like the light of an eclipsed sun. It is, I believe, the fact that the few popular ballads which exist celebrate the heroism of Richard.

Sir Clements Markham, however, has solid arguments of fact. The most solid, I think, is that Henry, when he had taken over the Tower, where the Princes were detained, and were supposed to have been murdered, issued an account of Richard's crimes in which he never mentioned the Princes at all. If he had found them gone it would have been the best "copy" he could get. The apparent deduction is that he found them alive and kicking. If that is so there can be little doubt under whose gentle and soothing influence they ultimately ceased to kick. And this is supported in a very strange and suggestive way by the incident of Perkin Warbeck and such pretenders. The revolts in their favour seem certainly to contradict the idea that there was any general and firmly established conclusion that the young Princes had been murdered in the last reign; certainly they tend to destroy the idea that Richard had grown seriously unpopular upon any such accusation.

I am fully conscious of the ignominy which is to be heaped upon any amateur or idle person who attacks the problems of history; I know that scientific historians have mysterious faculties which I myself lack. But I think I should be safe in saying this: that people would not first have dethroned Richard because the Princes were dead, and then afterwards have dethroned Henry because the Princes were alive. I cannot believe (such is my little faith) that they were dead before Bosworth and alive after Bosworth. I am, therefore, with some pain driven back upon the alternative that they were alive before Bosworth, and dead after it. The other charges against Richard III. seem already to have melted into air. He certainly did not kill Henry VI. If he did kill Henry the Sixth's son, it could only have been a case of one armed man killing another in the mêlée of Tewkesbury; he did certainly kill Hastings by due process of law, and

Figure 1.1. Amédée Forestier, halftone illustration for "Our Note Book," *Illustrated London News*, 5 January 1907, 4.

proceeds to interpret figures in the headpiece as representations of editorial staff. Chesterton identifies the writer sitting on the bench, "clad in that close and clinging fifteenth-century costume" and "ostentatiously" dipping quill into ink, as his own avatar – a claim carrying more than a hint of irony, given that the scribe is lithe and Chesterton was famously stout. He interprets the two classical busts appearing atop plinths on either side of the carved bench as depicting the magazine's editor – Bruce Ingram, grandson of *ILN*'s founder, Herbert Ingram – and a "trusty lieutenant."[2] A comparison of the header to the portraits of Ingram suggests that the busts resemble *ILN* producers in spirit rather than physical appearance, much like the writerly figure standing in for Chesterton. But whether or not the header's figures accurately depicted the *ILN* staff, Chesterton's nod to the new visuality of "Our Note Book" enhanced how readers engaged with this feature by entwining text and image – a rhetorical strategy that encapsulates the *ILN*'s raison d'être.

One of the earliest and most enduring illustrated magazines, with a print run beginning in 1842 and ending in 1989, the *ILN* established the guiding principle of illustrated journalism: the importance of pictorial representation as a way of documenting the world.[3] The evolving aesthetic and material processes through which the *ILN* did so at the fin de siècle constitute the focus of this chapter. The dialogue Chesterton creates between pictures and letterpress in "Our Note Book" suggests that the magazine's aesthetic transformation in 1907 was an extension of its long-standing efforts, as declared in the inaugural issue in 1842, to cover "every subject which attracts the attention of mankind, with a spirit in unison with the character of each subject, whether it be serious or satirical, trivial or of purpose grave."[4] At the same time that the *ILN*'s graphical transformation brought each topic's spirit and mode of representation into greater harmony, the new look unveiled in 1907 announced the *ILN*'s embrace of modern popular aesthetics. Influenced by non-print, mechanical media, these aesthetics were highly visual and multimodal in nature. In this and many other regards, the *ILN* was a paragon of evolving popular illustrated print conventions. The shift from verbally oriented to visually oriented, multimodal storytelling that is exemplified by the *ILN* was fundamental to the repositioning of the illustrated news weekly and other types of pictorial magazines in the new media milieu of the early twentieth century.

As briefly discussed in the introduction, media theorist Friedrich Kittler offers an insightful account of media culture's sea-change at the turn of the century, highlighting that non-print media such as the gramophone and film compelled people to reassess the materiality of communication practices. Kittler's account is an astute one, but his portrayal of the relationship between print and mechanical media is incomplete. Kittler posits a technological and ideological rift dividing new media from all print, which is typified, for Kittler, as the book.[5] However, the circulation history of print media indicates that although they were displaced from their position at the pinnacle of popular culture over the first decades of the twentieth century, they remained major communication platforms. More importantly, many print media cross-pollinated with new media in ways that indicate that the distinction between old and new was provisional and porous.

Print scholars have discussed this mutual influence; Sean Latham, Laurel Brake, and Anne Ardis, among others, have documented a dialogic relationship between periodicals and mechanical media at the turn of the twentieth century.[6] Scholarship on this subject has yet to fully account for the dialectic between new media and popular illustrated magazines specifically. The aesthetic evolution of the magazines is key to the uniqueness of this relationship: it was in response to the changing media landscape that popular pictorial print transformed at the turn of the century. Most historical narratives of print culture take for granted that illustrated journalism was already dominated by visual storytelling by this time. For example, scholars such as Richard Altick, Patrick Collier, and Sinnema hold that the *ILN* was influential in part because its editors had insisted on subordinating text to image from the magazine's inception.[7] However, I contend that the *ILN*'s text-to-image ratio and reliance on verbal exposition demonstrate that until the end of the century, this periodical – and other illustrated news weeklies that followed its lead – was an intermediary derivative, limited by long-standing journalistic conventions that privileged the written word.

This chapter proposes that it was not until the fin de siècle that pictorial news weeklies subverted print's established text-image hierarchy. This pivotal point epitomizes the changing status of illustrated periodicals in the turn-of-the-century new media milieu. I use André Gaudreault and Phillipe Marion's theory that a medium is always "born twice" to diagnose the development of the illustrated news weekly and popular pictorial print more broadly over the nineteenth and early twentieth centuries.[8] This medium's initial, "integrating" birth occurred in the 1840s when *Punch* and the *ILN* became the first weeklies to be densely populated with wood-engravings.[9] Its second, "constitutional" birth took place between 1885 and 1907, when the replacement of wood-engravings with new photomechanically reproduced images distinguished mass pictorial magazines as new media.[10] Combining statistical surveys with a close reading of *ILN* characteristics, I analyse evidence of this shift in the magazine's changing text-to-image ratio, its decreasing reliance on verbal apparatuses to interpret images, its comparative use of words and pictures in fictional storytelling, and its image frequency and variety.

Drawing on the media criticism of Kittler and others, I examine the implications that the rise of visual, multimodal expression in popular magazines had for reader engagement, using three *ILN* exemplars: the *Coronation and Procession* number (1902), "Stories without Words" (1906), and "Fairy Stories by Photography" (1907). The early twentieth-century *ILN* invoked readers' technological imagination through innovative visuals supplemented with verbal commentary that drew attention to illustrated journalism's unique mediation of the modern world. The last of the three case studies, "Fairy Stories by Photography," shows how the increasingly visual, multimodal character of popular pictorial magazines brought them into conversation with other visually oriented media, particularly new media. This cross-pollination with other media was key to the evolving status of popular illustrated print in the landscape of popular media and culture. Having previously occupied a central role in Victorian popular culture, these magazines maintained a leading place within the turn-of-the-century milieu of mass-media culture through aesthetic interconnectivity with new media such as photography and film. In other words, thanks in large part to the magazines, print remained a major medium of a popular culture, despite the increasing prominence of non-print communication technologies.

The case studies of this chapter also demonstrate that the increasingly visual, multimodal character of pictorial magazines encouraged readers to recognize the correlation between the production of a periodical and the meaning afforded by its aesthetic properties. This dimension of print media literacy requires readers to pay attention to mediation and the role it plays in interpretation. Such awareness became part of readers' technological imaginary, equipping them to scrutinize how the physical characteristics of periodicals and other media conditioned the representation of popular culture.

The Text-Oriented Pictorial Weekly, 1842–85

The use of pictorial storytelling has a long history in print journalism. In the eighteenth century, for example, illiterate members of the working classes could rely on images in the *Newgate Calendar* to learn the sordid details of recent crimes and executions. Beginning with *Punch: The London Charivari* and the *ILN*, the Victorians expanded the number and diversity of images in the pictorial press. It was not until the turn of the nineteenth century, however, that mass, cross-class illustrated news and entertainment magazines went so far as to privilege pictorial expression over text.

Gaudreault and Marion's theory of medium development offers a guide for examining the material aesthetics of the illustrated periodical and its relationship to other media as these evolved over the nineteenth and early twentieth centuries. According to their theory, a medium's initial birth is only one of several phases of its development. Once it has established autonomy within a culture, rather than functioning on terms derived from other, pre-existing media, it achieves its second, constitutional birth.[11] At the fin de siècle, the pictorial news weekly's new aesthetics distinguished it as a unique and pivotal medium of popular culture, repositioning it within print culture and the broader media milieu. This was part of a fundamental transformation through which all illustrated journalism extended its emphasis on visuality, mediation, and spectacle. The particulars of the transformation varied between periodical formats, each of which can be understood, according to Gaudreault and Marion, as one of the "cultural series" that constituted the formation of medium identity for popular illustrated magazines.[12] As a cultural series, the evolving *ILN* encapsulates how illustrated magazines became autonomous media and repositioned themselves within the fin-de-siècle media ecosystem.

Popular illustrated magazines began to develop into a fully fledged medium during what Gaudreault and Marion term *appearance*, the first of three phases – appearance, emergence, and constitution or advent – through which media are gradually constituted. Each of the phases involves different "social agents."[13] In the appearance phase, a new technology integrates with "legitimate types of existing media, practices and genres" for socio-cultural use.[14] In the case of popular illustrated magazines, a cluster of processes for illustrated weekly newspaper production constituted this new technology. As a means for large-scale image reproduction, wood-engraving was foremost among these processes. In its inaugural address to readers the *ILN* declared its intention to use wood-engraving to intervene in British journalism. Having watched the "progress of illustrative art" for "the past ten years," the *ILN*'s editors deemed May 1842 the right moment for "launching the giant vessel of illustration" into the "broadest" and "widest" channel "that it has ever dared to stem." The *ILN* suggests that the very words "illustrated news" are tokens of "a fresher purpose" and an "enlarged design" for "the world of newspapers."[15] These turns of phrase suggest a new take on established practices. Indeed, Mason Jackson, an *ILN* engraver and editor, later contended that although the idea of illustrated journalism was "as old as the newspaper itself," it was most fully realized through the *ILN*.[16] In accordance with Gaudreault and Marion's theory, the *ILN*'s appearance required its producers to "come to grips" with the "codes" of established genres, conventions, and institutions of the existing print media culture.[17] Herbert Ingram and Henry Vizetelly, the *ILN*'s first proprietors, innovatively synthesized such codes and conventions to produce a middle-class weekly that combined text and illustration to report both serious news items and entertaining diversions.[18]

During pictorial journalism's second phase, *emergence*, pre-established codes of print journalism shaped the use procedures that formed around the processes of illustrated magazine production, giving rise to what Gaudreault and Marion call a "proto-medium."[19] During its first decades in print, the *ILN* promoted circulation, reading, and appropriation practices consistent with established print culture. Like other weeklies, the *ILN* had a publication schedule, format, and content that reflected its status between the dailies and the monthlies: it offered more sophisticated visuals than a daily news format could offer,[20] and more up-to-date information about current events than a monthly format could provide. Like other periodicals issued on the weekend, the *ILN* had a Saturday release date that made the magazine eligible reading material for Sunday's leisure hours.

In keeping with the conventions of periodical culture, the *ILN*'s weekly seriality shaped its depiction of annual and ongoing current events. For example, the world news summaries and illustration commentaries situated updates on any ongoing stories within the context of previous and forthcoming numbers. Ongoing or recurring events were reported under a recurring header; for example, the headers "The Transvaal War" and "The Transvaal Crisis" regularly introduced reports on the Second Boer War (1899–1902). Visual style also gave a sense of continuity to the periodical's representations of ongoing events; often, the same special artist or artists sent multiple field sketches to *ILN* engravers over long stretches on a battlefront.[21]

The *ILN*'s promotional schemes also adapted conventions established by other magazines. For example, the *ILN*'s introduction of special Christmas and Summer numbers in the 1870s was a response to the use of this practice by other popular periodicals targeting middle-class readers, such as the monthly *All the Year Round* and the weekly *Graphic*. The *ILN* similarly followed the widespread practice of including supplemental, full-page or double-page images, available only to subscribing readers, that were designed to be pulled out and appropriated as personal mementos or adornments.

Although the *ILN* inherited many established conventions of journalism, modifying those conventions only in lockstep with other Victorian periodicals, its editors considered its pictorial approach to be ground-breaking because the magazine championed the representational fidelity of visual storytelling. As Andrea Korda notes, the *ILN* presented its illustrations of contemporary events as "objective transcription[s] of reality."[22] The magazine's careful attention to visual details, image reproduction, and verbal accompaniments to illustrations indicates that pictures carried epistemological weight. The *ILN* also participated readily in broader visual culture, cross-pollinating with other pictorial media such as paintings, public spectacles, and photography.[23] Indeed, the *ILN*'s role in visual culture was distinctive enough to prompt rebuke from William Wordsworth in a sonnet, "Illustrated Books and Newspapers," written in 1846 and published in 1850.[24]

Despite championing pictorial communication, the *ILN* demonstrated in its text-to-image ratio and its reliance on verbal apparatuses to contextualize its pictures that for most of the Victorian era the magazine relied on letterpress as the primary mode of communicating information about topical events and culture. This verbal orientation derived partly from limitations of printing technology and partly from socio-cultural conventions. In general, educated readers considered words superior to images. Victorian culture was highly visual, but class-based educational bias supported the status of the written word as the primary means of communication. Indeed, in "Our Address," the *ILN*'s own descriptions of the relationship between words and pictures capitulates to this bias. The article frames the confluence of image and text as a wedding in which "Art" becomes "the bride of literature."[25] This figure bestows supreme communicative status on the written word, enforcing a textual patriarchy.[26] From this perspective, images supplemented letterpress. As long as images held a supporting role, illustrated journalism remained a derivative medium – what Gaudreault and Marion describe as "a simple auxiliary to existing genres."[27]

The Rise of Pictorial Storytelling

Viewed through the lens of Gaudreault and Marion's theory, the relationship between images and words is key to the pictorial news magazine's transition from the second phase of medium development, in which it remained a derivative proto-medium, to the third phase, in which it became autonomous. This second birth began at the end of the nineteenth century and was made possible by advances in print technology and changing attitudes towards visual communication.

Pictorial journalism transformed in response to technology and a changing visual culture, while also contributing to the way these aspects of the media landscape were perceived by readers. Investigating specific aspects of the *ILN*'s change from a verbal to a pictorial orientation as evidence of this process reveals insights about reader engagement and the illustrated periodical's status in turn-of-the-century mass culture.

One method for comparing the magazine's reliance on verbal and pictorial modes of expression is to compare the amount of physical page space that pictures and letterpress occupied in a series of samplings over the crucial decades of transition, 1880 to 1907. This ratio markedly changed during the period of the *ILN*'s second birth. It can be approximately tracked by documenting the percentage of pages in which images occupy at least half of the space (figure 1.2).[28] In the *ILN*'s inaugural number of 14 May 1842, images occupy at least 50 per cent of page space in only 19 per cent of the number's sixteen pages. Most of the *ILN*'s pages are therefore spatially dominated by text. A random sampling of editorial content from regular *ILN* numbers of every decade (i.e., non-supplementary, non-special weekly issues) demonstrates that the spatial presence of pictures in the *ILN* increased significantly over the course of the nineteenth century. By the 1880s, four decades after the *ILN* had first appeared, the proportion of image to text in the magazine had almost equalized, marking the beginning of pictorial news journalism's second birth. In a sample number from 10 January 1880, images occupy at least 50 per cent of page space on 42 per cent of the number's twenty-four pages. All 42 per cent of these image-heavy pages are exclusively pictorial: at this stage of its development, the *ILN*'s printing technology allowed for large pictures, but these were often segregated from text for printing ease.

Ten years later, images predominated in the pages of the *ILN*. In a sample number, from 11 January 1890, pictures occupy at least half of the page in 63 per cent of the number's pages. By this time, the *ILN* frequently integrated photomechanically reproduced and wood-engraved pictures inset in various ways in columns of type. Even the text-heavy pages often included one or more illustrations. The greater frequency and page occupancy of images attest to the *ILN*'s increasing reliance on the visual representation of news topics, as well as its increasing use of pictorial advertisements (discussed in more depth in chapter 2).

By the turn of the century, pictorial matter had eclipsed text on the printed pages of a weekly issue. In a sample number of the *ILN*, printed on 13 January 1900, images occupy at least half the space in 76 per cent of thirty-eight pages. The presence of visuals increased throughout the early years of the twentieth century: in the number for 12 January 1907, for example, images occupy at least half the space in 85 per cent of forty pages.

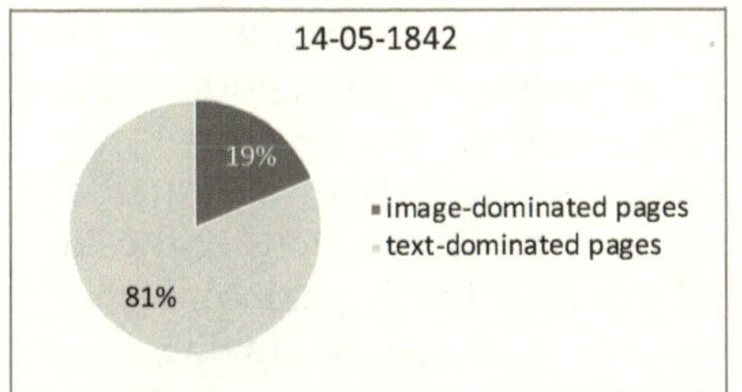

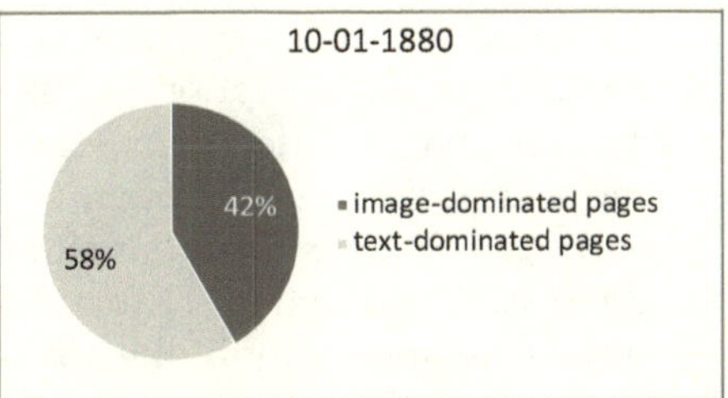

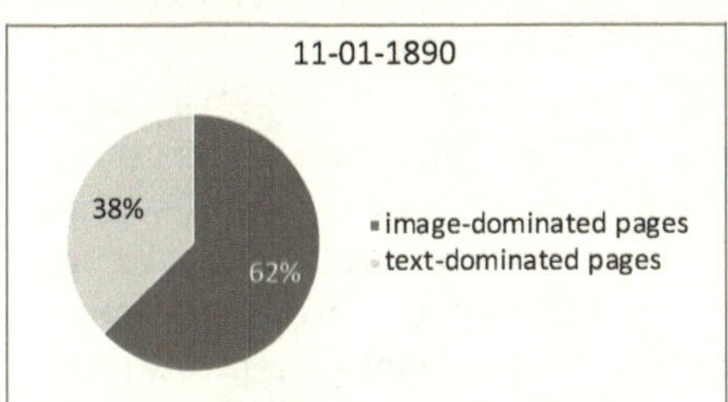

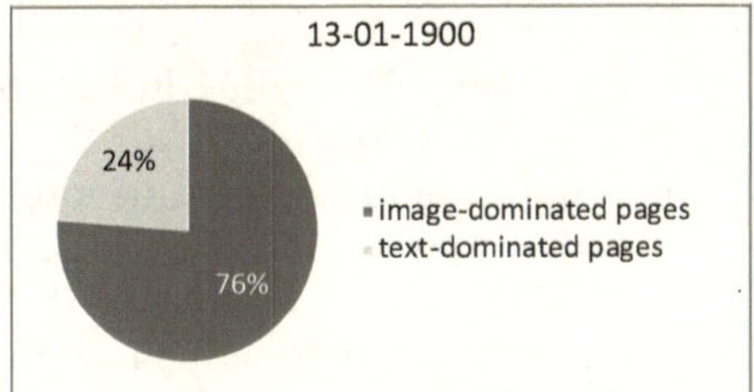

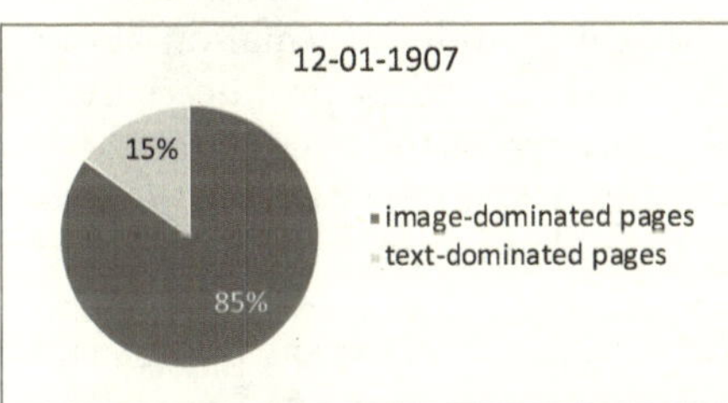

Figure 1.2. Visualization depicting the ratio of illustration to letterpress in the *Illustrated London News*, 1842–1907. The dark-grey area of each pie chart represents the number of pages in which images occupy at least 50 per cent of page space. The light-grey area represents the number of pages in which letterpress occupies at least 50 per cent of page space.

Indeed, quantitative analysis of the *Graphic*'s text-to-image ratio between 1870 and 1900, conducted by Paul Fyfe and Qian Ge, suggests that this trend extends beyond the *ILN* to other major illustrated news weeklies.[29] The marked increase in the *ILN*'s visuality between 1842, when only 19 per cent of pages were substantially pictorial, and 1907, when 85 per cent of pages were substantially pictorial, affirms the news weekly's transition from emergence to advent by the early twentieth century.

Tracking the *ILN*'s use of verbal apparatuses to support reader interpretation of images offers another way to trace the development of pictorial news media. Throughout the nineteenth century, *ILN* images appeared within a contextual verbal framework that typically included a headline and a caption. An issue's top editorial, news, and supplemental images, often showcased as full-page pictures, required even more exposition in the form of an article. These articles appeared as early as the *ILN*'s first year (for example, "Our Illustrations of the Afghan War," printed on 11 June 1842). Even after the magazine's second birth was underway in the 1880s and pictures began occupying more space than did letterpress, the *ILN* continued to rely on such explanatory summaries to supplement its visual information.

For a time, beginning in the 1890s, such exposition was formalized into a regular feature, "Our Illustrations" – an elaborate editorial apparatus to help readers interpret pictorial news and situate it within broader biographical, geographical, technological, and political contexts. This feature addressed the events depicted in a number's most prominent pictures, which might be full-page images or multi-page series of smaller images depicting aspects of the same news item. In a given number, "Our Illustrations" might include information about the circumstances in which the *ILN*'s special artists produced their sketches; the historical or political significance of the events depicted; and a description of what, exactly, is happening in the pictures. For example, during the Second Boer War, "Our Illustrations" often included commentary on the war's developments as well as narratives of the circumstances resulting in the scenes depicted in the *ILN*'s pages. The iteration of the feature for 9 September 1899 explains the South African Republic's ongoing preparations for battle. It outlines the typical conscription and training process, mentioning details that appear in a double-page illustration of conscripted soldiers meeting on horseback in a marketplace.[30] The narrative oscillates between general observations about the war and particulars of the illustrated scene, encouraging readers to interpret illustrations as faithful depictions of specific events and symbolic representations of larger patterns beyond the documentary scope of a pictorial weekly. The article also provides more detailed information about the illustration's temporal, geographic, and political contexts than the double-page image's caption can provide.

"Our Illustrations" reveals an underlying logic that was at work in the *ILN* for most of the nineteenth century: the larger the visual range and detail of an illustration, the greater the verbal apparatus required for its interpretation. But this logic was already waning by the time the feature was formalized in the early 1890s; the increasing predominance of images was not accompanied by a corresponding increase in verbal apparatuses per number. Tellingly, "Our Illustrations" quickly died out, disappearing from the *ILN* in 1903.

The *Coronation and Procession* Number: Showcasing the Spectacular

The changing text-to-image ratio and use of verbal apparatuses show that the *ILN*'s reliance on letterpress to aid pictorial interpretation gradually diminished at the turn of the twentieth century. The magazine increasingly used images to convey most of the information, with text playing a comparatively minor role. The *ILN*'s *Coronation and Procession* number, published on 14 August 1902, exemplifies this shift. *ILN* special numbers such as this one contained larger quantities of images than regular numbers did and were often the inaugural sites of new journalistic practices, visual or otherwise.[31] In the case of the *Coronation and Procession* number, this innovation involved undermining established journalistic practices by using few verbal apparatuses to aid the interpretation of complex images.

The *Coronation and Procession* number documents the coronation of King Edward VII on 9 August 1902, serving as a counterpart to the *ILN*'s *Coronation Record Number* published in June of that year. The two numbers are part of a succession of special publications that the *ILN* published throughout its run to commemorate auspicious royal milestones. In terms of their form and subject matter, the nineteenth-century commemorative numbers shared much in common with other *ILN* special publications of the same era. For example, the thirty-four-page Golden Jubilee number of 1887 was similar in format to the *ILN*'s annual Summer and Christmas special numbers, interweaving long columns of text about the history of Britain and its monarchy with images ranging from small initial letters to full-page portraits and advertisements. The fifty-eight-page Diamond Jubilee number of 1897 was a more elaborate publication, combining colour decorations and illustrations with full pages of text. Just as the *ILN*'s Summer and Christmas numbers focused on entertainment instead of news, the 1887 and 1897 jubilee numbers recounted Queen Victoria's life and reign, rather than reporting on the actual events by which they were occasioned. The rites of the royal jubilees were depicted in the *ILN*'s regular numbers. The *Coronation Record Number* published in June 1902 upholds the conventions evident in the Victorian jubilee publications, celebrating King Edward's coronation with an overview of British coronation history and its ceremonies.[32] However, the *Coronation and Procession* number breaks with tradition, combining the pomp of an auspicious royal milestone with extensive on-site reporting that is primarily visual in nature.

Under a blue-and-red cover, the *Coronation and Procession* number is made up of twenty-four full-page illustrations, bookended by advertisements, and concluding with a double-page, pull-out image. Each page depicts a stage of Edward VII's procession from Buckingham Palace to Westminster Cathedral; his coronation at Westminster Abbey; and his triumphant return to the palace as Britain's formally inaugurated sovereign. Unusually for the time, the number exclusively uses halftone reproductions of artwork created by the magazine's top special artists to document these scenes. By 1902, photographs reproduced by the halftone process had become the magazine's primary image type. The work of special artists had been the mainstay of news illustration until wood-engraving was supplanted by photomechanical processes in the 1890s; by the time the *Coronation and Procession* number was published, artwork was usually reserved for non-news features such as fiction and supplements. The *ILN*'s choice to report on a news story exclusively through artist-rendered images at this time aesthetically conveyed the historic event's import and linked the traditions of Britain's monarchy to those of its popular print culture. Each image is signed by its artist, sometimes prominently. A more explicit effort to draw attention to the number's celebration of both monarchic and journalistic tradition can be found on the first page of editorial content, which boasts that the images are the work of the *ILN*'s top special artists: "NOTE. – The Illustrations for this Number have been specially drawn by R. Caton Woodville, A. Forestier, Ralph Cleaver, T. Walter Wilson, R.I., S. Begg, A.M. Faulkner, Allan, Stewart, and others, our Special Artists in the Abbey and on the line of route."[33]

The detailed images interact with supplemental titles and captions to convey the aspects of the coronation and procession deemed most significant by the artists and editors of the *ILN*. The illustrations draw attention to the most important figures and activities of each scene through detailed documentation, particularly of faces, clothing, setting architecture, and ritual accoutrement such as the royal orb, staff, and crown. Where featured, the faces of the king and queen are recorded in particular detail. The titles and captions add various kinds of context for the pictures, ranging from temporal and geospatial to sensory. For example, the image on the third page, by Richard Caton Woodville, depicts a royal coach surrounded by guards on horseback; against a backdrop of trees, foot soldiers stand at attention nearby. The image title offers context for this scene and names the carriage's invisible occupants: "The Start of the Coronation Procession: Their Majesties in Their State Coach Leaving Buckingham Palace." The subsequent caption identifies the groups surrounding the coach as a "bodyguard of Colonial and Indian cavalry and the first division of the Sovereign's escort of Royal Horse Guards."[34] This supplementary information guides readers' exploration of the pictures. Although such use of letterpress was familiar to the *ILN*'s regular readers through apparatuses such as "Our Illustrations," it is used more sparingly in the *Coronation and Procession* number.

The *Coronation and Procession* number's images are composed so that readers look upon each scene from the point of view of a spectator positioned on a balcony, a stand, or the ground near the event's main action. The contextual letterpress makes each visual story a more tangible approximation of first-hand experience. For example, the caption for an image by Woodville of the coronation procession's aides-de-camp reads: "The Nobility of India in the Empire's Coronation Procession: The Indian Honorary Aides-De-Camp to the King Passing Up St. James' Street ... This drawing was made from the stand in front of the Royal Societies Club."[35] Londoners could draw on their own visual knowledge of St. James's Street to reconstruct this stage of the procession, albeit through the gaze of the *ILN*'s special artist looking out from the Royal Societies Club.

Although the *Coronation and Procession* number evokes the interwoven traditions of Victorian society and print culture, this publication ultimately showcases not only King Edward's coronation but also the *ILN*'s transition away from the letterpress orientation of Victorian print journalism. Compared to the *ILN*'s previous numbers, special and regular alike, this publication is most distinctive for its reliance on graphical representation. Image titles and captions of a few explanatory lines constitute the only text in the otherwise wholly pictorial contents.

Fully embracing spectacularity, the *Coronation and Procession* number underscores one of the coronation's major cultural functions, to make a grand show of British imperial power. Each page of the number remediates a display of ritual pomp carried out by agents of the British Empire and lauded by cheering crowds. The captions reinforce this spectacle by describing the trappings of ceremony in luxurious detail (for example, the king's stagecoach is drawn by "eight cream-coloured horses in their gorgeous trappings of scarlet and gold") and non-visual sensory information essential to the impact of the display (for example, the "boom of salute from the Tower," cheering multitudes, and trumpeting fanfare).[36] Unsurprisingly, the nation's aristocracy and its religious and political leadership are positioned in the centre of the imperial spectacle. Illustrations depict members of the upper class in detail, while rendering anonymous guards and crowds as vaguely homogenous. The captions consistently emphasize social status, signalling the importance of individuals and groups by listing their complete titles and offering contextual information about their contributions to the glory of the British Empire.

By using pictorial exhibition to recreate the coronation procession's spectacle of imperial power, the *ILN*'s procession number underscored the potency of pictorial journalism's increasingly visual orientation. A promotional page at the end of the issue extends this work by drawing attention to the number's storytelling techniques. The page functions as both supplement and advertisement, offering a final overview of the *Coronation and Procession* number while encouraging readers to purchase the complementary *Coronation Record Number*. Tellingly, the supplement describes the latter's mode of expression as "a popular and interesting pictorial method."[37] While the promotional page does not elaborate on the nature of this method, the preceding pages embody its outputs.[38]

As modelled by the *Coronation and Procession* number, this "popular and interesting pictorial method" epitomizes some of illustrated journalism's long-standing techniques: it assembles detailed news images with additional context, relayed in titles and captions, to record the sequence of the coronation procession and to place readers within each scene. At the same time that it establishes a high watermark of Victorian illustrated journalism, the *Coronation and Procession* number exemplifies the visually oriented, multimodal storytelling that was gaining prominence in regular numbers and transforming the practices of weekly illustrated news. The number requires no text-heavy editorial apparatus. Although the captions provide some contextual information, they also encourage readers to focus on pictorial details and relate the illustrations to their own embodied visual experience. The number's opening and closing pronouncements draw readers' attention to the confluence of the reproduction methods and journalistic practices that produced it. Through this range of techniques the *Coronation and Procession* number both responded to and stoked a popular enthusiasm for visual culture, showcasing a public spectacle in a format that was itself spectacular to advance illustrated journalism's visual mandate. The number self-referentially signposts its sophisticated use of images, increasing the visibility not only of the *ILN*'s pictorial news but also of visual storytelling itself.

The dominance of visual storytelling in the *Coronation and Procession* number in 1902 and the demise of "Our Illustrations" in 1903 suggest that, by the turn of the century, illustrated journalism's readers no longer required advanced verbal exposition to interpret images. For a time, "Our Note Book" absorbed the other contextual functions of "Our Illustrations" by including condensed overviews of the historical, political, or cultural context of a number's most prominent image series. However, by 1907, "Our Note Book" had largely ceased to offer commentary on the *ILN* pictures.

For most news images from 1903 onward, titles and short captions offered adequate verbal supplements to aid a reader's visual interpretation. The pictures themselves conveyed much information through visual detail and their proximity to related contents. Where an image may have lacked meaningful context on its own, the *ILN* used layout strategies such as placing the picture close to another pertinent news item. For example, a page of the 13 April 1907 *ILN* presents a wash-drawing portrait by Samuel Begg, depicting a cabinet minister, Lewis Harcourt, addressing the House of Commons, surrounded by a border containing pen-and-ink sketches that catalogued his various physical poses at the scene of his legislative duties (figure 1.3).[39] A brief caption describes Harcourt's position within the cabinet. Across from this page, a snippet of "The World's News in Brief" verbally introduces the new cabinet minister by declaring, "Mr. Lewis Harcourt has disproved the popular belief that a humorous speaker can never get on in the House of Commons." The remainder of the snippet does not unpack this declaration, instead praising Harcourt's leadership abilities and noting that he has "followed the prevailing fashion of marrying a beautiful American."[40] The limited verbal information about Harcourt's "humorous" speaking meant that readers had to depend on the image on the facing page to interpret the news item. Without explicit pointing, then, the snippet and the illustration evidently inform one another; the tidbit from "The World's News in Brief" offers context about the picture of the new cabinet minister, while the image conveys information about Harcourt's body language that cannot be captured in a few lines of copy.

"Stories without Words" and the Disappearance of Illustrated Fiction

Tracing the comparative roles of image and text in the *ILN*'s fiction offers another way of profiling the magazine's transition in its regular numbers to an autonomous medium. Between the early 1880s and the turn of the century, the *ILN* was "among the most prestigious metropolitan outlets" for illustrated serial and short fiction.[41] Fiction typically occupied two full pages or six columns of letterpress, interspersed with up to three illustrations that took up 10–40 per cent of the page space allotted to this feature. Some illustrations doubled as decorative headers that incorporated the title's text in a relevant landscape or background that might be populated by the story's characters. Other illustrations depicted key moments in the story, such as a first encounter, a conversation, or a confrontation. A caption excerpted from the story's text appeared below each picture to signal its context; on their own these images are semantically cryptic, yielding little information about the story's plot unless read in tandem with the verbal narrative. For example, F.H. Townsend's illustrations for "The Planters," by Shan Bullock

THE MANNERISM OF THE MEMBER.—I.: THE TWENTIETH CABINET MINISTER

DRAWN BY OUR SPECIAL ARTIST, S. BEGG.

THE NEW CABINET MINISTER

S. BEGG

THE RIGHT HON. LEWIS HARCOURT, M.P., FIRST COMMISSIONER OF WORKS, RECENTLY PROMOTED TO CABINET RANK.

Figure 1.3. Samuel Begg, "The New Cabinet Minister." Halftone and line-block illustration, *Illustrated London News*, 13 April 1907, 550.

(1897), depicts an expressive trio of characters without suggesting the nature of their fraught interactions with one another. Townsend's illustration encapsulates the social dynamics between its three main characters and visually reinforces the emotional distress of Lizzie, the female figure in the foreground.[42] However, without a caption linking each image to a specific moment in the story, the significance of the illustrations would remain opaque. Only by reading the letterpress can Lizzie's expression be recognized as evidence of her longing for a marriage proposal from one of the image's other subjects.[43]

As the semantic role of Townsend's illustration suggests, the *ILN*'s illustrated fiction consistently privileged the expressive power of letterpress over that of images. Available evidence indicates that this verbal orientation was a contributing factor in the demise of *ILN* fiction after the second birth of the illustrated news weekly. In the 1880s and 1890s the *ILN* published serial and short fiction in almost every regular number, as well as all Summer and Christmas numbers. The magazine's inclusion of illustrated stories became more erratic in the early 1900s. By 1906, fiction required more sustained attention to letterpress from the reader than did any other feature in the *ILN* – not because fiction's format had changed but because all other content had. The verbal orientation of fictional narrative made the genre inconsistent with the *ILN*'s changing conventions for expression. Tellingly, the last appearance of fiction in a regular number of the *ILN* was at the end of December 1906. By no coincidence did the first number of 1907, discussed at the opening of this chapter, unveil a new, more pictorial look for the *ILN*, at the same time that it silently ceased to publish fiction. These developments assured the dominance of visual storytelling over verbal narrative in the illustrated news magazine.

"Great Novelists' Suggestions for Stories without Words"

Just prior to the *ILN*'s aesthetic pivot in January 1907, an item titled "Great Novelists' Suggestions for Stories without Words," appearing in the 1906 Christmas number, modelled an innovative approach to fiction that aligned with the magazine's increasing use of visual, multimodal storytelling. Although this approach was not adopted in regular numbers of the *ILN*, "Stories without Words" presents instructive evidence of how a visual orientation prompted the *ILN*'s staff to push the boundaries of convention – in this case, by subverting established rules for constructing illustrated fiction. Like the *Coronation and Procession* number, "Stories without Words" uses interpretive pictorial techniques that significantly depart from previous conventions of pictorial journalism, fostering readers' awareness of mediation in the process. The *Coronation and Procession* number uses visual storytelling to cover a major news story, King Edward's coronation, whereas "Stories without Words" uses it to reconfigure illustrated magazine fiction.

"Stories without Words" employs the recognizable talents of the *ILN*'s artists and short-fiction authors to showcase a series of scenes depicting adventure, mystery, and love plots. Ten full-page images are followed by two pages of corresponding notes that offer highlights of each story's plot. Image titles and captions, as well as the notes corresponding to the scenes, are the work of several "famous novelists." These include authors previously published in the *ILN*'s regular numbers, such as Mayne Lindsay, Flora Annie Steel, Max Pemberton, and Seumas MacManus. The special feature's images are the work of artists who are also familiar to readers as illustrators of the *ILN's* fiction, including W. Russell Flint and Gunning King, as well as R. Caton Woodville and Amédée Forestier, who illustrated the *Coronation and Procession* number.

Like the short-story illustrations in the *ILN*, the images of "Stories without Words" are tonal artworks reproduced by the halftone process. Each one depicts a salient moment of action or discovery in a fictional story. For example, the first page of the series displays Woodville's dramatic image of sailors trying to free their boat from the clutches of a frozen sea. The page's header, "Walter Wood's Suggestion for a Story without Words," appears in bold above; the picture's title, "Foiled by King Frost," and a caption appear below (figure 1.4).[44] A chaotic jumble of bodies in action is the picture's focus; the sides of the boat appear near the periphery. Little image space is devoted to the sea itself, although the strange tilt of the boat, relative to the other ship and the frame of the image, suggests a violent storm. More prominent than the sea is a thick layer of ice that has covered the boat's entire surface; the men struggle to wrench the treacherous-looking shards away from their vessel. At the bottom of the page the ice has subsumed not only the boat's exterior but also the legs of a crewman who, as the largest figure in the image, offers a compositional focal point. Partly visible in the left foreground, another sailor holds a bucket of what appears to be steaming water; he is poised to counteract as the ice threatens to envelop his comrade. The interaction of the two men encapsulates the dangerous conflict between humanity and natural phenomenon – personified, in the picture's title, as King Frost – that is thematically central to this image.

The note for "Foiled by King Frost," written, as the header for this image suggests, by the author and journalist Walter Wood, offers a narrative fragment that begins at the moment depicted in the image and reveals the conclusion to its central conflict.[45] Wood's text takes the point

Figure 1.4. R. [Richard] Caton Woodville, "Foiled by King Frost." Halftone illustration for "Stories without Words," *Illustrated London News Christmas Number*, December 1906, 20.

of view of a crewman on the steamboat depicted in the upper-right corner of the picture. This narrator relates the struggle of the smaller ship's crew to wrest it free of ice, which culminates in the vessel's envelopment by the "towering, broken sea." The crewman ominously concludes that "Death, whose pace is swift ... has run the faster race."[46]

The meaning of "Foiled by King Frost" emerges from the interaction of the image and the text, supplemented by details that each mode offers independently and by the readers' imaginations. While Wood presents readers with the story's climax and dénouement, his note leaves much of its exposition and rising action to readers, including only a handful of contextual details – for example, the sea is described as the "Dogger," which may be shorthand for the Dogger Bank of the North Sea. Interestingly, although Wood focalizes the story from the perspective of a rescuing crewman on the steamboat, Woodville centres the action on those in the frost-gripped ship. Readers had ample visual information with which to imagine their own narrative counterpart to Wood's note, taking the perspective of one of the ill-fated individuals on the icy ship. Wood's note thus supplements Woodville's image without over-determining how readers could interpret it.

Like the *ILN*'s illustrated fiction, "Stories without Words" presents images of pivotal narrative moments, reproduced from tonal artwork by the halftone process. Crucially, although image type, style, authorship, and function made for continuities between the *ILN*'s short fiction and "Stories without Words," the latter flips the dynamic between words and pictures. The notes appearing after the images in "Stories without Words" supplement the pictures' visual narratives with brief, fragmentary verbal narratives; in this sense, the words illustrate the images.

This relationship is underscored by the relative presence of the verbal and the visual on the magazine's pages: the article's full-page pictures precede the notes and take up more page space by a ratio of five to one. Even the notes section has prominent visual elements in the form of ornamental headers and decorative borders. Just as importantly, the presentation sequence and the relative page space of letterpress and image reinforce that, as the feature's title suggests, pictures are the main means of narrative expression. The ten-page image series requires no textual introduction aside from a simple heading: the first image, for Walter Wood's story, constitutes the first page.[47] Readers could infer the feature's logic by perusing the image series and by heeding an instruction at the end of each image caption to see a corresponding note on a subsequent page.

In its format, then, "Stories without Words" significantly differed from that of the *ILN*'s fiction. Typically, fiction's illustrations served to pique a reader's interest, conveying excitement and drama without giving away the story. Using the caption of each image as a guide for locating the pertinent moment in the story, a reader had to engage with the text to interpret the illustrations' significance. In contrast, the pictures of "Stories without Words" are imbued with primary narrative significance. The images are interpretively rich, enticing readers with many narratively revealing details. Letterpress is demoted to a supplementary mode of expression: each image's meaning has only slight dependence on the verbal support offered by the captions and following notes. Indeed, the relationship between the feature's two parts – the images and the notes – bears some similarity to the relationship between "Our Illustrations" and the news images in a regular *ILN* number. "Our Illustrations" added context to news images and offered an interpretive key. The notes for "Stories without Words" similarly inform the visual storytelling; however, because the images appeared before the notes, readers (at least, those who read the pages in a conventional sequence) had an opportunity to rely chiefly on pictorial interpretation before turning to the letterpress for contextual details.

In terms of its interpretive functionality, "Stories without Words" had the additional effect of facilitating readers' awareness of medium and mediation in two ways. First, by flipping the conventional dynamic between text and image, the article defamiliarized illustrated fiction, prompting readers to reassess the relationship between words and images in this periodical genre. Second, the separation of the verbal and pictorial constituents of storytelling effectively made each mode's affordances more visible to readers. While the notes provided background context that the images could not easily include, such as information about earlier or later events, the pictures provided most of the expressive details, such as tone and characterization, that shaped the stories. In the following years the *ILN* fostered this awareness of mediation through its increasingly spectacular aesthetics and complex communicative modes.

Photomechanical Images and Hybrid Aesthetics

The *Coronation and Procession* number and "Stories without Words" show just how pictorial news periodicals could be, thanks to the production scale and affordability of mass image-reproduction technology. A related development not evident in these examples was the diversification of visuals produced with the new print technology. The artist-produced wash-drawing method used for both the *Coronation and Procession* number and "Stories without Words" was just one of the many styles and types of images made possible by the photomechanical reproduction process. The expanding aesthetic range that photomechanical technology afforded was essential to the advent of illustrated journalism as an autonomous medium.[48]

Gaudreault and Marion note that a proto-medium undergoes its second, "distinguishing" birth once it has developed a unique way "of re-presenting, expressing and communicating the world."[49] For popular and avant-garde magazines alike, this process involved expanding the range and registers of graphical content. Magazines could reproduce fine art and photographs without the intervention of a wood-engraver's hand; at the same time, the art and craft of drawing images specifically for mass reproduction reached new levels of nuance, thanks to artists such as Phil May and Aubrey Beardsley. For illustrated news weeklies, the *ILN* foremost among them, the distinguishing second birth involved subverting print culture's hierarchy of text and image while also, like other late-Victorian illustrated periodicals, developing aesthetic practices that took advantage of the affordances of photomechanical reproduction. Halftone images from photographs became the *ILN*'s preferred form for visual news reporting, although line-block images continued to relay important news about events that were too rapid or volatile to be photographed. The *ILN* also used halftone images that reproduced artwork for certain kinds of content, particularly non-news entertainment features. Whether for news events or entertainment articles, the *ILN* used photomechanically reproduced images to convey both immediacy and mediality. These capacities sometimes contradicted and sometimes complemented one another; both were major facets of the unique aesthetic character that the *ILN* developed during its second birth, and both engaged readers' technological imagination.

Tracking image types in the *ILN* between 1880 and 1907 demonstrates the impact of photomechanical image reproduction on illustrated periodical media. As the *ILN* adopted the technology, the number and aesthetic variety of pictures in the news weekly increased. This is borne out by statistics on image types taken through the random sampling of issues (figure 1.5). Line-block and halftone images had almost entirely displaced wood-engraving in the *ILN* and virtually all other popular illustrated periodicals by 1900.

Although all types of halftone prints appealed to *ILN* producers and readers, halftones from photographs emerged as the preferred image form in the early twentieth century. Tom Gretton estimates that, by 1900, halftone images made up 93 per cent of all the *ILN*'s pictures; in 1910 this number had risen to 98 per cent.[50] The visualizations of *ILN* image-type

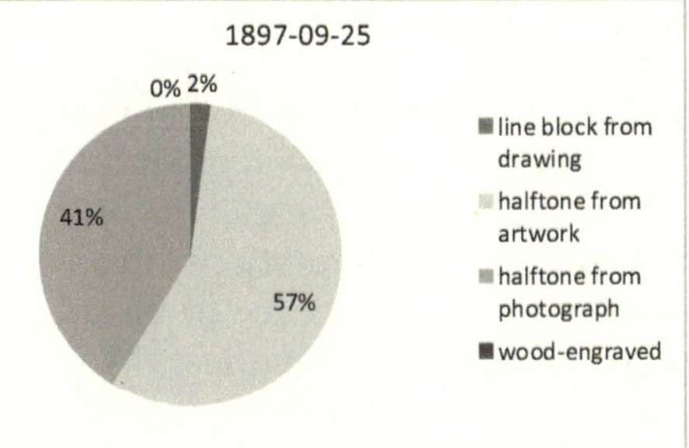

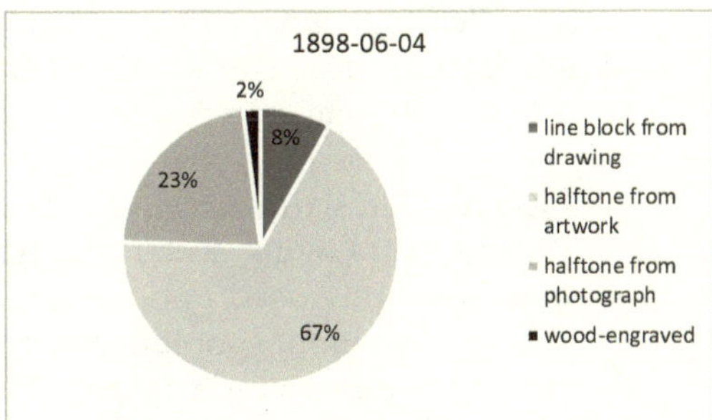

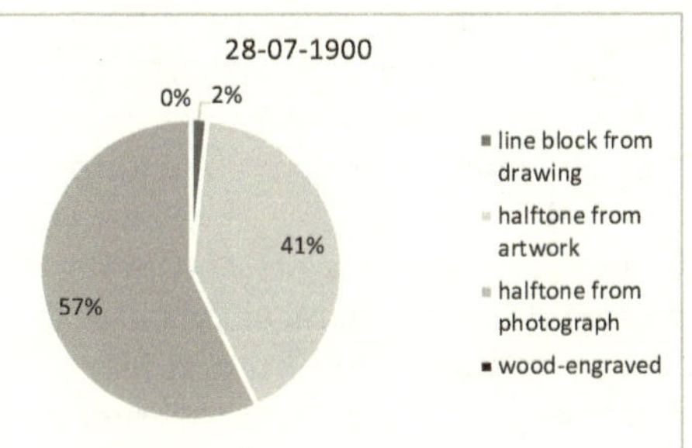

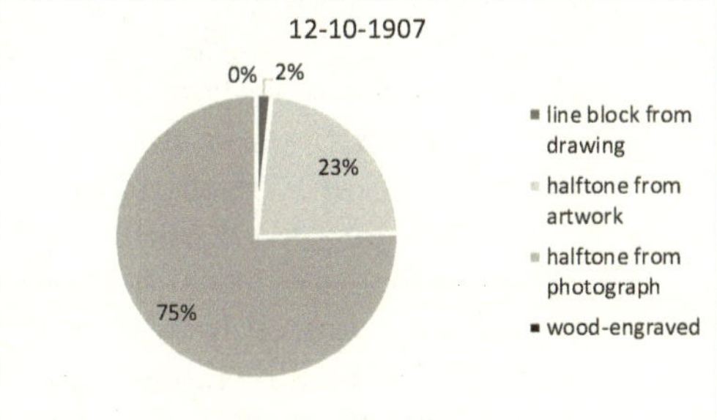

Figure 1.5. Visualization depicting the ratio of different types of images used in the *Illustrated London News*, 1897–1900 and 1907. Statistics were taken from random samples.

frequency in figure 2.5, taken from a random sampling between 1897 and 1907, suggest that the majority of halftone images were reproduced from photographs, although halftone images from artwork maintained a modest presence. The visualizations indicate that the *ILN* made little use of line-block images by the late 1890s, although these remained popular in less news-based periodicals, such as monthly miscellanies, and appeared more frequently to reproduce news-correspondent sketches during wartime. For example, in 1898, during the Second Boer War, the figure graph shows a slightly higher ratio of line-block images from special artists' drawings, and a lower ratio of halftone images from photographs. During this period, as Gretton notes, full- and double-page images reproducing work by *ILN* artists were still valued as editorial enhancements and supplements.[51] However, photograph-based news images far outnumbered images reproduced from artwork in a typical *ILN* number. By 1906, even the covers of *ILN* numbers included halftone images reproduced from photographs.[52] This public-facing display signalled the centrality of photographic halftones to the practice of illustrated journalism and the *ILN* brand.

Halftone images reproduced from photographs did not necessarily undermine the long-championed representational capacities of an *ILN* special artist's drawings, but they offered different advantages and affordances. Owing to technological and logistical limitations, news weeklies rarely used photography-based images as a source of visual information about spontaneous or chaotic events, such as battles.[53] Well into the twentieth century, reproductions of actual battles continued to be line-block and halftone reproductions of artwork, rather than reproductions of photographs, perhaps due to the limited capacity of turn-of-the-century cameras to capture precise images of moving action.[54] However, the weeklies used images from photographs to document more predictable and stable news subjects, such as military encampments, cultural events, and celebrity portraits.

Readers perceived both line-block and halftone images as having unique representational authority because photomechanical processes rapidly reproduced images of news events, with limited human intervention. As Lorraine Janzen Kooistra has noted, before the pictorial press adopted photomechanical reproduction on a large scale, those images of current events at which a special artist was not present were often "remediated verbal descriptions, rather than eye-witness reportage."[55] Once illustrated journals could print photographically reproduced images, stored visual news data could quickly be reproduced without an intermediate verbal report. Halftone reproductions of photographic images used a method of data inscription and storage that readers perceived as complementary to the line-block reproductions of a special artist's rapid, on-site, visual reportage. Photomechanical line-block engraving, suggests Gerry Beegan, appeared to offer a "direct conduit" for "an artist's individual vision" – including the vision of a special artist on site – by "removing the interpretive hand of the engraver."[56] Used in combination, photomechanical line-block and halftone processes closed what Kooistra describes as a "temporal disjunction" between the images and the texts of pictorial news during the era of wood-engraved reproduction.[57] The *ILN*'s use of images reproduced by these rapid and direct processes therefore boosted the weekly's journalistic authority in the eyes of readers.

While the *ILN* deployed halftone and line-block images to reinforce the sense of proximity to world events conveyed in its news reports, it also used them to invoke the hybridity of modern society, a technique appearing in many illustrated periodicals at this time. The use of multiple image and reproduction types resulted in aesthetic assemblages that reflected the diverse socio-technological "amalgamations" of modern life.[58] In this way, the *ILN*'s codes of expression imbued its content with a contradictory but ever-present subtext of immediacy (direct or near-direct contact between reader and subject matter) and mediation (the material conditioning of this contact by industrial practices). Both aspects of the *ILN*'s visually oriented, multimodal storytelling evoked the technological zeitgeist of modernity. The *ILN*'s aesthetic sense of immediacy suggested the simultaneity made possible, in the nineteenth century, by rapid transit and communication technology such as the railroad and the telegraph. The magazine's aesthetic sense of mediation resonated with the mechanization of culture wrought by industrialization.

In the *ILN*, hybridity manifested in the diversity of picture and ornamentation styles. Reader interpretation of *ILN* contents involved registering a wide array of image types, whether consciously or unconsciously. Through their diverse aesthetics, the images resonated with other hybrid facets of late-Victorian visual culture. For example, in the *ILN* number for 5 January 1907, the ornate header for the "Art Music & the Drama" [*sic*] page interweaves halftones from photographs and wash-drawings to invoke aesthetic authority (figure 1.6). The header includes the feature title, photographic portraits of some of the week's performing actors and artists, and small, artist-drawn fragments of society scenes set within a decorative frame. The halftone photographic portraits, reminiscent of cartes-de-visite, remediate the physical data that was photographically gathered from actual performances and sittings, evoking a trace of each celebrity's presence. The wash-drawings of historical art appreciation relate modern London's arts scene to upper-class traditions, suggesting continuity between *ILN* readers and historical aristocratic audiences. An art nouveau border frames traditional arts appreciation and current arts reviews within modern print aesthetics, emphasizing the *ILN*'s authority on cultural taste. Through such deliberate assemblages of varied images, the *ILN* aligned the illustrated weekly's personality with the sensibilities of contemporary life.[59]

New Media and Mediation in "Fairy Stories by Photography"

Conveying both immediacy and mediality in its diversifying array of images and layouts, the *ILN* exemplifies how illustrated periodicals reconstituted themselves as a new media outside the framework of non-pictorial journalism. The *ILN*'s hybrid, multimodal aesthetics also demonstrate how this second birth enabled pictorial print media to take on a unique role within the turn-of-the-century new media milieu:

ART MUSIC & THE DRAMA

EXHIBITIONS.

THE sculpture of Signor Medardo Rosso, to be seen at the galleries of Mr. Cremetti in Dover Street, is the most advanced and the most modern of advanced and modern sculpture. But it is a growth, a change, an exaggeration, rather than a discovered and new art. And it may be best understood, indeed Signor Rosso's method will seem most reasonable, if it be approached from the classic standpoint — if it be regarded as the outcome of following to a just conclusion the principle which made the greatest Greek sculptors efface detail in the treatment, for instance, of hair. We take it — this power of effacement—as the sign of a great style. And Signor Rosso has carried the convention of effacement to what to-day we regard as its extreme limits. These limits are the more interesting because he is an artist of extraordinary talent; and that which might be an extreme and annoying mannerism in the work of a lesser sculptor is human and normal in his work, because of his sincerity of aim and his mastery of expression.

Signor Rosso works with a painter's sense of the importance of what the eye sees, rather than with the average sculptor's sense of the importance of what the actual form is, or what the hand could feel. Thus his sculpture will render you the vague look of a face at the far end of a rather dim room; and he is more concerned with what a certain aspect of lighting may make of certain forms than with their actual shape. Thus if his model sits before him in a light beating straight upon her features so that there are few shadows, and consequently little indication of the relief of the features, he will slur those features in his modelling. Such is a crude statement of an elaborate convention, beautifully practised.

Much has been written of Signor Rosso's kinship to M. Rodin, and there has been invented a rivalship between the French master and the Italian. But how little need is there for anything but the peaceful conjunction of two names greatly representing one art and one period, and therefore one development, of that art? And if these two have followed, for some distance, the same path, it is because the way of it has been made

SINDBAD AT DRURY LANE: MISS QUEENIE LEIGHTON.

ABDALLAH AT DRURY LANE: MISS FLORENCE WARDE.

THE GERMAN OPERA.

NOW that we are near enough to the short season of German Opera to have a definite idea of the programme and to consider the work of those who will interpret it, we remark that no really modern composition awaits a hearing. Weber, Beethoven, Smetana, and Wagner are the composers represented. Wagner himself has been dead nearly a quarter of a century, Weber and Beethoven passed away some eighty years ago, and Smetana was a contemporary of Wagner. It is well that "Der Freischutz" and "Fidelio" should be revived, and special interest attaches to the last-named opera because the performance will be conducted by one of the greatest living violinists, Eugène Ysaye. There are many who

THE EMPRESS OF ALL THE SAHARAS AT DRURY LANE: MR. FRED EMNEY.

All the photographs on this page are by the Dover Street Studios.

would call him the greatest player of our time, though he is not heard in London nowadays. Perhaps he finds that our audiences have devoted so much attention to those who have passed and those who have yet to arrive that they cannot spare sufficient for ripe achievement. They are a little intolerant of work that has no suggestion either of undeveloped spring blossom or changing autumn leaf. Of course, Ysaye is a famous conductor; perhaps because he is such a great violinist, he can get wonderful effects from the stringed instruments of an orchestra.

We wish that Peter Cornelius' "Barber of Baghdad" could have been included in the repertory of the coming season. This opera, which is now about forty years old, and shows in every scene the influence of Wagner's methods and teaching, was received with great favour when it was produced in the last spring season at Covent Garden. Only the unfortunate recall to Germany of one of the leading singers kept London from becoming better acquainted with a really fascinating work. The opera is well known to most of the company that is coming to Covent Garden, as it has been mounted no great expense would have been incurred, and it would have made a very welcome and reasonable addition to the programme. "The Barber of Baghdad" was produced in 1858, when "Lohengrin" had been given at Weimar under Liszt, at a time when "Tristan" was nearly finished, but was some seven years removed from performance.

only need working up. The antics of the middle-aged Sindbad's family and friends who from distrust of his stories resolve to share his voyage as disguised members of his crew, the buffooneries of two British tars who fool with an elastic dog and dance a delirious breakdown, the behaviour of the whale on whose back the shipwrecked party camp, the burlesque brutality of the Saharan Empress who sells her guests into captivity, the droll misadventures of would-be passengers who fail to board a motor-'bus—all these laughter-moving elements are going to delight the children when Mr. Passmore feels more at home as Sindbad, when Mr. Randall has got used to the rôle of Mrs. Sindbad—played so well at short notice on Boxing Night by Mr. Arthur Conquest—when Mr. Fragson broadens his methods and relies less on his piano, and when more scope is given to Messrs. Drew and Alders, two most amusingly grotesque comedians. Meantime, Miss Queenie Leighton makes an ideal "principal boy," and Miss Marie George, with two taking songs to sing, is as dainty a pantomime heroine as could be desired.

"THE TREASURE-SHIP," AT THE HIPPODROME.

A truly dazzling spectacle is that which the London Hippodrome management is offering just now in the series of adventures which form the subject of the dramatised story of "The Treasure-Ship in Fairy Seas." Down to the depths of the ocean the spectator is carried, to be shown a coral cave, divers at work raising a sunken ship, an octopus attacking the divers, mermaids and sea-monsters floating through the expanse of sea, a flying fish ballet performed by the Heiderich troupe of aerial dancers, and curious kaleidoscopic and phosphorescent illuminations of the real water. No scenes so uncommon and so full of imaginative appeal have ever been presented even on the Hippodrome stage, which has quite a reputation for marvellous pictorial effects.

"THE FORTY THIEVES," AT THE CORONET.

Several beautiful stage-pictures, full of the right Oriental colour, claim attention in Mr. Robert Arthur's pantomime of "The Forty Thieves," which was presented on

Figure 1.6. Halftone illustration for "Art Music & the Drama" [*sic*]. *Illustrated London News*, 5 January 1907, 56.

illustrated print facilitated the capacity of readers to recognize the physical and aesthetic characteristics commensurate with mediation and, in turn, to assess media critically as such.

The evolution of illustrated print came at a critical time for print culture. A defining feature of the turn of the century was an influx of multimodal, mechanical media, including the hand camera, gramophone, film, and radio. Unlike print, these media did not inscribe, store, and disseminate written language. Not conforming to existing means of expression, they destabilized the media landscape.[60] These technologies also complicated the established understanding of meaning as transcendent, channelled through oral and written language, and commensurate with mimesis.[61] Whereas the words of a printed text gestured towards symbolic meanings, photography, the gramophone, and film functioned by recording and expressing physical phenomena as sensory data.[62] These mechanical media effectively denaturalized the writing process, reducing it to one of many forms of data recording and storage, and challenged the established criteria for evaluating cultural expression.[63]

This challenge to pre-existing views about communication galvanized another defining feature of the turn-of-the-century media milieu: an increasing conceptual awareness among audiences of media and mediation as such. As new media adapted cultural expressions that had previously existed in print and oral forms, they raised collective awareness of communication's materiality. This change of perception engendered the conception of communication media that prevails today.[64] Indeed, the *Oxford English Dictionary* documents various uses of the term *medium* that emerged in the late nineteenth century to describe the materials of a creative or communicative technique and signify a channel of communication.[65] It was shortly thereafter, in the early twentieth century, that the *OED* added the two definitions of *medium* that have become the most widely used in popular Western discourse: "Any of the varieties of painting or drawing as determined by the material or technique used," and a "channel of mass communication, as newspapers, radio, television, etc."[66] Taken together, as John Guillory observes, these definitions of media describe "a domain of cultural production that assimilates the traditional fine arts to the larger category of what later comes to be known as mass communication."[67]

As discussed in the introduction, pictorial journalism initiated readers' media literacy by showcasing periodicals as manufactured objects that exhibited traces of their own production. Throughout the Victorian period, articles on periodical production encouraged readers to view these traces as part of a periodical's meaning, implying that the technologies of production conditioned that meaning. At the turn of the century, the innovations in image reproduction that transformed the aesthetics of print also drew readers' attention more closely to the relationship between visual design and meaning. This factored into reader engagement with all manner of print books and periodicals, ranging from aesthetic little magazines and scientific trade journals to newspapers and general-interest miscellanies. In addition, as the variety, methods, and subject matter of mass image reproduction expanded, cultural attitudes towards pictorial communication became more complex.

I have already discussed how "Stories without Words" drew readers' attention to mediation by subverting the relationship between words and images. Another, particularly rich example of how the *ILN* facilitated readers' awareness of medium and mediation is "Fairy Stories by Photography: Grimm Illustrated," an item from the *ILN*'s 1907 Christmas number. As noted at the outset of this chapter, the first magazine number of January 1907 embodied a significant moment in the *ILN*'s development of unique, hybrid codes of expression for the pictorial news weekly. Demonstrating how the *ILN* adopted a hybrid aesthetic to depict entertainments, as well as news, "Fairy Stories" presents another telling example, from November of the same year. The *Coronation and Procession* number and "Stories without Words" stimulated readers' consciousness of the distinct aesthetic affordances of the *ILN* as an illustrated periodical. By recognizing the techniques that illustrated-magazine producers developed to exploit this pictorial medium, readers were implicated in the weekly's advent as a new medium. "Fairy Stories" advanced this development with aesthetic techniques that made a spectacle of the magazine's *intermediality* – its cross-pollination with other media. Through its use of and relation to other media, "Fairy Stories" encouraged readers to imagine the illustrated periodical as part of the new media milieu.

"Fairy Stories" comprises six full-page images that combine halftone images from photographs and artists' drawings to depict scenes from *Grimms' Fairy Tales,* a cultural wellspring that influenced many nineteenth-century texts and images.[68] Each tale's major character is reproduced in halftone from a photograph and appears at the centre of the scene, carefully posed as the focal point of a fantastic tableau. The scene's peripheral characters and background are rendered through a combination of sketched lines and wash tones.

Like the *Coronation and Procession* number and "Stories without Words," "Fairy Stories" encourages readers to regard images as the primary vectors of meaning. Each picture's tableau encapsulates a central theme or moment of its fairy tale, and the accompanying letterpress sketches the tale's plot points. The images are not given the titles of their respective fairy tales but, rather, descriptions of the moments they depict – for example, "The Prince Climbing the Golden Ladder of Rapunzel's Hair."[69] These titles reference the recognizable fairy-tale titles while framing the pictures as visually salient moments from those tales, rather than as condensed depictions of whole stories. The caption under each title summarizes the plot of the depicted fairy tale but offers little narrative. Most Edwardian readers would have been familiar with these stories; spared the challenge of piecing together a new narrative, they could attend instead to the fairy-tale remediation itself. The images add emotional depth and semantic texture to the familiar tales. Each scene expresses an aesthetically rich moment that foregrounds important aspects of the tale's story – a prince's desire for a beautiful princess, a heroine's care for her brother, the weird calm of an enchanted castle. Presented with a spare plot outline, a pithy image, and prior knowledge of the Grimm Brothers' fairy tales, readers had abundant interpretive material.

"Fairy Stories" advanced the illustrated weekly's second birth with a hybrid aesthetic that used halftone images to explore a new kind of intermediality. According to Gaudreault and Marion, after a medium's advent it loses its former, derivative intermediality and acquires one that reflects its new character. The medium "negotiates" this intermediality in "interaction with its own potential."[70] Victorian periodicals drew on the practices and remediated the contents of many old and new means of expression, from manuscript illumination to oil painting and even older forms of periodical illustration. This range of practices increased dramatically with the introduction of photomechanical technology at the end of the century. [71] "Fairy Stories" leveraged this range to innovative effect, juxtaposing old and new aesthetic techniques to foreground its own unique intermediality.

The feature combines photographs and hand-drawn or painted images, both reproduced by the halftone process, into imaginative composites. The contrast between the photographed foreground figures and the hand-drawn backgrounds is visually striking (figure 1.7). The artist, "A.C.T.," touched up some clothing details of each photographed figure and added shading to integrate these figures in the drawn scenes. The dark, heavily graded tones of the their faces, skin, and hair are virtually free from such line work, rendering them distinct from the backdrops on which A.C.T.'s pencil sketched fine outlines and shadows over light-grey tones.

Given illustrated journalism's long-standing practice of documenting its own production processes, many readers of "Fairy Stories"

FAIRY STORIES BY PHOTOGRAPHY: GRIMM ILLUSTRATED.

THE PRINCE CLIMBING THE GOLDEN LADDER OF RAPUNZEL'S HAIR.

Once upon a time there lived a poor man and a poor woman, and the woman, coveting the fine lettuces in a sorceress's garden, bade her husband fetch some of them. Now, the sorceress caught the man thieving, but released him on condition that his baby-girl should be given her. This child the witch called Rapunzel, and, as soon as she reached the age of twelve, locked her up in a high tower that had no door, and only one window. When the sorceress wished to enter the tower she stood beneath this window, and croaked "Rapunzel, Rapunzel, let down thy hair that I may climb without a stair," and the beautiful child would unbind her golden tresses, so that the locks hung down the walls of her prison. One day a King's son came into the forest, and saw the witch's strange stairway. Next day he came to the tower again, and sang the rhyme he had heard. In answer to it, the golden ladder was let down, and the Prince climbed up. Love came at first sight, and the pair arranged to escape together. The witch, however, learnt of the Prince's visit, banished Rapunzel, and caused her lover to be blinded. So for a year he wandered in misery. Then he came upon Rapunzel, and her tears, falling upon his eyes, gave him sight. Thus the two were enabled to travel to the Prince's country.

SETTING BY "THE ILLUSTRATED LONDON NEWS"; PHOTOGRAPHS OF MISS VALLI VALLI (RAPUNZEL) AND MISS GLADYS COOPER (THE PRINCE) BY BASSANO.

Figure 1.7. A.C.T., "The Prince Climbing the Golden Ladder of Rapunzel's Hair." Halftone illustration for "Fairy Stories by Photograph: Grimm Illustrated," *Illustrated London News Christmas Number*, December 1907, 24. Courtesy of Clara Thomas Archives and Special Collections, York University.

possessed a print media literacy, detailed in this book's introduction, that contributed to their interpretation of this special feature's intermedial aesthetics. The materiality of the figures in the images attests to their reproduction from photographs of real individuals. Other pictorial and verbal characteristics underscore the technological hybridity of the fairy-tale illustrations, boosting the visibility of their production history. Under each caption is a brief statement giving information about the staging, model(s), and photographer of the original photograph used for the picture – for example, "Setting by 'The Illustrated London News'; Photograph of Miss Gladys Archbutt by Bassano."[72] The art nouveau borders around the pictures are printed in clean lines of green or red that attest to a different original image type (pen and ink) and reproduction method (line block). Perhaps to set off the visual and material differences between the pictures and the borders, the decorative figures that populate the line-engraved borders also thematically differ from those of the fairy stories, more directly invoking the number's Christmas theme.

In addition to its material and technological hybridity, "Fairy Stories" conveys intermediality by imbricating a wide range of old and new media practices and artistic forms. The most prominent visual techniques manifest in this special feature – halftone images from photographs and artists' drawings – were associated with conventional illustrated journalism, but they also borrowed from illustrated fiction, ephemera, scrapbooks, photography, and various performance arts. Like fiction illustration, most of the pictures in "Fairy Stories" focus on moments of interaction between two characters, emphasizing individualizing details such as facial expressions and physical gestures. Like illustrations for fairy tales and romance fiction specifically, the images in "Fairy Stories" depict their alternate worlds in elaborate detail, underscoring the narrative's removal from a contemporary British context.[73] The aesthetics of "Fairy Stories" also evoke the medium of the Victorian scrapbook; the pictures of this special article can be classified as photocollage, or the practice of combining photographs with typography and non-photographic imagery.[74] Photocollage was a familiar aesthetic of mainstream culture by this time, though news weeklies such as the *ILN* made little use of it normally.

"Fairy Stories" invoked, in addition to illustrations and scrapbooks, contemporary forms of photographic manipulation practised by professionals and elite amateurs. The pictures of this article bear some resemblance to spirit photography: like the artist-drawn settings and background figures, the fantastical figures of spirit photographs appeared lighter and more ethereal than the sitters in the foreground, an effect often created through double exposure.[75] However, many viewers believed that spirit photography documented real phenomena, whereas the "Fairy Stories" pictures are framed as fictitious.[76] In this regard, the article resembles the mid-century composite photography of Oscar Gustav Rejlander and Henry Peach Robinson, who assembled figures and sections of multiple photographs to create artistic pictures (see figure 1.8). As Jordan Bear has argued, the success of Rejlander and Robinson depended on viewers' capacity to recognize and appreciate the "fundamentally mediated status" of their photography.[77] Indeed, the composite nature of Rejlander's work was a main point of attraction for viewers, and Robinson was successful in part because he gave viewers the opportunity to identify how his images were fabricated.[78] The appeal of "Fairy Stories" is similarly due to its visible fabrication. Like the composite photographs of Rejlander and Robinson, "Fairy Stories" engaged viewer interest by reimagining real phenomena in augmented scenarios. While Rejlander and Robinson achieved this effect by editing negatives into improbable constructions, the creators of "Fairy Stories" achieved it by incorporating photographic figures into artist-drawn images of fantasy.

Blending photocollage with other multimedia sensibilities, "Fairy Stories" offered a site for readers to speculate about the illustrated weekly's potential to merge photographic data from real life with fantastic artistry and performance media, as well as fairy tales. In particular, "Fairy Stories" imbricated traditional and innovative performance art practices. Like scrapbook photocollage, it used theatrical staging techniques for its scenes.[79] In mid-century photocollage, such staging evoked the long-standing use of fairy mythology across a spectrum of British performance entertainment, from music hall to theatre, as well as the era's enthusiasm for tableaux vivants. In "Fairy Stories" the continuum of fairy lore from print to performance media is implied through the theatrical staging of the images, as well as the feature's casting: the women photographed for the images were actresses recognizable to many *ILN* readers through their performances (including fairy-tale roles) on some of London's most well-known stages.[80]

The theatricality of "Fairy Stories" also evoked the novel performance medium of the cinema. By 1907, when the *ILN* published "Fairy Stories," Britons (and particularly Londoners) of all classes could regularly attend film showings at local shops converted into penny cinemas.[81] Many turn-of-the-century films were based on fairy tales – for example, George Méliès's *Cendrillon* (1899) and *Barbe-bleu* (1901). These stories were ideal subjects for new media because they circulated through oral retelling and had no single origin or author; to remediate a fairy tale was to participate in a long-standing tradition of adaptation.[82]

Figure 1.8. Oscar Gustav Rejlander, "The Two Ways of Life." Photographed in 1857, printed in 1925. © Victoria and Albert Museum, London.

Additionally, widespread familiarity with the tales meant that a cinema audience, like the readers of "Fairy Stories," would recognize the visual tokens of each well-known story. The use of an unfamiliar format was therefore not a hindrance to audience understanding of the narrative.

As I have implied, the combination of intermedial aesthetics and fairy-tale subject matter in "Fairy Stories" was almost certainly intentional. Producers of Victorian and Edwardian popular culture were often drawn to fairy tales because they provided an opportunity to exploit a medium's capabilities to depict the fantastical and magical. In illustrated fiction a writer's text and an artist's images wove a world aesthetically distinct from reality. In photocollage, photorealistic elements interacted with figures and settings drawn or painted from imagination. Trick photography and film manipulated records of physical reality to create fantastical scenarios with aesthetically realistic figures and settings. "Fairy Stories" drew on all these aesthetic techniques to engage readers' technological imagination. Aesthetic allusions to this array of media practices situated the *ILN* within the evolving media milieu of the early twentieth century.

Intermedial aesthetics are evident across fin-de-siècle print culture, particularly in illustrated monthlies, where a more leisurely publication schedule created space for innovations in design. However, the *ILN* and other popular news weeklies were unique in the new media milieu because of their expressive specificity. In their subversion of the text and image hierarchy they differed from non-pictorial journalism. Unlike smaller, more avant-garde visual periodicals, they exhibited a mass-culture orientation and mass-produced, hybrid aesthetics, and they circulated more widely and dependably than did photographs or films. Aesthetically positioning their news and entertainment content in conversation with new media, the *ILN* and other pictorial news weeklies subtly reminded readers that their format and subject matter remained timely and relevant in an accelerating world.

Fiction's Fall and Rise in Twentieth-Century Illustrated Print

In focusing on the *ILN* to make my case for how popular pictorial print more broadly adapted visual, multimodal storytelling, I have argued that the disappearance of fiction from this magazine, as well as its main competitor, the *Graphic*, offers evidence of that change. However, in many similarly transformed weeklies and monthlies, fiction continued to thrive well into the twentieth century. David Reed reports that in the weeklies that focused on instruction and entertainment, rather than news and current events, fiction continued to constitute about 20 per cent of editorial content between 1900 and 1910.[83] While fiction's presence in the weeklies remained stable but modest, it actually increased in the general-interest monthlies, as a growing number of magazines, hoping to replicate the success of the *Strand Magazine*, gave fiction pride of place among a cornucopia of subject matter and a wealth of images.[84] Indeed, Mike Ashley characterizes the period between 1880 and the First World War as the golden age of popular periodical fiction.[85]

Clearly, although fiction's letterpress orientation no longer aligned with that of news weeklies, it remained relevant to other popular print media. How did fiction adapt to and engage with the visual, multimodal nature of early twentieth-century popular culture and its own print environments? Although this subject begs a comprehensive study of its own, I can offer a few observations on the changing position of fiction in popular print culture relative to this book's case studies.

Although fiction remained a defining feature of illustrated monthly miscellanies, it did not exhibit the dynamic multimodal aesthetics that put other editorial content in conversation with new media. Within the media context of the magazines, fiction remained necessarily a more letterpress-oriented form of expression than many other types of content, including the advertisements, population journalism, and novelty journalism that are examined in subsequent chapters of this book. Fiction illustrations had a unique set of interpretive functions not comparable to the images accompanying journalism about real-world persons and events, such as the graphics of the *Coronation and Procession* number, or visually rich fantasies, such as "Fairy Stories by Photography." That fiction's pictures were shaped by a different set of print conventions is underscored by how little illustrated fiction adapted the multimodal aesthetics evident elsewhere in the magazines in the early 1900s. Fiction was rarely illustrated with images reproduced from photographs. As demonstrated by, for example, Sidney Paget's artwork for Arthur Conan Doyle's Sherlock Holmes stories in the *Strand*, magazine fiction's artwork capitalized on the print technology that made it possible to lay out images and text in interesting formats on the page. However, in their style and subject matter, the images did not evolve greatly beyond late-Victorian conventions.[86]

One of the most significant trends in popular fiction at the turn of the century was the rise of short fiction. This can be interpreted as a response to an evolving mass culture, although it did not engage directly with visual media. Serialized novels diminished in frequency, replaced by series of interconnected stories – a technique successfully used by Arthur Conan Doyle in his Sherlock Holmes fiction.[87] By the early twentieth century, the term *short story* was in common usage.[88] This form of verbal storytelling reflected the rapid pace and momentary character of modern, consumerist culture. It did not always engage directly with the increasing visuality and multimodality of its media milieu, but its format appealed to readerships engaging with media on an accelerated cycle of consumption; in this sense, short fiction responded to aesthetic sensibilities fostered by the pace of modern industrial life and by new media. Its increasing popularity was also due to a number of the same factors that contributed to the aesthetic transformation of the magazines, including readership growth and periodical diversification.[89]

Another significant innovation in popular magazine fiction was the rise of all-fiction publications, such as the *Novel*, launched in 1905, and the *Story-Teller*, launched in 1907.[90] The fact that these went unillustrated suggests that fiction's role in popular culture was not in the realm of visual intermediality. In fact, the all-fiction magazine offers an interesting complement to the twice-born illustrated periodical: both occupied prominent positions in early twentieth-century popular culture, but for very different reasons. In a sense, each medium enhanced and specialized long-standing practices – the illustrated periodicals by more fully realizing the visual, multimodal affordances they already possessed, and the all-fiction periodicals by stripping down to verbal narrative alone.

Conclusion

The *Coronation and Procession* number, "Stories without Words," and "Fairy Stories" demonstrate that at the turn of the century, illustrated print journalism's mediality was essential to the way in which it engaged readers and positioned itself within mass culture. The *ILN* engaged readers' technological imagination to increase their understanding of the illustrated magazine's unique techniques of representing popular culture. During its second birth, the *ILN* repositioned itself within the new media milieu, effectively ensuring that print remained essential to popular culture well into the twentieth century even as this culture's ecosystem continued to diversify. The aesthetic transformation of illustrated journalism encouraged readers to become more conscious of how different material characteristics and storytelling techniques shaped their interpretation. Consequently, awareness of mediation became a significant aspect of their technological imagination. The visibility of mediation in turn-of-the-century numbers of the *ILN* and other pictorial magazines created new possibilities for readers to exert agency. As I will show in the next three chapters, their awareness of mediality enabled readers to scrutinize and respond to the aesthetic strategies of the magazines with an array of tactics for making meaning.

Chapter Two

Imagining Consumer Culture: Reading Advertisements in the *Illustrated London News* and the *Graphic*, 1885–1906

Advertising has become recognized as a means of communication not only for the conveniences of trade, but for political, lovemaking, fortune-hunting, swindling, and the thousand and one other purposes which are always ready to assert themselves in a large community.

Henry Sampson, *A History of Advertising from the Earliest Times* (1874)

Ubiquitous in the public landscape of late-Victorian Britain, advertisements took many forms, including signs, bills, posters, leaflets, trading cards, sandwich boards, tram tickets, chalked and painted murals, and even theatre safety curtains.[1] Henry Sampson's effusive commentary about advertising's "thousand and one" social functions reflects his era's fascination with the increasingly visible role that advertisements played in popular culture. However, few media brought advertisements into the private sphere. Since periodicals had this privileged access, they were particularly important to the promotion of goods and services in an emerging consumer culture. As print journalism grew in scale, diversity, and aesthetic sophistication, so, too, did its advertisements. Within a few decades the typical advertising page in an illustrated weekly evolved from a block of dense, minimally illustrated letterpress columns to a visual bazaar of images and slogans. How did the metamorphosis of advertising have an impact on periodical readers? How did its extravagant aesthetics facilitate their engagement at the intersection of print and consumer culture?

Taking as exemplars two illustrated news weeklies, the *Illustrated London News* and the *Graphic*, I argue that periodical advertisements played a crucial role in fostering readers' active participation in mass culture between 1885 and the early 1900s. During this period British popular culture significantly expanded in scale and developed a consumerist orientation. As dynamic interpretive environments, periodicals facilitated advertisers' representations of mass culture, but they also presented opportunities for readers to respond to such strategies with subversive tactics. Through their visual, textual, material, and spatial characteristics, periodicals engaged the technological imagination to encourage readers to conceive of themselves as consumers of mass culture. At the same time, this engagement of the technological imagination created opportunities for readers to exert agency as appropriative producers of that culture.

Following Margaret Beetham's ground-breaking analysis of the relationship between context, text, and aesthetics of periodical advertisements in *A Magazine of Her Own?*, periodical scholars have identified many ways that the medium-specific characteristics of advertisements can teach us about the cultural functions of periodicals. For example, Laurel Brake points out that advertisements, other so-called ephemera, and editorial content provide important information about a work's history as a circulated print commodity.[2] Priti Joshi demonstrates that the heterogeneous content and layout of advertisements amplified the polyvocality of newspapers and that studying these characteristics improves our understanding of historical readers' engagement with specific periodicals.[3] Scholars have also studied the rhetorical effects produced by the interaction of words and images in advertising to learn how late-Victorian periodicals treated cultural topics such as imperialism, women's rights, and, most prominently, consumer capitalism.[4] As Robert Scholes and Clifford Wulfman argue, advertisements show us "how the rhetoric of commerce is mixed with that of politics and art" in popular print.[5]

The emphasis that I place throughout this book on how aesthetics and media literacy shaped reader engagement informs my perspective on this discussion about advertising in historical print. As I related in the introduction, Victorian readers possessed a print media literacy by which they could interpret the material traces of a print object's production and situate it in its real and imagined socio-technological contexts. The case studies in chapter 1 show that illustrated journalism encouraged readers to interpret its aesthetic elements as technological signifiers, as well as visual and textual expressions of cultural discourse. As popular periodicals transitioned from a verbal to a pictorial orientation at the turn of the twentieth century, advertisements played a key role in the magazine's second birth as a medium and its participation in the new media milieu of commodity culture. I now turn my attention to changes in the advertisement aesthetics of the *ILN* and the *Graphic*, the most widely circulated illustrated news weeklies of the fin de siècle and two of the richest archives of periodical advertisements available today. This chapter traces the evolving techniques through which periodical editors and advertisers sought to influence readers' engagement with interacting editorial and commercial contents.[6] The present study also identifies ways that readers could appropriate or subvert the meaning of those techniques. To delineate evidence of the power dynamic at work in this and the rest of the book's case studies, I use Michel de Certeau's theoretical characterization of the interaction between the *strategies* of cultural producers and the *tactics* of consumers.[7]

As demonstrated in this chapter, periodical advertisements employed multimodal aesthetic strategies that encouraged readers to view their own engagement with the magazines, and with popular culture broadly, as an unending cycle of consumption. However, the same aesthetic conditions enabled readers to develop tactics for producing, as well as consuming, periodical meanings. Illustrated magazines in the new media milieu enabled what N.K. Hayles calls "hyper-reading": interpretive practices such as scanning, skimming, fragmenting, and juxtaposing.[8] For Hayles, these practices are born of the information excess of the digital age,[9] but I posit that they were just as essential to navigating an earlier age of information superabundance, which began in the late-Victorian period as print achieved mass circulation.[10] Periodical hyper-reading encompassed a diverse set of tactics through which readers could simultaneously consume and produce representations of mass print culture. Ultimately, the dynamic between print producer strategies and reader-consumer tactics influenced how readers engaged with broader mass culture. Through the interpretive process facilitated by magazine advertisements, readers became simultaneously consumers and producers of this culture.

Periodical Advertising Strategies

By the late nineteenth century, advertisements had become highly lucrative for and increasingly prominent in illustrated magazines. British periodical advertising dates back to journalism's early modern origins.[11] Governmental taxes curtailed periodical advertisements from 1712 until the early nineteenth century, but after the British government had repealed so-called knowledge taxes on stamps, advertising, and paper between 1830 and 1861, the increasing periodical size and decreasing advertisement constraints enabled periodicals and advertisers to establish a mutually beneficial dynamic.[12]

Over subsequent decades, the advertisements proliferating in the magazines celebrated a new, spectacular consumer culture in which shopping was a pleasurable, status-building activity of the expanding middle classes. These advertisements used sophisticated pictorial and verbal strategies to promote luxury household goods.[13] Economist Thorstein Veblen famously described this phenomenon as "conspicuous consumption" in his 1899 treatise, *The Theory of the Leisure Class.* Inspired by Victorian exhibition culture and stimulated by advances in print reproduction technology, magazine advertisements gradually moved away from heavy copy and sparse stock images in favour of concise slogans, visually distinctive branding, and imaginative promotional displays.[14] Technological developments such as photomechanical image reproduction enabled advertisers to take their representations of conspicuous consumption to new heights at the turn of the twentieth century.[15]

As advertising practices were generally consistent across different periodical formats, the commercial contents of the *ILN* and the *Graphic* are representative of these practices; Thomas Richards observes that the *ILN* is "the closest thing we have to a concordance of Victorian advertising," and the *Graphic,* the *ILN*'s nearest rival, serves as a complementary second source on the aesthetic strategies of advertising in the period.[16] During the initial expansion of periodical advertising, from approximately 1860 to 1885, regular weekly numbers of the *ILN* and the *Graphic* typically presented all advertisements in the text-heavy, column-organized style that we now associate with classified advertisements. As an advertising page from an 1882 number of the *ILN* shows, such segmented organization restricted advertisements to a rather static format (figure 2.1). The relatively small graphics used on this page are chiefly stock images, rather than unique representations of commodities.[17] Four separate advertisements for Louis Velveteen appear in the bottom half of the page, illustrating that, due to print production constraints, periodical advertisers had to rely on repetition, rather than variety, for visual impact.[18] Other common strategies included repetition of the same copy or a simple repetition of the company name down the page.

Relatively few single advertisements occupied more than one column of a page, although an advertisement for Eno's Fruit Salt offers such a case. This advertisement repeats the name of its product several times; indeed, although it differs in size from other advertisements on the page, it uses the same promotional techniques, assembling small blocks of promotional copy around a central image – in this instance, a lighthouse. The image relies on words for its promotional impact: the text, superimposed on waves breaking on the lighthouse, declares that "140,000 persons every year die unnatural deaths." The text inscribed upon the lighthouse itself indicates that Eno's Fruit Salt is the solution to this "waste of life."[19] While the image metaphorically conveys the

APRIL 22, 1882 THE GRAPHIC 411

WISDOM IS THE ONLY SOURCE OF REAL HAPPINESS, AND THE ONLY GOAL WORTHY OF A MAN'S AMBITION.

THE GREATEST BLESSING

THE HUMAN MIND CAN CONCEIVE.

A ROYAL and NOBLE EXAMPLE!!!

"REFERRING to the continued manifestations of interest in sanitary science by members of the Royal Family—in short, in all matters affecting the health of the people—he remarked that if all the owners of cottages in the Empire exercised the same sanitary care that had been exercised in the cottages on Her Majesty's private estates, the general sickness and death-rate would be reduced one-third; in other words, it would be as if on every third year there were a Jubilee.

AND NO SICKNESS.

AND NO DEATHS!!! An Address by Dr. W. R. Richardson, F.R.S., &c., &c., at the Ladies' Sanitary Association.

WITH EACH BOTTLE of FRUIT SALT is wrapped a Large Illustrated Sheet, showing the best means of stamping out infectious diseases, Fevers, and Blood Poisons, &c.

IMPORTANT TO ALL.—Especially to Consuls, Ship Captains,

ENO'S FRUIT SALT is particularly valuable. No Traveller

FOR BILIOUSNESS or SICK HEADACHE, GIDDINESS,

ENO'S FRUIT SALT

IS A BLESSING IN ALL AILMENTS

BOAST OF LIFE IN ENGLAND

140,000 PERSONS every year DIE unnatural deaths

PREVENTIBLE DEATH.—Why should fever, that vile slayer of millions of the human race,

A NATURAL WAY of RESTORING or PRESERVING HEALTH

TO EUROPEANS WHO PROPOSE RESIDING IN OR VISITING HOT CLIMATES,

IMPORTANT to TRAVELLERS.

TORPID LIVER.

HEADACHE and DISORDERED STOMACH.

CHRONIC DYSPEPSIA.—"A gentleman called in yesterday.

SUCCESS IN LIFE.—"A new invention is brought before the public,

CAUTION.—LEGAL RIGHTS ARE PROTECTED IN EVERY CIVILISED COUNTRY.

Examine each Bottle, and see the Capsule is marked "ENO'S FRUIT SALT." Without it you have been imposed on by Worthless Imitations. Sold by all Chemists, price 2s. 9d. and 4s. 6d.

Prepared only at ENO'S FRUIT SALT WORKS, HATCHAM, LONDON, S.E., by J. C. ENO'S PATENT.

CULTIVATION OF THE AURICULA.

A DECADE OF VERSE. 5s.

CHAPMAN, NOTTING HILL, W.

LOUIS VELVETEEN, IN BLACKS AND ALL COLOURS SPECIALLY CHEAP PRICES.

BRIDAL TROUSSEAUX.

HENRY GLAVE'S ENGLISH AND FOREIGN FANCY DRESS PRODUCTIONS.

VALUABLE FAMILY LACE.

LOUIS VELVETEEN.

F. CATER and CO., 133 to 139, FINSBURY PAVEMENT,

CELEBRATED VELVETEEN.

COURT DRESSMAKER'S STOCK, AMOUNTING TO SEVERAL THOUSAND POUNDS, PURCHASED BY PUBLIC TENDER FOR CASH

STAGG, MANTLE, AND CO.

STAGG, MANTLE, and CO.,

"LOUIS VELVETEEN."

BLACK AND ALL COLOURS.

GOODE, GAINSFORD, and CO.,

THE STANDARD LIFE ASSURANCE COMPY.

LIFE ASSURANCE AT HOME AND ABROAD.

19 Millions Sterling.

5½ Millions Sterling.

3½ Millions Sterling.

CHAS. CODD'S ORANGE CHAMPAGNE

WORTH ET CIE., ARTISTES EN CORSETS.

WORTH et CIE.,

21s., 25s., and 30s. per pair.

GRATEFUL—COMFORTING.

EPPS'S (BREAKFAST) COCOA.

EPPS'S CHOCOLATE ESSENCE.

LACES COPIED FROM THE ANTIQUE,

FREMINET'S CHAMPAGNE,

CHARLES MEEKING and CO., HOLBORN,

"LOUIS" VELVETEEN

ROUND THE WORLD YACHTING

JOHNSTON'S CORN FLOUR IS THE BEST.

"Is decidedly superior."—The Lancet.

REFUSE OTHER KINDS WHEN OFFERED INSTEAD.

SAMUEL BROTHERS, MERCHANT TAILORS, BOYS' OUTFITTERS, &c.

"WEAR RESISTING" FABRICS (Regd.) for GENTLEMEN'S, YOUTHS', AND BOYS' CLOTHING.

THE "LOUIS" VELVETEEN

HENRY GLAVE, 534, NEW OXFORD STREET.

IMPROVED SPECTACLES.—Mr. HENRY LAURANCE,

FOR ARMS and CREST send

LAYETTES.

Figure 2.1. Advertising page, *Graphic* 25 (22 April 1882): 411.

product's special status as a beacon of healthy living, the words inscribed upon the lighthouse and the waves below it offer a verbal apparatus for interpreting this pictorial symbolism. Even in this unusually pictorial advertisement, then, text takes semantic precedence over image.

Beginning in the mid-1880s, advertisements began to increase in number and pictorial sophistication in the *ILN* and the *Graphic*. The typical size of an advertisement grew, resulting in significantly fewer advertisements per page, but the number of pages devoted to advertisements increased, and single full-page advertisements became more common.[20] Advertisement sections also migrated from the front and back of each issue to integrate with editorial contents in the weeklies. At first, this took the form of additional advertising pages that followed the main news and event listings of the week. Additionally, starting in the mid-1880s, half- and quarter-page advertisements began to share editorial pages with letterpress and pictures.

Thanks to the tandem development of visually oriented consumer culture and mass image-reproduction technology, the advertisements that appeared in the *ILN* and the *Graphic* between 1885 and the early 1900s exhibited increasing visual creativity. Conventional advertising practices such as the use of stock images and verbal repetition continued into the twentieth century, but new techniques extended the aesthetic spectrum. Periodical advertisements developed a variety of eye-catching strategies, including the use of headlines set in display type, copy set across column rules, large picture blocks, and full-page displays.[21] Reliance on letterpress content also decreased. By the early 1900s, many advertisements were using a bold, unornamented, and highly pictorial style that prevailed well into the twentieth century. Advertisements integrated varied images, catchy verbal slogans and product endorsements, striking spatial composition, and otherwise provocative aesthetic strategies to lobby readers.

These developments in advertisement aesthetics functioned as strategies in de Certeau's sense of the term. A strategy, according to de Certeau, is a mode of "force-relationship" that a dominant social power exerts on a weaker "other" based on presupposed distinctions between proper and improper behaviour.[22] Strategies are representations of culture that reinforce the dominant social mode. In modern consumer culture the proprietors of capitalist enterprise strategically employ advertisements that target consumers in order to influence their understanding of what constitutes proper social behaviour within a capitalist framework.

Kitsch and mélange were two multimodal aesthetic strategies through which late-Victorian periodical advertisers sought to shape readers' understanding of consumer-oriented popular culture. A product of bourgeois consumerism, kitsch was first identified as such in 1860s Germany as an attribution of cheap, art-like consumer products.[23] As Richards notes, the aesthetic exaggeration involved in kitsch de-emphasizes a commodity's unremarkable production history and renders it an emblem of spectacular or sentimental experience.[24] This strategy lends mass-produced goods an affective aura that makes them feel personally meaningful. The term *kitsch* did not see wide use until the early twentieth century, but it encompasses techniques of gaudy amplification that are evident in a wide array of products from the nineteenth century onwards that were designed to appeal to mass-market consumers.[25]

At the turn of the twentieth century, purveyors of household and cosmetic soaps often used strategies commensurate with kitsch in their advertisements. Products such as Swan Soap and Sunlight Soap were closely associated with personal, domestic activities that, when hyper-aestheticized in print images, could conjure sentimental feelings, leveraging the readers' emotional memories to increase product appeal.[26]

Advertisements for Pears' Soap particularly relied on such strategies in their depictions of children at play, as demonstrated by an 1891 *Graphic* advertisement entitled "Our Baby." The promotional space of the advertisement is halved, with a halftone print on the left and text on the right (figure 2.2). The picture block uses little text. "Pears' Soap," in rough handwriting, is visible over the shoulder of a pale, angelic child, apparently scrawled on one of the dark boulders behind a brook over which he perches. A caption below the image suggests its culturally distinctive status: "OUR BABY. From the original picture by the Honorable John COLLIER. The property of the Proprietors of PEARS' Soap."[27] Beside the image, a flurry of letterpress promotes Pears' Soap in a conventional, typographical style. Manicules and underscoring compel the reader to heed the boastful text: "HIGHEST AWARDS EVERYWHERE!" In multiple fonts the letterpress proclaims the long history and award-winning reputation of Pears' Soap. While the picture block innovates by aesthetically aligning itself with editorial content and fine art, the typographic section falls back on familiar methods for engaging readers.

The Pears advertisement not only reimagines its product as a catalyst for sentimental reverie – an innocent child bathing in a pastoral setting – but also foregrounds its aestheticization of this moment. The advertisement capitalizes on Collier's reputation as a popular Pre-Raphaelite artist, appealing to consumers by declaring the advertisement's culturally authoritative origins – a strategy that Pears first used with

Figure 2.2. Pears' Soap advertisement, *Graphic* 43 (7 February 1891): 167.

"Bubbles," its adaptation of *A Child's World* by John Everett Millais (1886).[28] For art-based kitsch advertisements such as "Bubbles" and "Our Baby," this strategy involved redefining original artworks as being of the moment rather than for posterity. Richards argues that as "instant souvenirs, kitsch objects belong to one moment, becoming passé immediately upon consumption.[29] Late-Victorian advertisers capitalized on this momentary nature of hyper-aestheticized mass objects. If the perceived aesthetic value of the sentimental moment depicted in "Our Baby" was enduring, it would conflict with consumerism's continual turnover. The momentary value of this advertisement sits at the intersection of several cultural elements: the Victorian idealization of the "Child of Nature," associated with what critics have termed the cult of the child; Collier's popular appeal as a sentimental genre painter; and the recent trend of adapting artworks into advertisements.[30] The popularly perceived value of these individual elements is not necessarily fleeting, but the appeal of their combination in a soap advertisement is specific to one cultural moment.

The kitsch of "Our Baby" is also a function of the advertisement image's own production history that invokes readers' technological imagination. The caption for the advertisement associates the print with a unique original (Collier's painting), but the materiality of the halftone image attests to its mass multiplication. This use of modern reproduction technology serves dual purposes. First, the halftone image's subtle visual texture and graduated shadings invoke the rich detail of the original painting, thereby aestheticizing the consumption of Pears' Soap. Second, as many magazine readers would know from their periodical education in print production, the advertising image's representation of tonality was made possible through the relatively new technology of photomechanical reproduction. Using cutting-edge technology to reproduce its promotional materials, Pears encouraged readers to associate their product with modernity and to view Pears as a cultural authority.

As the dual significance of the advertising image's halftones suggests, hyper-aesthetic kitsch was complemented by the modern visual hybridity of mélange. Both techniques appealed to readers in part by making apparent the status of images as modern mass replications.[31] But while kitsch strategically evoked nostalgia, mélange evoked the spectacular technological future. In periodical advertisements, it did so by reproducing various types of photomechanically produced images and by drawing on a variety of aesthetics, including photorealism, art nouveau, and even the pen-and-ink style of the news weekly illustrators known as special artists.[32] Mélange became pronounced in periodical advertisements of the 1890s and early 1900s as advertisers found new ways to incorporate photomechanical image-reproduction techniques. This aesthetic strategy aligned consumerism with the cultural hybridity that Gerry Beegan identifies as a trait of late-Victorian modernity familiar to British consumers.[33]

In late-Victorian periodicals, the effect of mélange was produced from the contrasting discourses, images, and use of space within a single advertisement, or within a cluster of advertisements sharing page space. A 1906 advertisement for Savory and Moore's Peptonized Cocoa and Milk in the *Graphic* demonstrates how mélange creates a sense of modern hybridity that, like kitsch, could boost an advertisers' cultural authority (figure 2.3). The advertisement uses photomontage (assembling multiple photographs into a composite image) to convey an amusing and thoroughly modern spectacle. A halftone from a photograph of an open product tin sits under the brand's banner. A block of text in the bottom left corner of the advertisement invokes pseudoscientific authority, asserting that the "nutritive value of Cocoa … depends on its digestibility," and boasting that Savory and Moore's "peptonized" cocoa has the distinction of being digestible "even by those who cannot take any other form of Cocoa."[34]

At the edge of the advertisement's border two pairs of hands, reproduced in halftone from an artist's rendering, reach out to the tin in a supplicating gesture. Their respective sizes and sleeves suggest a heteronormative couple, reinforcing the domesticity of the scene. A tiny woman, represented in halftone from a photograph, perches over the rim of the cocoa tin, the fairy-like sleeves of her dress draped over part of its label. The figure directs a blank but receptive gaze in the direction of the large, disembodied hands as she holds out a cup of cocoa. The difference in size between the woman and the hands reaching towards her yields an effect at once humorous and ominous.

The cocoa server's incongruous size may amuse readers, but it also strategically reinforces Savory and Moore's association with modern technological convenience. The woman's receptive stance reinforces the advertisement's messaging about the product's ready nutritional availability. The visual play is distinctly modern in nature, making innovative use of the photomechanical halftone process to reproduce a photocollage combining photographs and drawn figures. The Savory and Moore's image is the only halftone photocollage on a page full of advertisements; indeed, few other illustrated advertisements in the *ILN* and the *Graphic* used photocollage in the very early 1900s, although photocollage was a popular aesthetic at this time.[35] Associating its brand with the latest in print technology was consistent with Savory

Figure 2.3. Savory and Moore advertisement, *Graphic* 73 (27 January 1906): 120.

and Moore's strategy of marketing its product as a staple that was modernized – and, presumably, improved – through the mysterious process of peptonization. The photorealism of the hands emerging from beyond the advertisement's margins also encourages readers to put themselves in place of the disembodied consumers reaching for cocoa. In effect, the advertisement aims to be as easily digestible as the company claims its cocoa to be. Through the mélange of photocollage, Savory and Moore invokes the authority that late-Victorian society bestowed on modern technologies and signals the company's participation in modern cultural sensibilities.

Mélange also manifested in advertisements as an intertextual hybridity produced by the clustering of diverse promotions on a periodical page. This type of mélange was typically an indirect strategy on the part of advertisement producers: the placement of adverts was ultimately determined by periodical staff, rather than by the advertisers themselves. However, the mélange effected through advertisement assemblage could still be intentional. Advertisers used all aesthetic methods at their disposal to distinguish their advertisements from others; in this way, most advertisements were developed in conversation with related promotional materials already in print.

An advertising page taken from the *Graphic* in 1900 exemplifies this intertextual type of mélange (figure 2.4). Four advertisements divide the page into equal quadrants. An advertisement for Hennessy's Brandy in the upper left is striking for its use of negative space: a decorative art nouveau border frames the white of the un-inked paper with a black floral pattern. In contrast to the border's flourishes, the advertisement's main text, "Hennessy's Brandy," is printed in modern sans serif with large, bold lettering. Eight lines of copy underneath, in a smaller font, constitute the rest of the advertisement's contents. The image's use of white space, coupled with the border's flat black decoration, evokes the modern aesthetic of line-block engraving that Aubrey Beardsley famously produced for periodicals such as the *Yellow Book* and the *Savoy* in the 1890s.

In the page's diagonally opposite quadrant, the lower-right-hand corner, a promotion for Keystone Burgundy complements the aesthetics of the Hennessy advertisement, evoking art nouveau sensibilities but using a layout that imitates the conventions of editorial magazine content. A tall, narrow image depicts three fashionably dressed women at dinner. A wine bottle sits at the centre of the table; behind the seated women a male servant stands ready with a second bottle on his tray. The line illustration relies chiefly on black and white for contrast but makes use of detailed patterns in the women's clothing and in background

January 13, 1900 THE GRAPHIC 61

HENNESSY'S BRANDY.

Messrs. Jas. Hennessy & Co. have at their stores at Cognac the largest stock in the world of genuine old Cognac brandy made from grape wine.

Their brandy can be taken at any time with absolute safety, whilst for medicinal purposes it is now almost universally prescribed by the medical profession.

WILLIAMS' SHAVING SOAP

When you see that sign at a hairdresser's "Williams' Shaving Soap used here," you need not hesitate to enter. You may be sure of a good, clean, comforting shave. Above all you are safe from the dangers which lurk in cheap, inferior shaving soaps.

WILLIAMS' SHAVING SOAPS are used by all first-class Hairdressers.

WILLIAMS' SHAVING STICKS, 1s. WILLIAMS' LUXURY SHAVING TABLETS, 1s.
WILLIAMS' AMERICAN SHAVING TABLETS, 6d. WILLIAMS' "JERSEY CREAM" TOILET SOAP, 6d.
Trial Tablet WILLIAMS' SHAVING SOAP for 1d. stamp, by addressing—
The J. B. WILLIAMS CO., 64 Gt. Russell St., LONDON, W. C., or 161 Clarence St., SYDNEY.
Chief Offices and Laboratories—GLASTONBURY, CONN., U. S. A.

THE GOPHIR DIAMOND CO.,
95 & 176, REGENT STREET, LONDON. W.

Keystone Burgundy

We are the proprietors of Hall's Wine, and have an unquestionable reputation for medicated wines.

Keystone Burgundy is not medicated, but a natural wine solely controlled by us; and it is not particularly for invalids. It is not to battle with illness, but to combat the wear and tear of every-day life; to supply the system with a maximum of nourishment and natural stimulant at a minimum cost.

For the same reason, and on same occasions, as you drink beer, stout, burgundy, or claret, you should drink Keystone Burgundy.

The questions of whether it is better and cheaper you can decide for yourself at our risk. We will send one bottle or twelve bottles, and if you do not like Keystone Burgundy you may send it back, and we will refund your money in full.

Keystone Burgundy is ferruginous; that is, it contains iron naturally, which it acquires by the grapes being grown on soil with iron and limestone in it.

It is a pure, natural wine. Delicious in flavour; not the least inky, although it has iron in it; and it is free from acidity.

18/- per dozen bottles, carriage paid.
Single bottle, 1/6.

Stephen Smith & Co., Limited, Bow, London, E.

Figure 2.4. Advertising page, *Graphic* 61 (13 January 1900): 61.

interior décor. The combination of stark black and white with minute, repetitive detail associates the advertisement with modern print aesthetics. The product's name, displayed as a headline in bold type, and a column of advertising copy offer textual counterpoints to the image. The layout subtly implicates editorial importance through this combination of pithy headline and letterpress with illustration, a typical formula of the *Graphic* and other pictorial magazines.

Above the Keystone Burgundy advertisement, in the upper-right quadrant, a halftone image of a handsome, mustached man looks at a shaving and hairdressing establishment's door on which proudly hangs a sign, "Williams' Shaving Soap Used Here." The Williams' Soap advertisement relies on long-standing graphic tropes such as a variety of text forms and fonts, an emphasis on brand quality, the familiar symbol of a barber's pole, and an attractive but conventional Everyman figure (only partly visible, perhaps to encourage a female reader to imagine her own husband in his place).

In the diagonally opposite quadrant of the page, the bottom left, an advertisement for the Gophir Diamond Company similarly pairs long-standing promotional techniques with modern visual sensibilities. The company name tops the advertisement in a conventional, square display font, accompanied by a brief tag line boasting about the quality of the product. A photographic halftone of Gophir Diamond's jewellery occupies approximately nine-tenths of the advertisement, with detailed descriptions of the pictured imitation pearls below. Offering a tidily organized exhibition of products against the blank backdrop of the page, this advertisement differs little from those of previous decades in terms of its concept and layout. However, it is made aesthetically distinctive by its use of a halftone image from a photograph, rather than a more conventional wood-engraved illustration of wares. By invoking the fidelity of the photographic camera, the Gophir Diamond advertisement offers readers an approximation of its real products, as if presenting an accurate representation of the jewellery would imbue the company's pearls and diamonds with authenticity even though they are, as the advertisement indicates, imitations. The halftone image adds credence to the advertisement's claims about the "absolutely perfect" colour, shape, and weight of the pearls.

Taken together, these advertisements destabilize image categories and display the hybridity of modern culture. The advertisements use old and new aesthetic strategies, presenting multiple, sometimes contradictory, cultural narratives, styles, and image-reproduction methods. The Gophir and Hennessy advertisements showcase items on their own, letting consumers imagine their own contexts of use. The

Keystone advertisement places its product at the centre of a modern lifestyle of privileged leisure to which savvy consumers – particularly women – may have aspired. Gophir bestows authenticity and credibility on an imitation product by combining an old-fashioned concept and layout with the modern look of photography. Just as the product's imitative construction made it affordable to the middle class, the halftone's rendition of a photograph makes the product available for viewing. Williams Soap is a more quotidian, less visually interesting commodity, so its advertisement emphasizes themes of stability and tradition by incorporating the enduring symbol of a barber's pole. The Hennessy advertisement similarly relies on an aged name and product ("genuine old Cognac brandy") to appeal to readers who are initially attracted by its novel use of white space. This advertisement's compositional emphasis on text, adorned with a black ornamental border, stylistically evokes an era before large, detailed images became ubiquitous in advertising; yet its use of an art nouveau border reflects modern sensibilities. The Keystone advertisement also uses a black-and-white aesthetic, but its image has been reproduced with a line-block from a pen-and-ink drawing – a technique that popular periodicals had only recently adopted in reproducing their illustrative contents. This material characteristic reinforces the advertisement's unequivocal embrace of another aspect of fin-de-siècle culture, the New Woman – the fashionable women in the image keep their own company over wine as a man stands aside, ready to assist when called on.

As advertisements became more aesthetically hybrid, so too did the contents of the *ILN* and the *Graphic*, due to many of the same social and technological factors, as well as the cross-pollination of periodical advertisements and editorial content. Over the turn of the century, the characteristic miscellaneity of Victorian periodicals mutated into aesthetic hybridity, fostered by the blend of consumerism and cultural narrative employed by the magazines. The seriality of the magazines, another defining characteristic, took on a quality of continuous ephemerality as mass print production and circulation continually relegated existing periodicals to old news, imbuing each number's content with a sense of impermanence.[36]

The evolving characteristics of the magazines were both cause and effect of an accelerating cycle of print consumption. Through hybridity and continuous ephemerality the *ILN* and the *Graphic* encouraged readers to imagine mass print culture as an infinite proliferation of diverse goods to be purchased and momentarily consumed. The interacting aesthetic characteristics that developed in the advertisements and periodical contents formed a strategic matrix that served commercial periodical interests. Within this matrix the distinction between advertisements and other magazine contents blurred, effectively conflating reading and consumption. The aesthetics of periodical contents, as well as advertisements, therefore served as strategies for grooming readers to participate in popular culture as statistical consumers (a ramification that chapter 3 addresses in depth).

Periodical Reader Tactics

Although the strategies of periodical advertisers and editors conditioned how readers encountered periodicals, they could only influence the interpretive process so far. It was ultimately up to readers to make meaning of advertisements – individually and in relation to other advertisements, periodical contents, and broader contexts. The multimodal aesthetics through which advertisers engaged readers' technological imagination also enabled what de Certeau characterizes as tactical resistance. De Certeau posits the individual tactic as a complementary social mode to the commercial strategy. A tactic "insinuates itself" in social "force-relationships" to create fragmentary, transitory, and heterogeneous elements through which the tactician achieves momentary liberation from the dominant cultural narrative.[37] De Certeau contends that many everyday activities that are improvisational and creative, including talking, reading, and walking, are tactical in character. These subversive cultural practices are "quasi-invisible" because they are ongoing but clandestine, never achieving sustained control over dominant cultural strategies.[38] Since they are transitory, tactical responses to social force-relations leave little evidence behind.[39] However, given that tactics depend on the possibilities offered by circumstances, it is possible to identify the opportunities for subversion that periodicals afforded readers through their aesthetic strategies.[40] Accordingly, what follows is a sketch of potential ways in which readers could tactically interpret the cultural representations mobilized by the advertisements in the *ILN* and the *Graphic*.

Readers could resist periodical advertisers' strategies through two main types of tactics, curation and counter-interpretation. Curatorial tactics involved reusing select periodical advertisements and contents in personalized contexts. For example, readers pasted select magazine cuttings and pull-outs to the walls of their homes, adjoining personal space to the magazine environment on their own terms. This practice was sufficiently widespread to surface in popular-culture discourse. In Olive Schreiner's *The Story of An African Farm*, for instance, the walls of Gregory Rose's one-room house are "profusely" covered with *ILN* prints.[41]

Through related curatorial practices such as photocollage, readers could incorporate figures from a magazine into their own original drawings or, alternatively, insert hand-drawn figures into scenery taken from repurposed advertisements or news illustrations. Readers cut out aesthetically or topically striking elements from advertisements, articles, and supplements to paste into new print environments, creating visual narratives organized by their own aesthetic purposes or thematic categories.[42] Such practices were both creative and critical.[43]

An anonymous scrapbook from the Harry Page collection at Manchester Metropolitan University illustrates how curatorial tactics enabled readers to recontextualize and remediate consumer culture according to a personal hierarchy of values. This scrapbook, identified only by its number in the collection, 157, consists of a series of stories and vignettes told through elaborate pictorial scenes accompanied by handwritten narratives. The album's compiler populated each scene with items clipped from illustrated print. The paper quality, image types, and subject matter suggest that most of these graphics derived from periodical advertisements printed sometime between 1875 and 1885. The scrapbook maker tactically assembled these items into sardonic representations of middle-class domesticity: the narratives make fun of dominant socio-cultural mores while the illustrations render consumer materialism into a series of ludicrous spectacles. As Alexis Easley argues, the maker of this scrapbook used satire to foreground "the vacuity of fashion and consumer culture, as well as the material, commercial nature of … domestic relationships."[44] For example, one page displays the interior of a library where the fashionable guests of an evening party congregate after dinner (figure 2.5). Crown mouldings adorn the far wall; in front of a bookcase and fireplace five figures stand around several articles of furniture and a portfolio on display. The scrapbook maker's handwritten commentary undercuts the scene's sense of aesthetic pleasantry, telling us that the party "is hardly a success" and that one of the attendees, an elderly cousin, privately critiques the materialistic display, wondering disdainfully "why old Tomkinson was such a fool as to invest capital in all these books!" The scene's protagonists, Tom and Polly, declare the party "delightful" nevertheless, oblivious to the narrator's assessment. The gap in perceptions suggests that it is the display of fine furniture, clothing, and social ritual by which conventional members of the middle class such as Tom and Polly judge their own success, choosing not to peer beneath a pleasing bourgeois veneer.

Another page of scrapbook 157 offers more subversive commentary on consumerism specifically. Part of a story about the unfortunately single Mr. Brown and a couple in his acquaintance who are getting

Figure 2.5. Excerpted page from scrapbook 157, Harry Page Collection. © Manchester Metropolitan University Special Collections.

married, the page illustrates some of the couple's many wedding gifts. Seven groups of items are distributed evenly across the space of the page. Each group has been cut from an advertisement and clearly displays a commercial brand. Indeed, in terms of its visual layout and accompanying text, the page mimics a page of magazine advertisements. The text parrots some of the language of advertising copy – the bride's sister, who "is extremely careful of her complexion," has given the couple a bar of soap – as well as cultural idioms; Aunt Selina, who considers needlework "a far more profitable occupation than reading silly novels," has given the bride supplies for this handicraft. Products marked with the Pears logo have been coloured in with red paint to enhance their visual impact. Although the display fetishizes these consumer products, its reverent attitude towards consumerism is ironic.

The page is one of several successive displays of household products, a Great Exhibition of wedding gifts rendered absurd by their excessiveness. The scrapbook maker's sarcastic observations enhance this sense of absurdity. For example, on a page filled with timepieces, the compiler simply comments, "A few friends with original minds give clocks.—" As Easley argues, the plethora of similar gifts assembled on these pages draws attention to consumer culture's tendency towards homogeneity.[45]

Scrapbook 157 demonstrates how curation enabled Victorian readers to tactically appropriate commercial magazine content in order to create personal aesthetic objects and subvert popular culture. Assembling and enhancing advertisement illustrations to suit personal taste, the compiler of this album recontextualized print consumerism to satirize middle-class life, highlighting the disparity between appearances and reality while poking fun at excessive materialism. Drawing awareness to disparity and excess, the compiler critiques the consumerist values championed by the advertisements that provided the scrapbook's materials.

Like tactics of curation, tactics of advertisement counter-interpretation involved the appropriation of print culture objects. While tactical curation reconfigured print media, counter-interpretation involved a more itinerant activity that de Certeau calls "poaching."[46] He argues that in everyday acts, individuals poach elements of the "dominant cultural economy" by making "innumerable and infinitesimal transformations" that adapt it "to their own interests and their own rules."[47] For de Certeau, reading is a key site of poaching, and therefore of cultural resistance. To read is to wander unpredictably through an imposed system and select where to place attention and bestow value. This often involves formulating an idiosyncratic interpretation counter to the dominant narrative suggested by a given system – in other words, the poaching of meaning. Given that turn-of-the-century illustrated weeklies encouraged readers to conflate reading and consumption, readers could transform the act of reading-as-consumption into reading-as-poaching.

Techniques of hyper-reading exemplify the kind of poaching that illustrated magazine advertisements made possible. Late-Victorian readers developed these techniques in response to information superabundance. By the late nineteenth century, literate British citizens of all classes had daily access to more print images and letterpress than they could possibly read; with the expansion of the periodical press, the body of knowledge proliferated at an unprecedented rate. The sheer volume of print matter demanded hyper- and heterogeneous engagement in order to keep up with the "news." Such techniques were especially necessary for readers of pictorial magazines, which featured newly abundant letterpress, ornamentation, and illustration, and even more indispensable for readers of magazine advertising pages, which were often the most graphically complex portions of a number. As Tom Gretton contends, late nineteenth-century magazine readers had to learn how to look at newly spectacular advertisements and advertising sections and decide where to place their attention.[48] While, as Gretton notes, interpreting advertisements involved a somewhat different skill set than that of interpreting editorial contents, the interaction of these contents within a magazine environment encouraged readers to engage with them simultaneously.[49] The heterogeneous format of illustrated magazines lent itself to hyper-reading, which allowed readers to identify quickly which textual and pictorial features across the barrage of editorial and commercial text and images deserved more sustained attention.[50]

Skimming and scanning were two of the main hyper-reading techniques encouraged by the abundance of aesthetic information in the turn-of-the-century *ILN* and *Graphic* numbers. Few articles and even fewer advertisements required a reader's sustained, linear engagement to glean a basic understanding of form and content. Readers could gather much general information about a number's editorial and commercial contents by scanning headlines, icons, banners, and photographic spreads. As they covered a large number and variety of news items each week, the *ILN* and the *Graphic* relied on an editorial brevity that further enabled skimming. The caption of an image-oriented news item rarely exceeded three lines. The weeklies often presented verbally oriented news items as a series of short summaries organized by a geographic or topical logic, which was indicated by a headline in different type – for example, "Home and Foreign News."[51] Scanning was further facilitated by the visually oriented, multimodal storytelling techniques used in advertisements and editorial content. Readers could glance at several news images and advertisements before deciding which deserved closer attention based on topic, tone, complexity, and aesthetic appeal.

Fragmentation and juxtaposition are two other hyper-reading practices within which reader activities of selection and isolation also fall. Wandering idiosyncratically through a magazine's pages of editorial and commercial contents, readers could select multiple expressions to juxtapose and compare. As Beegan observes, late-Victorian magazine readers took pleasure in "assembling and using fragmentary information in order to feel that they knew what was happening at that moment."[52] This knowledge could be collected across periodical numbers, titles, and print media types. Design techniques used in the editorial contents of periodicals fostered such reading behaviours; for example, both the *ILN* and the *Graphic* often used layouts that mimicked the look of a photograph album in order to display multiple images on the same topic (figure 2.6). The composition might invite a reader's eye to focus on some images more than others, but this set of information offers no conventional linear sequence through which to proceed: a reader need not interpret the images in sequence from left to right or top to bottom. Readers could select, isolate, and juxtapose the information based on what they thought most interesting or useful.

The layout of the advertising pages, which presented multiple promotions side by side, also readily encouraged hyper-reading. In the *Graphic*'s page of advertisements for Hennessy, Williams, Gophir, and Keystone, for example, readers could counter-interpret the exhibited aesthetic strategies in myriad ways. A reader might choose to isolate and focus on only the images, meaning that the highly pictorial Gophir and Williams advertisements would garner the most attention; the Hennessy's promotion would recede into the background, and the Keystone advertisement's attempt to imbue its content with journalistic credibility would be moot. Alternatively, a reader could use juxtaposition to construct a hierarchy among the advertisements, perhaps interpreting the Gophir advertisement's display of abundant jewels as ostentatiously hollow in comparison to the confidently minimalist strategy used by Hennessy's Brandy. A reader might use selective attention to medium and mediation to navigate the page based on techniques of visual display or image type that piqued personal interest, focusing, for example, on the Keystone and Williams pictures because they reproduced original artwork. Indeed, responding to the advertisements' efforts to invoke the technological imagination, a reader might focus exclusively on the hybrid aesthetics of the advertisements, ignoring the commercial messaging altogether.

The subject matter of advertisements in the *ILN* and the *Graphic* also encouraged juxtapositional hyper-reading across editorial and commercial contents. Topical references were one way that the advertisements signalled visual and verbal intertextuality. For example, multiple advertisements for Ogden's Guinea Gold Cigarettes make references to the Second Boer War between 1899 and 1900, when the *ILN* and the *Graphic* were covering this conflict extensively. One *ILN* advertisement features a box of Ogden's cigarettes skewered on a bayonet, accompanied by the slogan "Carried at the Point of the Bayonet into Great

Figure 2.6. "The Close of the Campaign in Northern Nigeria." Halftone illustration, *Illustrated London News*, 29 August 1903, 310.

Popularity." Another Ogden's advertisement in the *ILN* depicts a solider lighting a cigarette in night-time darkness, with the declaration, "It's risky! But Ogden's 'Guinea Gold' are worth it" (figure 2.7).

Both of Ogden's advertisements entwine the brand with British courage and imperial power through implicit references to the South African war documented elsewhere in the magazines. The first advertisement displays a gesture without context: although the item's notched border suggests the castellations of a battle-ready fort, it does not include a battle-field or even the individual presumably holding the bayonet, thereby figuring the depersonalized, collective character of citizens upholding imperialist values. At the same time, the advertisement's use of hand-drawn letters, rather than standardized typography, imbues it with a sense of individuality. The unlikely visual combination of bayonet and cigarettes lends a sardonic tone to the image that is underscored by the declarative but equally ambiguous text. Indeed, lacking any supporting evidence, the statement "Carried at the Point of the Bayonet into Great Popularity" begs the question. However, while the premise of the advertisement makes little practical sense, it exudes symbolic potency; the visual intersection of Ogden's cigarettes with a symbol of military might associates the brand with stout British nationalism.

The second advertisement calls attention to itself by depicting a human figure and a familiar gesture within an unusual, largely implied context. Like the advertisement with the bayonet image, the second example avoids depicting the chaos of an actual battle-field. Instead, it evokes the Second Boer War through the lone figure's military uniform and the text's reference to the risk a soldier takes by making himself a visible target for the enemy at night. Imperialism is personalized through the image of an Everyman who risks death to practise the familiar ritual of smoking a cigarette. The soldier's brashness is displaced on the page by his loyalty to a specific British cigarette brand, Ogden's Guinea Gold, displayed in large, hand-drawn letters just above the figure. The advertisement's heavy inking underscores the symbolic power of lighting a match in the darkness; the soldier's branded ritual of home brings light into the dark circumstances of war.

Intertextuality and topicality are essential to what each Ogden's advertisement conveyed. The advertisements reference events reported in the *ILN*'s editorial content, thus framing their promotions in terms that resonated with the magazine's readers in September and October 1899. Linking their brand to ongoing news reports that spoke urgently to British nationalist sensibilities, the advertisements signalled the cultural currency of their brand. They also left the intertext sufficiently ambiguous to require readers to connect the advertisement themes and

Figure 2.7. Ogden's Guinea Gold Cigarettes advertisement. *Illustrated London News*, 21 October 1899, 181.

the *ILN* news contents themselves. For example, the name Guinea Gold evoked the Witwatersrand gold mines that regular *ILN* readers associated with Britain's colonial and military presence in South Africa.[53] Instead of making this link explicit, the Ogden's advertisements encouraged readers' awareness of their own processes of juxtaposition, and through this process created an opportunity for readers to make the connection themselves and take pleasure in being able to decode the cultural subtext.

The hyper-reading techniques that readers could use to engage with illustrated periodicals enabled them to produce new knowledge that took forms such as summary and synthesis. Navigating back and forth through a periodical, readers could assemble meaningful narratives based on select images, articles, advertisements, and other heteroglossia. For example, readers of the *ILN* on 29 March 1902 might assess the diamond-studded jewellery illustrated in a Mappin and Webb advertisement in relation to the sartorial values that Florence Fenwick Miller advocated in the "Ladies' Pages" directly above the advertisement.[54] Readers might even extend this interpretive work across the number, drawing on a photographic spread depicting the Cape Town residence of diamond magnate Cecil Rhodes to consider how fashion was implicated in the British imperialist project.[55] Readers could also synthesize information across magazine elements to extrapolate a counter-meaning. For example, a reader might sympathize with the desperate Boer War soldier who risks his life to smoke Ogden's cigarettes, and consequently revile the military leaders such as General Sir George White and Admiral Colomb whose portraits were published as part of the *ILN*'s war coverage.[56] Many Britons did not support the war and might have viewed the suggested correlation between Guinea Gold cigarettes and gold mines in the Ogden's advertisements as crass.[57] Even here, the technological imagination could play a role in interpretation. The hand-drawn aesthetics of the Ogden's advertisement of October 1899 make its lone figure, with his wary expression, more idiosyncratically individual and therefore, perhaps, more familiar and "poachable" than the regularized, photographic indifference of the military portraits.

Conclusion

Focusing on advertisements in the *ILN* and the *Graphic*, this chapter has demonstrated that the format of illustrated weeklies in the modern media milieu evoked specific hermeneutic behaviours, including curatorial poaching and counter-interpretive hyper-reading. The technological imagination contributed to both the aesthetic strategies of producers and the responding tactics of readers. While periodical producers invoked the technological imagination to garner authority and position readers as consumers, readers could employ it to become both producers and consumers of cultural meaning. Focusing on advertisements, an increasingly prominent category of content in an increasingly consumerist print culture, I have linked the changing periodical aesthetics to the changing possibilities for producer strategies and reader tactics. Chapter 3 focuses on another type of content, a genre of illustrated statistical narrative that I describe as population journalism, to show how producers used aesthetic strategies to mobilize political values that were in lockstep with the mass consumerism promoted by the magazines.

Chapter Three

Imagining Subjectivity: Reading Data Visualizations in *Pearson's Magazine*, 1896–1902

Of late years our magazines have been overrun by the statistical fiend.

J.G. Grant, "Statistics Gone Mad: With Apologies to the Statistical Society and Mr. Holt Schooling" (1899)

In "The Mathematics of Marriage," an 1898 article in *Pearson's Magazine*, T.D. Denham observes: "There is much of interest in ... figure-facts ... if they can but be set forth in picturesque form."[1] The "figure-facts" to which Denham refers are statistics; shown in "picturesque form," they become data visualizations – that is, graphical displays of abstracted, quantitative information.[2] Data visualizations began to appear in general-interest periodicals during the second half of the Victorian period in the form of thematic maps, technological diagrams, and weather charts. At the end of the century, popular illustrated periodicals introduced a new way to make figure facts interesting to readers, a genre of data-visualization articles that used photomechanical image aesthetics to exploit more fully the potential of the "picturesque form." This genre, which I term *population journalism*, combined entertaining data graphics with narrative analyses of vital statistics about human populations. While its heyday was brief, population journalism marked an important phase in the history of popular data visualization. It also exemplified how the new magazine aesthetics discussed in previous chapters could be used in the service of a dominant cultural politics. Representing the British nation as a managed population body and its citizen readers as population units, this genre intersected popular culture with Victorian Britain's politics of population life, what Michel Foucault terms "biopolitics."[3] So exactly what role did print aesthetics play in reader engagement with population journalism? How did they facilitate readers' understanding of population politics?

This chapter focuses on the population journalism printed between 1896 and 1902 in one of the most widely circulated illustrated monthlies, *Pearson's Magazine*, to consider how photomechanical aesthetics facilitated readers' engagement with biopolitics in the magazines. Chapter 2 demonstrated how the new aesthetic affordances of illustrated magazines at the turn of the century were used by periodical producers to foster specific conceptions of consumer subjectivity. Chapter 3 investigates how popular magazine aesthetics fostered specific conceptions of *political* subjectivity. Just as medium-specific characteristics conditioned how readers interpreted consumerism in advertisements, they shaped how readers interpreted biopolitics in data visualizations. Like the visually elaborate periodical advertisements of the era, population journalism engaged the print media literacy and technological imagination of readers in order to condition their interpretation of its depictions of the citizen subject. At the same time, readers could use their print media literacy to critique and repurpose such representations.

Scholarship on data visualization indicates a growing interest in its social and cultural history, but little attention has been given to how specific types of visualization were popularized in print media as such. The existing histories of data graphics that are most often cited by humanities scholars, including print historians, offer high-level surveys of its nineteenth-century development. Michael Friendly, Edward Tufte, and Johanna Drucker affirm that the field of statistical visualization expanded and diversified significantly in the second half of the nineteenth century; [4] Friendly even describes this period as visualization's "golden age."[5] These histories focus on the use of data graphics in specialized fields, such as political economics and geology, making little to no mention of how data visualizations were circulated for non-specialized audiences.[6] Similarly, the accounts of specific visualization techniques developed by historians of science and scholars of visual studies tend to focus on how data graphics were used in particular scientific and mathematical domains. One notable exception is the work of Klaus Hentschel, which includes data visualization in a survey of characteristics shared across the visual cultures of historic scientific domains.[7] Other scholarship in the history of science and the visual gives some consideration to the ways in which visualization made scientific information accessible to general readerships. For example, because the nascent field of meteorology was an important front of Victorian public engagement with the sciences, Katharine Anderson's account of its history addresses the role of graphics in general-audience weather journalism.[8] On the popularization of statistical graphics in particular, little work has yet been done, although a relatively recent study by James Thompson has shed light on the relationship between statistical thinking and visualization in the print matter used to promote Victorian election campaigns in the public sphere.[9]

Scholarship on the Victorian history of popular data visualization has yet to adopt the focus on medium and materiality that has been so generative for the field of print history. [10] Although it was one of the major genres through which readers encountered data visualization at the fin de siècle, population journalism has been sorely under-examined to date. I seek to reduce these gaps with this chapter, investigating population journalism in *Pearson's* by using an approach that emphasizes the genre's interacting material aesthetics and biopolitics.

Foucault's biopolitical theory offers a useful framework for studying population journalism because it centralizes premises that were essential to how data visualization was used to share statistics with Victorian general audiences. As Drucker notes, statistical data visualization emerged in tandem with two modern institutions, the bureaucratic state and the field of statistics, which took population management as an essential facet of their mandates.[11] In the eighteenth and nineteenth centuries, scientists and social thinkers began conceptualizing humanity as a species, and its "basic biological features" became "the object of ... a general strategy" that Foucault calls "biopower."[12] At the intersection of political arithmetic and statistical reasoning, the field of vital statistics emerged, advancing practices for measuring the biological features that function as indicators of biopower, such as size, health, and wealth.[13]

Population health was a major preoccupation of Victorian politics and culture. The view that a government's legitimacy depended on its capacity to foster the well-being of the people gained prominence as a response to concerns about class disparity, urbanization, and the circulation of disease engendered by industrialization.[14] Victorian biopolitics are characterized by pride in Britain's status as an industrial power, paired with concern about the impact of the modern age on the moral, physical, and economic vitality of the population. Additionally, as Britain expanded its imperial reach in the second half of the century, biopolitical discourse acquired a New Imperialist emphasis on Britain's vigour as the beating heart of a major global empire.

Biopolitical discourse found expression in not only the letterpress but also the images of popular print journalism, particularly statistical graphics. Although Foucault's own biopolitical analysis focused on verbal cultural expressions, and much scholarship on Victorian biopolitics has followed suit,[15] the genre of population journalism attests to the important role that images played in the press's promotion of biopolitical values to general readerships. In this chapter I analyse two distinctive aesthetics used by the population politics in *Pearson's* to represent political subjectivity: abstract and photorealist data visualization. Population journalism transformed biopolitics into a *spectacle* – in Guy Debord's sense, an aesthetic phenomenon that mediated social relations.[16] This spectacularity signalled population journalism's authority in the arena of fin-de-siècle popular culture, which was highly visual on many fronts, including exhibition culture and print media, as discussed in chapter 1, and consumerism, as discussed in chapter 2. As I demonstrate in my analysis of J. Brand's "Is Suicide a Sign of Civilisation?" (1896), the minimalist aesthetic of abstract visualizations, which were reproduced by line-block engraving from linear black-and-white originals, encouraged individual readers to conceive of themselves as statistical units within a delineated sociobiological population, the British nation. Photorealistic visualizations such as those in T.D. Denham's "The Mathematics of Marriage" (1898), which reproduced figures from photographs or drawings in tonal greyscale, were less strictly quantitative than abstract visualizations, but these graphics enacted a more complex biopolitics through their spectacular, multimodal aesthetics.

Through their respective aesthetic strategies, abstract and photorealistic population visualizations linked modern image-reproduction technology with modern statistical methods, encouraging readers to conflate population politics with popular culture. However, as in periodical advertisements, these aesthetic strategies presented indeterminate interpretive possibilities, effectively creating opportunities for readers to exert agency through a variety of tactics. The article "Statistics Gone Mad," published in *Harmsworth Magazine* in 1898, offers evidence of a journalistic counter-discourse that readers were equipped to adopt and extend through their media literacy and technological imagination. The case of population journalism demonstrates how print media literacy and technological imagining contributed to readers' engagement with and appropriation of popular visual expression and the political implications of this interaction.

Victorian Data Visualization and Population Journalism

Although humans have been expressing data in images for thousands of years, it was in the sixteenth and seventeenth centuries that scientists and mathematicians introduced what Friendly calls "the beginnings of visual thinking" in Europe.[17] In the eighteenth century, political efforts to organize information about land, taxes, goods, and populations focused this surge in "visual reasoning" at the intersection of statistics, governance, and biopolitics.[18] This marked the beginning of modern practices of large-scale data gathering and analysis. Indeed, one of modern data visualization's foremost pioneers was a political economist, Scotsman William Playfair.

In order to identify patterns in datasets too large to be manipulated in tabular format, Playfair and Swiss mathematician Johann Heinrich Lambert developed visualization formats such as the line graph, the pie chart, and other relational graphics. The late eighteenth-century work of Playfair and Lambert paved the way for a rapid expansion of statistical graphics and thematic mapping in nineteenth-century Europe, although British statisticians tended to favour the use of tables over more pictorial graphics until late in the century.[19] A marked increase in the appearance of data visualizations in specialized statistical publications, such as the *Journal of the Statistical Society of London*, confirms that by the fin de siècle it was widely practised among British statisticians.[20]

Print media are central to the history of modern data visualization, not only because they offer evidence of its advancement between the sixteenth and twentieth centuries but also because the evolution of visual reasoning was entwined with the development of image-reproduction technologies such as wood-engraving in the sixteenth and seventeenth centuries and coloured etching in the eighteenth century.[21] The same technological advances that enabled popular magazines to increase and diversify their techniques for visual storytelling made it possible to reproduce some types of data graphics on a mass scale. Periodical producers could visually aestheticize the statistical reporting that had already appeared regularly in the press,[22] often pertaining to topics of trade and the census.[23] For example, volume 4 of Charles Mayhew's serialized "London Labour and the London Poor" features maps that display the distribution of poverty-related characteristics across the nation. Mayhew's use of graphics was unusual when this essay was first printed in 1851, but by the end of the century such images had become familiar to readers of general-interest and news publications. Data graphics were not as ubiquitous as mimetic illustrations of news and fiction, but a small array of information graphics appeared regularly in periodical pages, including diagrams, thematized cartographic maps, and weather charts.[24]

Photomechanical reproduction further widened the horizons of possibility for sharing data visualizations, especially statistical graphics, with the masses.[25] Perhaps the most notable trend of information display was population journalism. Population articles covered a wide array of statistics-based topics, ranging from annual food consumption per capita to changes in average lifespan over time to military power compared across European nations.[26] Although its visualization techniques tended to lack

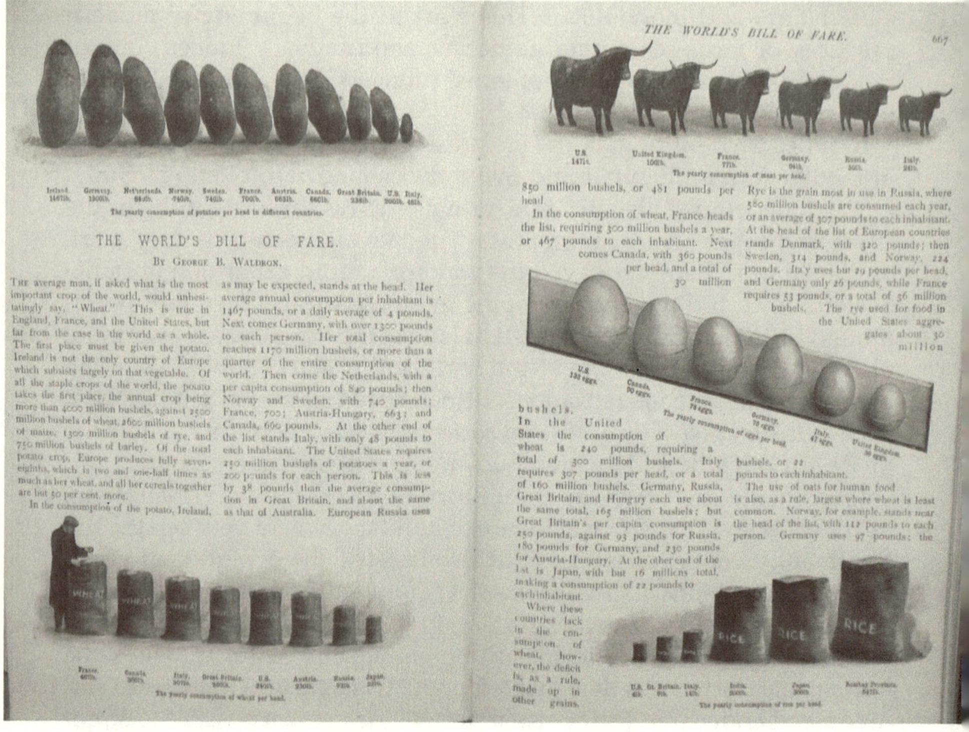

Ireland. 1467lb. Germany. 1300lb. Netherlands. 840lb. Norway. 740lb. Sweden. 740lb. France. 700lb. Austria. 663lb. Canada. 660lb. Great Britain. 238lb. U.S. 200lb. Italy. 48lb.

The yearly consumption of potatoes per head in different countries.

THE WORLD'S BILL OF FARE.

By George B. Waldron.

The average man, if asked what is the most important crop of the world, would unhesitatingly say, "Wheat." This is true in England, France, and the United States, but far from the case in the world as a whole. The first place must be given the potato. Ireland is not the only country of Europe which subsists largely on that vegetable. Of all the staple crops of the world, the potato takes the first place, the annual crop being more than 4000 million bushels, against 2500 million bushels of wheat, 2600 million bushels of maize, 1300 million bushels of rye, and 750 million bushels of barley. Of the total potato crop, Europe produces fully seven-eighths, which is two and one-half times as much as her wheat, and all her cereals together are but 50 per cent. more.

In the consumption of the potato, Ireland, as may be expected, stands at the head. Her average annual consumption per inhabitant is 1467 pounds, or a daily average of 4 pounds. Next comes Germany, with over 1300 pounds to each person. Her total consumption reaches 1170 million bushels, or more than a quarter of the entire consumption of the world. Then come the Netherlands, with a per capita consumption of 840 pounds; then Norway and Sweden, with 740 pounds; France, 700; Austria-Hungary, 663; and Canada, 660 pounds. At the other end of the list stands Italy, with only 48 pounds to each inhabitant. The United States requires 250 million bushels of potatoes a year, or 200 pounds for each person. This is less by 38 pounds than the average consumption in Great Britain, and about the same as that of Australia. European Russia uses

France. 467lb. Canada. 360lb. Italy. 307lb. Great Britain. 250lb. U.S. 240lb. Austria. 230lb. Russia. 93lb. Japan. 22lb.

The yearly consumption of wheat per head.

THE WORLD'S BILL OF FARE. 667

U.S. 147lb. United Kingdom. France. 77lb. Germany. 64lb. Russia. Italy. 24lb.

The yearly consumption of meat per head.

850 million bushels, or 481 pounds per head.

In the consumption of wheat, France heads the list, requiring 300 million bushels a year, or 467 pounds to each inhabitant. Next comes Canada, with 360 pounds per head, and a total of 30 million bushels.

In the United States the consumption of wheat is 240 pounds, requiring a total of 300 million bushels. Italy requires 307 pounds per head, or a total of 160 million bushels. Germany, Russia, Great Britain, and Hungary each use about the same total, 165 million bushels; but Great Britain's per capita consumption is 250 pounds, against 93 pounds for Russia, 180 pounds for Germany, and 230 pounds for Austria-Hungary. At the other end of the list is Japan, with but 16 millions total, making a consumption of 22 pounds to each inhabitant.

Where these countries lack in the consumption of wheat, however, the deficit is, as a rule, made up in other grains.

Rye is the grain most in use in Russia, where 580 million bushels are consumed each year, or an average of 307 pounds to each inhabitant. At the head of the list of European countries stands Denmark, with 320 pounds; then Sweden, 314 pounds, and Norway, 224 pounds. Italy uses but 29 pounds per head, and Germany only 26 pounds, while France requires 53 pounds, or a total of 56 million bushels. The rye used for food in the United States aggregates about 30 million bushels, or 22 pounds to each inhabitant.

The use of oats for human food is also, as a rule, largest where wheat is least common. Norway, for example, stands near the head of the list, with 112 pounds to each person. Germany uses 97 pounds; the

U.S. Canada, 90 eggs. Italy, 47 eggs. United Kingdom, 36 eggs.

The yearly consumption of eggs per head.

U.S. 4lb. Gt. Britain. 9lb. Italy. 14lb. India. Japan. Bombay Province.

The yearly consumption of rice per head.

Figure 3.1. Excerpted pages from "The World's Bill of Fare," by George B. Waldron. *Pearson's Magazine* 6 (1898): 666–7.

quantitative rigour, the genre's statistical basis enabled it to claim the objective authority that Victorians attributed to empirical, quantitative evidence; at the same time, its diverse, unusual visuals gave the genre a novelty that made its articles entertaining. Population journalism's peak of ubiquity was brief, but its distinctive look and subject matter made its data-visualization techniques effective for modern popular culture.

The basis of appeal for population journalism was its innovative use of visual forms to represent the people to themselves. For example, in "The Modern Mercury" (published in the *Strand Magazine* in 1896), J. Holt Schooling reports on "a vital factor" of the "social life and national activity" of Britain, the circulation of mail by post.[27] The article is supported by several data visualizations. In "The World's Bill of Fare" (published in *Pearson's Magazine* in 1898), George B. Waldron compares the food and beverage consumption of different nations (figure 3.1).[28] Both articles use data graphics to support a narrative emphasis on the British nation's abundant production and consumption. In "The Modern Mercury," a proportional area chart compares Britain's volume of circulated mail to that of other nations, and a set of circle clusters visualizes the quantity of British mail sent to each corner of its empire. In "The World's Bill of Fare," a series of data measures embody mimetically the food and drink they represent: row upon row of eggs, cattle, and rice, depicted in ascending size, display European habits of consumption per capita.

Articles of population journalism appeared in several monthly miscellanies, including *Harmsworth Magazine* (later called the *London Magazine*), the *Pall Mall Magazine*, the *Strand*, and the *Windsor Magazine*, between approximately 1895 and 1902. Some magazines, such as the *Strand*, only featured one or two pieces of population journalism, while *Pearson's* and *Harmsworth* each published approximately a dozen articles in this genre. In the early twentieth century these articles disappeared from the monthlies, although statistical visualizations using similar design techniques and themes continued to appear sporadically in other illustrated periodicals, such as the *Daily Graphic* (for example, a heavily annotated line graph titled "Our Overseas Trade," printed on 8 January 1908).[29]

Abstract Data Visualization in *Pearson's Magazine*, 1896–8

Population journalism appeared with particular frequency in *Pearson's Magazine*, which was known for its exceptionally miscellaneous and visual character, as well as its wide distribution across British classes and the empire.[30] Launched in 1896 by Cyril Arthur Pearson, *Pearson's* typified late-Victorian popular magazines in its use of New Journalism's entertaining brevity, levity, and emphasis on human interest – strategies that Pearson had perfected while working for George Newnes and W.T. Stead, two of New Journalism's most renowned pioneers.[31] Although scholars have largely neglected *Pearson's*, it was the "crown jewel" of Pearson's publishing empire, achieving wide circulation thanks to its relatively low cost (at six pence) and its generous use of images.[32] Illustrated monthlies typically targeted middle-class audiences, but *Pearson's* had an exceptionally broad-based readership that included working-, middle-, and upper-class consumers in Great Britain and its empire.[33] Given *Pearson's* wide reach and high circulation (it sold 200,000 to 400,000 per number in 1898), the magazine's population journalism wielded considerable influence over readers' conception of society.[34] This meant that its population journalism was encountered by a wide spectrum of the persons that this genre documented in numeric and graphical forms.

Like most popular, family-oriented periodicals, *Pearson's* used its influence to promote patriotic and imperialistic values inflected by biopolitics. For example, a 1906 series, titled "Problems of the Day," dealt with issues detrimental to population health, such as infant mortality and insanity.[35] It is unsurprising, then, that *Pearson's* population journalism reinforced the magazine's nationalist views by framing biopolitical tenets, such as population health, normalization, and expansion, in terms of British citizenship.[36]

J. Brand's "Is Suicide a Sign of Civilisation?," from *Pearson's* initial year in print, was the magazine's first piece of population journalism. The article ostensibly educates its readers with an overview of scientific measurements of human life while showcasing a specific version of the British nation of which readers could be proud. It also encouraged readers to conceptualize individuals as quantitative units of a bureaucratically defined statistical mass.

As was typical of the genre, "Is Suicide a Sign of Civilisation?" combines statistics, visualization, and social commentary. Speaking to fin-de-siècle Britain's cultural preoccupation with the relationship between the mental and physical health of individuals and the success of the nation, Brand compares statistics on suicide in countries deemed civilized and uncivilized, reporting that "amongst savages suicide, as an individual act apart from the customs of the country, is almost unknown." In contrast, "every civilized country pays its yearly tribute to this terrible plague with a regularity that is appalling, and the tribute is steadily increasing."[37] Brand includes statistics on the number of suicides among men, women, and children, citing a few harrowing anecdotes before addressing the causes. He deems heredity the chief cause, but a pie graph offers more specificity: "insanity" causes 34 per cent of cases, followed by "various" at 28 per cent and "grief" at 23 per cent. Like most population journalism, the article does not cite the source of its statistics, encouraging readers to accept the author's interpretation of the numbers. Ranking European nations in order of suicide numbers, Brand observes that Germans, the "profoundest thinkers in Europe," are also "the most suicidal race." He interprets the correlation between suicide and intellectual activity as evidence of causation, concluding that "suicide is not an explicable social phenomenon, but inevitable in the process of civilization."[38]

Comparing statistics from multiple nations, as Brand does with the frequency of suicide, was one of the main techniques through which population journalism made numerical facts meaningful, and one that highlights how the genre's biopolitics were informed by New Imperialism. At the fin de siècle the British Empire was the world's leading economic and military power as a result of large-scale colonial expansion in Asia and Africa. The era's international relations were shaped by rivalries among several such empires with territory around the world. In population journalism, comparisons of quantified population behaviours reinforced an imperialistic sense of economic, military, and cultural rivalry. The comparators most often cited were other major world powers, particularly Western ones such as Germany, France, and the United States. Britain often ranked first in these comparisons. When it did not, an inferior ranking was always framed by an article's author in a way that would reassure readers that Britain was still a privileged global leader. For example, Brand suggests that Britain's third-place ranking in suicide frequency across several Western nations is neither too low nor too high: the nation is intellectually advanced, but not so much so as to suffer from the excessive temperamental "fierceness" of the French and Germans.[39]

When population journalism cited statistics about other nations that were not imperial or economic leaders, it did so to underscore their otherness. Brand's comment about the rarity of suicide among so-called savages offers one example of this strategy. Another appears in "The World's Bill of Fare": in a comparison of rice consumption per capita, the data measures for visualized Asian regions are over four times larger than those for Western global powers, underscoring the otherness of non-Western dietary practices. Through such comparisons, population journalism fostered a conception of the British citizen at the centre of not only the nation but also the imperial stage. Colonial and foreign populations, which were never individualized, were interesting only as foils to Britons. In this way, even though *Pearson's* and the other magazines in which this genre appeared were circulated around the world, population journalism both assumed and constructed its readers as residents of the British Empire's homeland.

In addition to a New Imperialist concern with the metropole's vitality, population journalism's biopolitics were shaped by recent developments in scientific and social thought, particularly regarding human evolution. Brand's statistical narrative takes for granted several premises that shaped Victorian scientific knowledge: that humans could be grouped into homogeneous masses in a hierarchical taxonomy; that quantitative information about them had special epistemological status as objective truth – what Mary Poovey has described as "the modern fact";[40] and that studying population data would reveal "natural laws" of social development.[41] Brand's rhetoric also invokes social Darwinism, positioning the hereditary factors and group behaviours identified through statistical analysis as evidence of a population body's trajectory of evolutionary improvement or decline.

Brand's statistical accounting of deaths as part of an evolutionary process invokes a sense of certainty, placing this seemingly irrational behaviour within a science-based narrative that identifies direct and indirect causes. The account offered by "Is Suicide a Sign of Civilisation?" manages to reassure readers by placing suicide within a rational framework and demonstrating the nation's privileged status within it. Britain's third-place suicide rate positioned it well above the supposedly unsophisticated geopolitical groups but below the most morbidly introspective ones. British readers could thus interpret their nation as modestly situated on a trajectory that supported the existence of suicide as a regrettable but inevitable side effect of social progress.

Abstract data visualizations aid Brand's efforts to reassure readers about the scientific basis of his narrative. These graphics connect the article with the magazine's visual landscape while distinguishing its science-based analysis. The letterpress of "Is Suicide a Sign of Civilisation?" does not directly engage with the visualizations, leaving the reader to undertake the interpretive work of relating text to images with the aid of descriptive captions (a practice that was typical of population journalism and, indeed, of many illustrated print genres of the nineteenth century).

The article's data visualizations – three pie charts and a bar graph – offer starkly simplified representations of society compared to the prevalent image types in this *Pearson's* number, which include artist-drawn illustrations, halftone images from photographs, and detailed technical diagrams. One of the article's pie charts divides a year's suicides by method – hanging, drowning, poison, and "various" – and displays them as percentages of the whole (figure 3.2). The chart reinforces the article's rationalization of seemingly irrational behaviour, containing self-violence in impersonal categories that form a tidy circle. Use of a large miscellaneous category, "Various," limits the pie chart to four sections, presenting readers with a reassuringly (if misleadingly) small array of suicide techniques. Any unusually bizarre or horrific methods are absorbed by this dark-grey, vaguely labelled slice of the pie, buffering readers from the distress of studying real suicides. The pie chart's circular form is also reassuring, aggregating and reshaping individual behaviours into a visual whole. A horizontal bar graph similarly reduces real instances of suicide, binarizing them by male and female gender. Male suicides dominate the visualization, making up 73 per cent of the graph. Given that the two categories derive meaning from their relation to one another, female suicides are visually marginalized. The graphical abstraction reiterates that women are not only socially marginal but also, following Brand's supposition, less civilized than

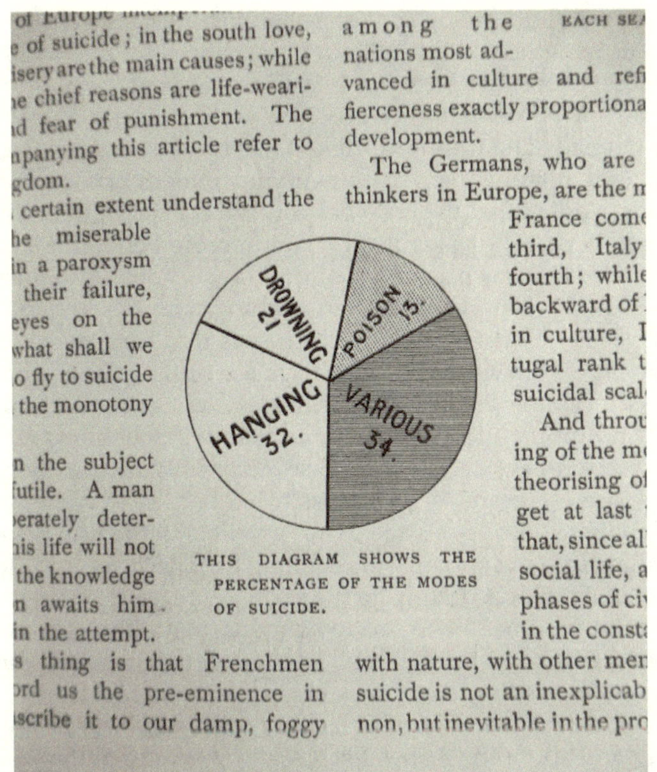
of Europe
e of suicide ; in the south love,
iseryarethe main causes; while
ie chief reasons are life-weari-
id fear of punishment. The
npanying this article refer to
gdom.
certain extent understand the
he miserable
in a paroxysm
their failure,
eyes on the
what shall we
o fly to suicide
the monotony

n the subject
futile. A man
erately deter-
his life will not
the knowledge
n awaits him.
in the attempt.
s thing is that Frenchmen
ord us the pre-eminence in
scribe it to our damp, foggy

among the
nations most ad-
vanced in culture and refi
fierceness exactly proportiona
development.
The Germans, who are
thinkers in Europe, are the n
France come
third, Italy
fourth; while
backward of
in culture, I
tugal rank t
suicidal scal
And throu
ing of the m
theorising of
get at last
that, since al
social life, a
phases of ci
in the const
with nature, with other men
suicide is not an inexplicab
non, but inevitable in the pro

Figure 3.2. Line-block illustration for "Is Suicide a Sign of Civilisation?," by J. Brand. *Pearson's Magazine* 2 (1896): 667.

men. This outlook resonates with population journalism's orientation to an average subject defined as such by middle-class, populist values.

Following Brand's "Is Suicide a Sign of Civilisation?," seven more articles of population journalism that included the same abstract graphical style appeared in *Pearson's*: "Which Is the Maddest Part of the Kingdom?" (1896), "The Lion's Share" (1896), "Is the Length of Life Increasing?" (1897), "To All Named Smith – Greetings!" (1897), "Land versus Sea" (1897), "Black Diamonds" (1897), and "Ourselves versus the World" (1898). These articles shared the same author, an actuary, statistician, and author named John Holt Schooling (1859–1927), who wrote and illustrated population journalism for a number of major periodicals, including the *Pall Mall Magazine*, the *Strand*, and the *Windsor Magazine*.[42]

Unlike Brand, Schooling consistently illustrated his own population journalism, as indicated typically in his authorial by-line, but his work nonetheless aligns with Brand's "Is Suicide a Sign of Civilisation?" article in form and content. In each article Schooling gives a narrative overview of uncited statistics concerning patterns of human characteristics and activities, relating them to the everyday lives of British citizens and reassuring readers that the statistics confirm the strength of the British population body. The visualizations underscore Schooling's narrative assessment of British social and political life. Schooling frequently celebrates British accomplishments, in keeping with the imperialist tone of *Pearson's*. In "The Lion's Share" he boasts that "one person in every four who crawl, walk, or ride on the surface of this planet is under the rule of Victoria, the greatest monarch in ancient or modern history."[43] The British Empire also looms large in many of Schooling's visualizations. A piece titled "Land versus Sea" ostensibly focuses on statistics that compare the planet's land mass to its bodies of water, but even here Schooling contrives a strategy for privileging the tiny British Isles. A visualization consolidates the United Kingdom as a hollow jelly mould that, if it reached down to the earth's core, could hold half of the ocean's total volume.[44] The image suggests that although the United Kingdom seems superficially small on the ocean's surface, it carries unseen weight. Schooling thus doses his narrative statistical reports with patriotic observations about England's superiority within the United Kingdom and about the British Empire's importance to the world.

I have highlighted a number of ways that abstract population-data graphics aesthetically reified Victorian biopolitics. Each article's figures quantify and re-present the British populace in clean geometric shapes and neat lines, visually and spatially colonizing human bodies and behaviours. The visualizations aggregate individual suicides into contained fractions of geometrically rationalizing shapes. Population-data visualizations contributed to the work of quantitative social management through material aesthetic strategies, as well as visual and spatial ones. For example, *Pearson's* graphic titled "Six Great Powers of Europe," in "The Lion's Share," demonstrates the linear aesthetic of the line-block process through which *Pearson's* reproduced the pen-and-ink originals of its abstract population visualizations (figure 3.3). This visualization uses only black (i.e., fully inked) and white (i.e., not inked) tones; fine, black lines on un-inked space produce a semblance of grey. This proportional area chart depicts the imperial powers as cross-hatched, uniformly sized cubes. Fully inked cubes representing imperial colonies and dependencies appear below, each joined to its respective nation by a line like a weight on a tether.

Figure 3.3. Line-block illustration for "The Lion's Share," by John Holt Schooling. *Pearson's Magazine* 3 (1896): 612.

The disparity between the size of the United Kingdom and the size of its colonies and dependencies – the largest such disparity in the visualization – suggests Britain's biopolitical prowess: among the six "Great Powers" it boasts an exceptional capacity to support a vast empire.

The material strategies through which abstract population graphics reified biopolitics extended to the graphics' production history, which readers could engage through their print media literacy. Slight idiosyncrasies of shape and the clean linearity of black-and-white forms attest to the status of abstract population graphics as reproductions of artists' drawings by line-block engraving. Victorian readers, informed by articles on illustrated print production, could account for such material factors as part of their interpretive processes. Readers who knew the production history of line-block images recognized them as the outcomes of cutting-edge mass print technology. Engaging the technological imagination, then, abstract data visualizations aesthetically rationalized the periodical page in two senses: they exhibited both its quantitative mapping by an artist's or statistician's hand and its systematic mediation by machine. Abstract visualization thus transformed individual subjects into units of mechanized mass print, as well as quantifying imperial and colonial populations.

Photorealistic Data Visualization

In 1898, *Pearson's* population journalism relinquished the abstract visualization style, with its suggestion of quantitative rigour, in favour of quirkier photorealistic visualizations. These used the halftone process to reproduce a composite of photographs and drawings as visually detailed, greyscale figures. The resulting aesthetics aligned less with political economics and more with scrapbooking and photocollage. At the same time that it dispensed with abstract data visualizations, *Pearson's* population journalism ceased to rely primarily on Schooling to write and illustrate these articles, further diminishing the genre's association with statistical integrity and scientific method. All nine population articles appearing between 1898 and 1902 incorporated photorealistic visualizations; of these, only one article was written by Schooling. The rest were written by less specialized journalists.[45]

The texts of *Pearson's* post-1898 population journalism upheld established biopolitical rhetoric, but the photorealistic graphics flouted conventional data-visualization values – presentational transparency, simplicity, and quantitative accuracy – in favour of New Journalistic visual novelty. Although their aesthetics undermined their own quantitative authority, photorealistic visualizations enacted more complex biopolitics than did the abstract graphical method. The latter reduced the individual subject's body to a quantified population unit, and the former remediated the individual subject's body as an aesthetic component of mass print.

T.D. Denham's "The Mathematics of Marriage" exemplifies *Pearson's* photorealistic population journalism, advancing the aesthetic strategies previously established by Brand and Schooling with a visual novelty that enacts more complex biopolitics (figure 3.4). Denham's data

THE MATHEMATICS OF MARRIAGE

By

T. D. Denham.

The blending of the most practical of sciences—mathematics—with the most romantic of our rites and ceremonies—marriage, may at first glance seem incongruous. But I hope to convince those who continue their reading beyond this first paragraph, that there is much of interest in the figure-facts of marriage, if they can but be set forth in picturesque form.

From the reports of the Registrar-General we extract the information that the annual birth-rate in the United Kingdom is thirty per thousand of the population, and the annual marriage-rate fifteen per thousand. So for every thirty births, fifteen people marry, and therefore for every twenty births, ten people marry.

This marriage-rate not only includes bachelors and spinsters who marry, but also widows and widowers who marry again: and out of 456,608 persons married in 1895, no fewer than 42,034, or not quite one in ten, had been married before.

But we have shown that for every twenty births, ten people marry, and we know that on the average one of those ten persons will already have been married: we are, therefore, left with nine spinsters or bachelors who

According to the last census twelve out of every twenty of the female sex were single, seven were married, and one widowed.

According to the last census twelve out of every twenty of the male sex were single, seven were married, and one widowed.

THE MATHEMATICS OF MARRIAGE. 397

Out of every twenty babies born into the world, nine (dressed in white) will eventually marry, eleven (in black) will not.

marry for every twenty births. And so the chances at birth that a baby will eventually marry are nine in twenty, or rather less than one-half. This result may seem surprising, but it is largely accounted for by the great mortality of persons under marriageable age, especially of infants up to the age of five. No fewer than 38 per cent. of babies die before they are five years old, and forty-four per cent of the whole population before the age of eighteen.

Though it may be a matter of common knowledge that the females outnumber the males in this country (the actual proportion is 106 to 100), the subdivision of the population into the three great classes, single, married, and widowed, and the figures relating to these subdivisions will be new to most of us.

Out of every hundred persons now living in this country, sixty are single, thirty-five are married, and five are widowed. So that, on the average, one person in every twenty you meet in the streets, in the train, or wherever it may be, will be either a widow or a widower, and three out of five will be unmarried.

This is the general average for all countries. In France, however, as many as forty in a hundred are married, eight widowed, and only fifty-two unmarried. People evidently

A woman's chance of marrying—half as great again in London, Notts, Yorkshire, Warwickshire, Lancashire, and South Wales, as it is in Rutlandshire, Middlesex, Cumberland, Surrey, Hertfordshire, and Herefordshire.

Figure 3.4. Excerpted pages from "The Mathematics of Marriage," by T.D. Denham. *Pearson's Magazine* 5 (1898): 396–7.

selections and diction enforce the cultural precept deeming marriage to be statistically normative and socially desirable – a view that was under attack from social and political dissidents at the fin de siècle but that many held to be essential to maintaining Britain's privileged cultural and political status. The article's "figure-facts," which are derived, like those in the articles by Brand and Schooling, from unattributed statistics, chiefly pertain to how many people marry (and remarry), at what ages they wed, and how many people remain single.

The illustrations for "The Mathematics of Marriage" complement the text by associating light shades with marriage, birth, and life and dark shades with singleness and death. A visualization of infants, appearing at the top of the article's second page, exemplifies how these two sets of associations are mapped onto distinctive population groups. In a queue of twenty babies, the eleven wearing black gowns, suggestive of funereal wear, represent the statistical likelihood of remaining single. The nine wearing white gowns, suggestive of baptismal and wedding dresses, represent the likelihood of getting married.[46] For every twenty births in England, Denham says, ten people marry; one of these ten "will already have been married," and "we are, therefore, left with nine spinsters or bachelors who marry": the eleven spinsters and bachelors who remain unmarried become the population's numeric and social remainder.[47] Curiously, the statistic that Denham cites does not appear to account for infant and childhood deaths, which were relatively high in late-Victorian Britain. Three of the eleven infants constituting the "numeric and social remainder" were statistically likely to be deceased by adulthood.[48] However, Denham sidesteps the difficult issue of infant mortality. Perhaps, in an era of preoccupation with the health of the nation, this issue was thought too volatile by Denham or the editors of *Pearson's* to be tidily contained through visual rationalization on the page in the manner of suicide and spinsterhood. As a general rule, *Pearson's* population journalism sought to reinforce the state's biopolitical values in a fashion that was both entertaining and reassuring to a general, middle-class audience; infant and childhood mortality did not readily lend themselves to such cultural work.

Throughout the article Denham expresses the marriage rate in terms of the "chances at birth that an infant will actually marry" in adulthood. Drawing a direct link from infancy to marriage – rather than, for example, citing the married percentage of the adult population – may strike readers as an unusual marriage statistic formulation. However, this article's framework posits birth and marriage as the quintessential characteristics of the biological trajectory and, correspondingly, of population life. Denham gives little attention to the statistical relationship between marriage and procreation; instead, the text and graphics of "The Mathematics of Marriage" emphasize the statistical relationship between being born and getting married. The population's marriage behaviours are only associated indirectly with the national body's reproduction. For example, the article header faces the row of babies heaped in visual abundance, a kind of fecundity itself.[49] The article limits its scope to one's own biological and cultural behaviour – one's own birth, one's own marriage – though neither birth nor marriage can be managed on one's own. The narrative thus places responsibility for population behaviours on individuals.

A pair of visualizations on the article's third and fourth pages reinforces this biopolitical individualization (figure 3.5). Two sets of images place four figures in sequence of size; these data visualizations use scale to express the comparative occurrence of marriage among different age

marry earlier and oftener in France than we do, whereas in Chili only twenty-six in a hundred are married, five widowed, and sixty-nine single. The disturbed state of the country, the constant insurrections, and the consequent killing off of young men of marriageable age are the chief factors of Chili's apparent aversion to married life.

From these inquiries we are naturally led to the question: How long does married life last? In England, an average husband and wife on their wedding-day may expect to live together for twenty-seven years, in France only twenty-six, in Holland and Belgium twenty-three, but in Russia thirty. If, therefore, you want to enjoy a long married life go to Russia. You may expect a period of thirty years to elapse before you are parted either by death or divorce.

Young people will be more particularly interested in our next problem:—Where to live if you want to be married? The highest marriage-rate for any European country is in Austria-Hungary. The average there is more than 17 per 1000 per annum. The lowest rates are in Ireland, only 10 per 1000, and Sweden with 11 per 1000. Consequently the chance of a person getting married is more than half as good again in Austria-Hungary, as it is in Sweden or Ireland.

To English people it will be more valuable to know which are the marrying counties of England, and which the non-marrying. The lowest marriage-rates in 1895—the most recent year for which the full and accurate returns are available, were 11·1 per 1000 in poor little Rutlandshire, 11·3 in Middlesex, 12·1 in Cumberland, and 12·2 in Surrey, in Hertfordshire, and in Herefordshire.

The highest marriage-rate, 17·2 per 1000, was in London, as one would naturally expect—so many of the fashionable marriages being solemnised in the metropolis. Next in order come Nottinghamshire, East Yorkshire, Warwickshire, Lancashire, and South Wales, with a marriage rate slightly in excess of 16 per 1000. Curiously enough, the same counties have been respectively at the top and bottom of the list for the previous ten years.

Let, then, all candidates for spinsterhood bury themselves in Rutlandshire, while intending brides and bridegrooms are advised to make for London with all speed.

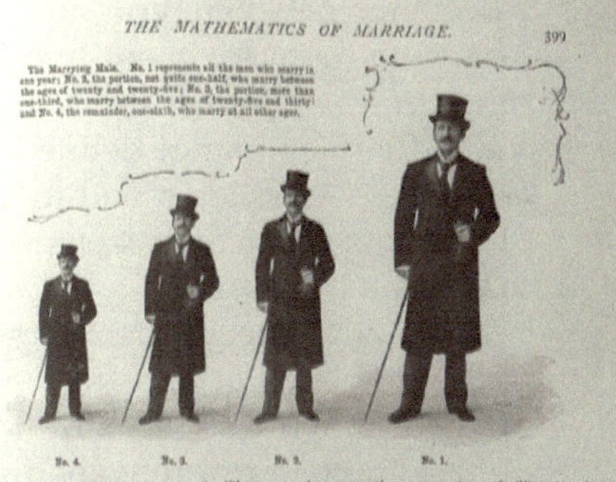

At what age do people marry? The most popular time for a woman to get married is from her twenty-first to her twenty-fifth year, inclusive. More than one-half of the women who marry at all, marry in these five years of their life, and another quarter marry between the ages of twenty-five and thirty. With men, not quite one-half marry between the ages of twenty and twenty-five, and more than a third between the ages of twenty-five and thirty.

The average age of marrying is just over twenty-six for women and just under twenty-eight for men. These figures include re-marriages. For spinsters only, the average age is twenty-five, and for bachelors, twenty-six and a-half. It is a noticeable fact that, in the last ten years, the average age of marrying has, for men and women alike, gone up half a year.

Quite an astonishing number of men and women in England and Wales still sign the Marriage Register with marks. The total in a recent year of 20,157 illiterates out of 456,408 persons marrying, was made up of 9239 men and 10,918 women, nearly one married person out of every twenty being illiterate! With the spread of education, however, the proportion of illiterates is becoming smaller each year.

There are quite a number of different ways in which a person may be married in this country. The most popular is by banns, according to the rites of the Established Church. Six hundred and thirty-three out of every 1000 marriages in England are solemnised in this way. One hundred and forty-seven per 1000 are civil marriages in a Registrar's office, 160 per 1000 in registered places of worship of other Christian denominations, including 40 in Roman Catholic churches, 39 by licence, 5 according to Jewish rites, and 3 *per 10,000* by the Quakers.

The most noticeable points in connection with these statistics are that in the last fifteen years the civil marriage-rate has increased five-fold from 29 per 1000 marriages to 147 per 1000, the total according to the rites of the Established Church has decreased from 896 per 1000 to 686 per 1000, and for other Christian denominations has increased from 73 per 1000 to 161 per 1000.

From 1864 to 1895, the marriage-rate in England has decreased to the extent of two per thousand of the population annually. In Scotland and Ireland it has remained

Figure 3.5. Excerpted pages from "The Mathematics of Marriage," by T.D. Denham. *Pearson's* Magazine 5 (1898): 398–9.

groups.[50] None of the images depicts a heteronormative couple: the pages spatially segregate married women, on the verso, from married men, on the recto. The data visualization encourages readers to imagine marriage as the behaviour of an individual and to group married individuals by age and gender. Readers might therefore categorize human bodies and behaviours within statistically determined demographics instead of the self-selected category of the married couple.

While "The Mathematics of Marriage" prompts readers to identify themselves as individual biopolitical units, it also encourages them to aggregate other citizens in demographic categories. Denham comments that "on average, one person in every twenty you meet in the streets, in the train, or wherever it may be, will be a widow or a widower, and three out of five unmarried."[51] He thus recasts the values by which readers can assess not only the behavioural normalcy or deviancy of themselves but also that of fellow citizens. The article's implied association between reproduction and the marriage of women and men leaves no room for these two activities to occur and relate to one another in other forms. Reproduction outside marriage, the birth of an individual who is not defined by marriage status, and same-sex marriage are not depicted within Denham's rubric. According to the logic of Denham's article, citizens who practise any of these behaviours deviate from the norm.

Although "The Mathematics of Marriage" maintains the biopolitical outlook of *Pearson's* abstract population journalism, its photorealistic aesthetic renders its visualizations not only less quantitatively accurate but also more interpretively opaque than the abstract visualizations of Brand and Schooling, which relied on simple but varied graphical techniques for accuracy and efficacy. Like much of *Pearson's* photorealistic population journalism, "The Mathematics of Marriage" makes frequent but haphazard use of small multiples. This technique involves multiplying the same graphical design structure to create a series of figures that are identical except for one aesthetic characteristic, such as size or colour. Small multiples enable the comparison of one variable across instances or populations. In photorealistic population journalism small multiples reflect what Thompson has described as iconicity: each visual unit is a synecdoche for its quantified subject.[52] In this regard, the small multiples of "The Mathematics of Marriage" are much like pictograms, a variety of small multiples popularized by Michael G. Mulhall's *Dictionary of Statistics* in 1884.[53]

In "The Mathematics of Marriage," figures of men, women, and children serve as the small multiples that quantify units of real populations. These figures perpetuate graphical distortion because their spatial proportions are supposed to but do not entirely correspond to the quantities they represent. For example, the two visualizations in figure 3.4 use disproportionate multiples to depict the comparative occurrence of marriage among men and women at different ages. Each visualization depicts the same figure four times (one male and one female), but the figures vary in size to express population quantities for the different age ranges of marrying citizens. Although size constitutes the main variable through which the visualizations convey data, the figures are disproportionately sized in relation to one another. In the series depicting "The Marrying Female," figure no. 2 supposedly represents slightly more than 50 per cent of the proportions of figure no. 1 but actually occupies closer to 75 per cent of her size on the page. Figure no. 3 represents 25 per cent of the total marrying female population in a year, and figure no. 4 represents less than this amount, but the two figures occupy identical quantitative areas.

This data visualization perpetuates what Tufte considers a serious error: distorting data measures to "make an editorial comment or fit a decorative scheme."[54] He contends that "graphical distortions" yield quantitatively dishonest data that "corrupt the display."[55] Distorted data visualizations mislead and confuse readers, "cloud[ing] the flow of information."[56] The epistemological principles assumed by Tufte in these comments are shared by most practitioners of visualization, dating back to Playfair. Offering the rationale for his influential 1786 work, *The Commercial and Political Atlas*, Playfair argued that the goal of data visualization should be to present information so that a reader can comprehend it as perfectly as possible.[57] Extending this view of data visualization's purpose, Tufte defines "graphical excellence" as visually offering a reader the greatest number of ideas in the shortest time with the least ink and in the least space.[58] According to Playfair and Tufte, data visualizations should not draw attention to themselves but should, as Drucker puts it, "mask the very fact of their visuality."[59]

Pearson's photorealistic population visualizations flout these ideals of perfect comprehensiveness and clarity. Their aesthetics distort statistical data, rendering them opaque. For example, the form and layout of the small multiples in "The Marrying Female" and "The Marrying Male" are determined more by editorial sensibilities than by visual perspective. The two sets of facing figures are arranged to create an aesthetically pleasing visual symmetry that undermines the interpretation of their data because the arrangement requires that one set of figures be sequenced in the reverse order of the other. A reader must interpret the figures in opposite sequence. In this way the visualizations privilege design over interpretive simplicity. Other characteristics of the two data visualizations transform graphical display into ornamentation: the figures in each visualization also exhibit quantitatively superfluous aesthetic data, such as facial features. Flourishes such as the inky shadows under each figure's feet and curlicues above their heads add irrelevant visual interest. Tufte dismisses such "interior decoration" as "chartjunk" that obstructs data visualization's true purpose: to "induce the viewer to think about the substance rather than about methodology" or design.[60]

According to the rubric first articulated by Playfair in the eighteenth century and theorized by Tufte in the twentieth and twenty-first centuries, *Pearson's* photorealistic visualizations are noisy and ineffective compared to their abstract predecessors. However, although photorealistic visualizations detracted from population journalism's statistical authority, they boosted the genre's visual interest and expanded its biopolitical authority. My analyses have already demonstrated that quantitative information was only one facet of the cultural data that population journalism mediated for readers. Indeed, the fact that *Pearson's* eventually replaced the work of Schooling with that of non-specialist authors suggests that statistical accuracy was not a top journalistic priority.[61]

Spectacular Normalization in "The Mathematics of Marriage"

I suggest that the quirky complexity of the visualizations in "The Mathematics of Marriage" and other photorealist population journalism was intentional and, in fact, contributed to the cultural work of the genre by making biopolitics itself a spectacle. Lauren Klein has argued that deliberately opaque data visualizations encouraged nineteenth-century readers to pay attention to the process of knowledge production itself.[62] Whether a visualization's complexity was the product of recursive design or simply poor execution can be hard to parse with certainty, but material and cultural contexts support an inference of the former in this case; still a novelty in mass print of the 1890s, halftone images were inherently spectacular.[63] As discussed in previous chapters, readers were equipped to recognize a halftone image as such and could situate it as the product of recent innovations in photomechanical mass image reproduction. I posit that the main cultural work of photorealist population visualization was therefore to enact an aesthetic spectacle of biopolitics that conveyed meaning in part by drawing readers' attention to the print production process.

The halftone images in *Pearson's* population journalism and other content distinguished the magazine as aesthetically modern – as a new media artefact in an era that made much of "new" cultural phenomena (for example, New Journalism, the New Woman, and New Realism). I have already suggested that the aura of modernity that surrounded halftone visualizations conditioned reader interpretation, imbuing with authority the cultural values expressed by those visualizations. The techno-material specificity of these graphics also conditioned reader interpretation. Halftone images that were reproduced from photographs, such as most of the images in "The Mathematics of Marriage," implicated the unique subjects of their originals: the real people, places, and events from which a magazine photographer captured physical data. Depending on the quality of paper and ink, the halftone could exhibit tonal details almost as minute as those of a photograph, seeming to represent life with more fidelity than did other print processes. However, all halftone images also implied their own mass multiplicity. A photograph, as a three-dimensional object, had unique materiality, but halftone images did not: the verso of a magazine page attested to the two-dimensionality of images materialized en masse in print culture. A photograph-derived halftone on a magazine page, regularized and flattened, was, as Gerry Beegan observes, simply "one ephemeral image among many contiguous texts."[64] A halftone image's miniscule dots recursively signified a production process that required remediating complex subjects as uniform bits of data and reproducing that data through a segmented, multi-stage photomechanical process evocative of the assembly line.[65] The halftone aesthetic suggested the increasing role of industrial, capitalistic automation in popular culture. Moreover, its tonal granularity implicated the material normalization of cultural information. Within the context of population visualization the normalizing effect of halftone reproduction acquired an additional dimension, imbricating it with the statistical thinking that informed Victorian population politics.

Through photorealism produced by the halftone process, population visualizations remediated the individual subject's body as an aesthetic component of mass print. Population journalism's textual, visual, and material elements constructed the reader as a unique individual but also, paradoxically, as a quantified, mechanized component of the population mass. For example, in the visualization of infants depicted in figure 3.3, the unique facial features and posture of each infant suggest that *Pearson's* sourced the image from a photograph of real babies. The halftone visualization thus invokes the putatively objective, documentary powers of the camera and the photograph. At the same time, the granular dots made by the halftone screen regularize the figures as products of mass mechanization. In keeping with *Pearson's* cultural imperialism, these mechanical replicas exhibit racial as well as material homogeneity. All the babies are white and fair, conveying a racialized view of the British nation and its future.

Similarly, a pair of visualizations at the bottom of the article's first page remediates individuals as replicated aesthetic components. Each visualization depicts three figures that respectively represent single, married, and widowed adults (female in the first visualization and male in the second). Each of the three figures bears the features of a perfectly average type: the figures are appropriately pleasing to the eye, but not exceptionally beautiful, with dress and posture that reflect conventional notions about how an individual should look and act at each stage of adult life. In the visualization that represents twenty females, twelve single maidens face the magazine's readers, clasping their hands and leaning inward with a smiling, dreamy expression that suggests playful but yearning hopefulness. Seven married women face away from the reader but look towards the right so readers can see their faces in profile. Their posture suggests the reserve that accords with social expectations for a matron in public. These figures also wear more elaborate dress than do the maidens, suggesting the economic security that a Victorian woman ideally achieved with marriage. One widowed woman faces towards the reader, but her serious expression and crossed arms keep her aloof. The dowager's unornamented, black mourning clothes further distinguish her from the other figures. Her posture and dress adhere to conventions for widowhood, rendering her stately, grave, and socially removed.

The detailed features of the visualization's figures suggest that *Pearson's* reproduced images of three real individuals in multiple. A line of units represents the proportion of each demographic in the population body. The queue progresses from left to right, evoking the progression of both a sentence and an assembly line. Maidens on the left of the line-up lean in towards the right, superseded by matrons who turn their faces in the same direction; the single dowager on the far right, with her face turned left towards the other figures, serves as a stalwart punctuation mark while illustrating the final stage of married life. This arrangement yields a simultaneously comical and dehumanizing effect, as each figure (the maiden, the matron, and the dowager) becomes synecdochic for a mass in which one shared population trait makes units self-identical.

Tactical Responses to Population Journalism

Through spectacularity, photorealistic visualizations foregrounded their own aesthetic mediation, encouraging readers to conceptualize themselves as units of mass, mechanized print and a normalized population body. However, in making their mediation visible, these visualizations also opened themselves to critical scrutiny. "Statistics Gone Mad," published in *Harmsworth* at the height of the population journalism vogue in 1898, attests to the existence of a critical backlash to population journalism. The author and illustrator, J.G. Grant, published no other articles in the mainstream press under this name, suggesting that the article's genesis may have been motivated by exasperation with popular data visualization rather than journalistic income.[66] In his article, Grant parodies the genre of population journalism by presenting a series of absurdly self-evident quantitative facts in visualized form and wryly insisting on their importance. His data visualizations include a circle diagram quantifying the instances of men with green whiskers (0%), a row of data measures depicting the number of beans that make five (5), and three multiples depicting the changing number of keyholes his neighbour Smythe sees on his front door over the course of a night (one at 5:00 p.m., two at 11:30 p.m., and none thereafter, a trend implying that alcohol is an unstated variable).

Grant frames each visualized fact as both a "startling" discovery and an obvious phenomenon that might be recognized by "anybody who would take the trouble," implying that while population journalism invokes scientific authority through its rhetoric and aesthetics, it does not reveal especially advanced empirical knowledge. His visualizations reinforce this suggestion. Grant has drawn a series of images in the abstract, pen-and-ink style of Schooling but has rendered them so simply that they hold little visual interest; the illustrations stylistically align more with the scribbles of a child than with the graphical expressions of a scientist. Rather than making accessible to the layperson the sophisticated principles discovered by the elite, then, Grant posits that population journalism affirms what readers would already know from personal experience. What previously unknown data this genre *does* reveal to readers is fundamentally useless – for example, the number of threepenny pieces that would have to be stacked on one another "to reach from Whitechapel to the Moon."[67] What is compelling about this genre, as Grant implies, is not its revelation of quantitative knowledge about the world but its use of visualizations to remediate the world. Indeed, Grant suggests that the spectacularity of data graphics, rather than galvanizing scientific discovery, masks the unremarkable nature of the statistical information they visualize. Grant thus critiques the aesthetic strategies employed by population journalism.

Magazine readers equipped with print media literacy and familiar with the kind of counter-discourse that Grant articulates could similarly scrutinize the production history of photorealistic population journalism. Although Grant focuses on abstract population journalism, *Harmsworth*, like *Pearson's*, published both abstract and photorealistic articles in this genre. Given that photorealistic population graphics were even more spectacular and less rigorous than the abstract visualizations that Grant scornfully parodied, his criticism is particularly relevant to photorealistic articles such as "The Mathematics of Marriage." Particularly where such articles drew attention to their own aesthetic and quantitative mediation of real individuals, readers could draw on both their media literacy and the counter-discourse denoted by Grant to critique the techno-material, aesthetic, and scientific processes that produced population journalism. Becoming aware of the interpretive processes that was involved in developing population journalism, readers could, for example, question the lack of methodological transparency for gathering data and calculating the statistics. Indeed, they might question whether the facts had any knowledge value at all. Recognizing that the visual display of quantitative data in a given article was not an objective expression of lived experience, readers would be able to scrutinize visualization techniques as design choices. In this light, population journalism would lose its aura of scientific authority, and readers could more readily engage with its aesthetic form and content in their own, idiosyncratic ways – in other words, they could poach it.

Conclusion

The biopolitical aesthetics of "The Mathematics of Marriage" illustrate that at the turn of the twentieth century, the reader-citizen had conflicting cultural roles as an individual and as a unit of the modern mass. By visualizing this duality as a spectacle, "The Mathematics of Marriage" and other population journalism articles that used halftone images encouraged readers to conflate population politics with popular culture. The changes to the aesthetic character of population journalism's biopolitics reflected the changing character of popular mass culture at this moment. By reducing the individual to a unit of mass print, population journalism's visualizations mirrored emerging mass culture's reduction of the individual to a unit of a consumer population that ultimately existed to circulate and proliferate capital.[68]

Like the advertisements in the *Illustrated London News* and the *Graphic, Pearson's* data visualizations exemplify the aesthetic evolution through which late nineteenth- and early twentieth-century illustrated periodicals responded to innovations in mass image reproduction and to an increasingly spectacular cultural landscape. Population journalism encouraged readers to conflate its population politics with popular culture. By making its mediation of bodies and behaviours visible to readers, however, photorealistic population journalism created space for readers to exert agency by critiquing biopolitical discourse and data visualization itself. Population journalism's aesthetic transformation generated new possibilities for reader engagement with data graphics in periodicals. What is more, it fostered opportunities for readers to recognize and respond to the biopolitics of visual popular culture. Within the pages of popular monthly miscellanies there is little evidence of reader criticism of population journalism and its politics. However, the article "Statistics Gone Mad" attests to a backlash against the population journalism craze. Whether this backlash originated among readers or periodical producers, it indicates a dialogue between popular journalism enthusiasts and critics that readers were equipped to extend through their media literacy and technological imagination.

My analysis of how readers could engage subversively with population journalism has necessarily been somewhat speculative, pointing to possibilities based on the available evidence. Although there are few traces within the magazines to indicate how historical readers appropriated this particular genre, readers left other records of their tactical responses to the cultural and political narratives promoted by magazine producers. Chapter 4 looks at how scrapbook makers appropriated periodical materials and practices to create unique paper media objects. As I show, the print media literacy and technological imagination fostered by the illustrated press shaped how individuals made these objects. Ultimately, producing their own media enhanced how scrapbook makers engaged with popular print and popular culture broadly.

Chapter Four

Imagining Print Production: Making Scrapbook Media, c. 1830–1918

Pro captu lectoris habent sua fata libelli.

(According to the capabilities of the reader, books have their destiny.)

Terentianus Maurus,
De litteris, de syllabis, de metris (c. 300)

As this chapter's epigraph declares, the fates of books are determined by their readers. Reflecting on the nature of book collection in the essay "Unpacking My Library," Walter Benjamin cites Terentianus Maurus to argue that the destiny of every book object is contingent on an individual reader's practices of knowledge production and storage. He points out that a textual artefact can be reborn through other modes of acquisition besides collection, such as personal decoration and scissors-and-paste editing.[1] The scrapbook I discussed in chapter 2 serves as one example of this; its anonymous creator transformed periodical advertisement images into a new visual narrative, enhancing them with watercolour paint and sardonic handwritten commentary. This object, scrapbook 157 (figure 2.5), can be classified as one of what Benjamin affectionately describes as the "booklike creations" that exist on the fringes of a home library: albums, tracts, leaflets, and periodicals.[2]

Book-like creations may have been peripheral to Benjamin's own print collection, but they were central to many readers' engagement with nineteenth- and early-twentieth-century print culture. This chapter is concerned squarely with the fates of periodicals that were appropriated by readers to suit personal practices of knowledge production and storage. Specifically, it focuses on how nineteenth-century periodical content was reborn in scrapbooks. Scrapbooks are *personal* media: they are produced by individuals and, as such, are inherently idiosyncratic. Scrapbooks are also *itinerant* media: compiled on a unique timeline, forever subject potentially to further revision, these objects are unsettled in nature. During the decades when illustrated magazines transformed into new media, scrapbook production was particularly prolific for many of the same reasons. These include the technological and economic factors that made print media more affordable, diverse, and pictorial than ever before, as well as the rise of consumer culture.[3] Initially popularized among middle-class women as a pastime of domestic leisure, scrapbook making was adapted for a wide range of purposes by men, women, and children of all classes across the Western world by the end of the nineteenth century.[4]

Previous chapters have focused primarily on the production and initial circulation of periodicals. I now turn to a later phase of circulation history in which readers deconstructed magazines and incorporated them, along with all manner of other print (and sometimes non-print) items, into heterogeneous text environments that followed idiosyncratic curatorial plans. While (as I showed in chapter 2) the distinction between magazine consumption and production blurred in illustrated magazines of the fin de siècle, it disappeared altogether in scrapbook media.[5]

So what can scrapbooks reveal about readers' engagement with popular illustrated print? Scrapbook makers used their albums to articulate their own subjecthood and represent specific domains of cultural knowledge important to them – in the words of Alexis Easley, to "create meaning from the ephemera of everyday life."[6] Although the aesthetics and interpretive affordances of scrapbooks are shaped by their uniquely personal orientation and limited circulation, their pages offer informative evidence of the ways in which readers appropriated periodicals. Additionally, striking parallels between scrapbook design and periodical design attest to the media literacy of album compilers. The products of this process thus offer archival evidence of the appropriative tactics discussed in chapters 2 and 3.

In recent years, print-history scholars have examined the cultural functions of many historical book-like creations and personal print media, including scrapbooks and other types of albums. Much of this work considers the technological and material specificity of media objects in order to understand how publics used them to remediate print and popular culture. For example, Elizabeth Siegel and Patrizia Di Bello have analysed the cultural and semantic work of mid-century British and European women's albums in relation to burgeoning photographic technology. Susan Tucker, Katherine Ott, and Patricia Butler argue that makers used scrapbooks to assemble their own interpretations of a fragmented modern world.[7] Ellen Gruber Garvey deems the scrapbook a "crucial technology" for interacting with print media and creating original expressions.[8] Garvey and Tucker, Ott, and Butler study American scrapbooking, which responded to a print culture distinct from Britain's. However, their insights about how scrapbook makers exerted subjectivity through material remediation apply equally to the British context. Indeed, Maria Damkjaer and Easley draw similar conclusions about scrapbooks in Victorian Britain, identifying within them abundant evidence of readers' heterogeneous engagement with print culture and consumerism.[9]

There is much more to be learned from the rich store of evidence that personal print media offer about how historical individuals and groups engaged with the cultures of a given time and place. Notably, the role of scrapbooks in the rapidly evolving media ecosystem of fin-de-siècle Britain has received little scholarly attention. Drawing on the insights offered by existing scrapbook histories, chapter 4 takes as its premise that scrapbooks offer evidence of changing perceptions of and engagements with popular print. Such itinerant personal media challenge analysis by their very nature, defying fixed interpretation, as Damkjaer observes.[10] But my focus here is not on *what* scrapbooks mean so much as *how* they mean it: how individual scrapbooks model information through characteristics of design. Tucker, Ott, and Butler note in passing that scrapbooking enabled makers to cultivate visual literacy and design proficiencies.[11] This chapter analyses evidence of those processes in depth by contextualizing them in relation to the dominant print media with which scrapbooks interacted.

My theoretical framework for this chapter draws on digital humanities thinking about the relationship between design and argumentation in order to study scrapbooks as *models* through which makers organize cultural knowledge. Designing a knowledge model is a process of critical inquiry, as digital humanities scholars have frequently observed.[12] Model design involves two interrelated facets: interpretation of the subject matter being modelled, and interrogation of the modelling process itself. This chapter's case studies provide material evidence of such interpretation and interrogation of popular print culture.

To analyse scrapbooks as models that interacted with popular print, chapter 4 focuses on a series of individual case studies from three institutions: the University of Manchester, Manchester Metropolitan University, and the Library of Birmingham.[13] The albums were made by men and women of various socio-economic classes and occupations, although all three collections skew towards the middle classes. All of the scrapbooks are British; most, if not all, are English, although the exact provenance of some is unknown. All of the scrapbooks discussed here include content originally printed between 1885 and 1918, but many also contain materials printed in previous decades, going back as far as the advent of popular illustrated journalism in the early 1840s.[14] Indeed, this chapter necessarily takes a broader historical scope than does the rest of the book because scrapbook construction often spanned decades of the maker's life.

Following a brief overview of the late-Victorian scrapbooks as an object categorically distinct from but related to a number of print and personal paper media, I identify scrapbook characteristics that show how their makers applied knowledge of periodical media and production to select and assemble their materials. My analyses reveal how scrapbooks extended the hermeneutic process of simultaneous consumption and production that was fostered by Victorian periodicals. Pulling material "out of the flow of the print marketplace" and fixing it in codex form for a highly localized readership,[15] scrapbook makers left material records of the local, domestic, and heterogeneous priorities of magazine readers as they engaged in the tactics of appropriation that Michel de Certeau describes as poaching.[16]

Having analysed periodical practices that scrapbook makers incorporated into their own production practices, I examine album features that demonstrate how makers imagined new horizons for print media production, augmenting the existing techniques of design and modelling that conditioned how readers engaged with content. Scrapbooking enabled Victorian readers to become familiar with the constraints and possibilities of producing codex-structured print media for themselves. Through this process, scrapbook makers produced new knowledge about print mediation itself. Readers drew on their print media literacy and technological imaginations to determine the destinies of periodical artefacts. In so doing, they enhanced their own understanding of and ability to intervene in popular print culture.

Victorian Print Culture and Scrapbooks

Although scrapbooks can be hard to distinguish from other personal media and eclectic print objects in practice, they are a subcategory of album dedicated primarily to material gleaned from a variety of other print sources.[17] Victorian scrapbook makers often harvested material from purpose-made sheets of scraps sold commercially. Particularly from the mid-century onward, they also mined newspapers and illustrated periodicals for items to paste into their albums. Blank scrapbooks and newspaper-clipping albums were marketed as distinctive items in the nineteenth century, and archives today often classify them as different types of objects. However, album makers tended to reject the distinction in practice, so the present study does not distinguish between late-Victorian scrapbooks and newspaper-clipping albums.

Like all models, Victorian scrapbooks drew on the pre-existing practices and conventions of forms other than periodicals; a brief review will establish these as reference points against which to identify the scrapbook construction techniques that were shaped by periodicals in particular. Most of these forms were print and personal paper media, although, as Jennifer Lei Jenkins points out, non-print cultural objects such as the curio cabinet, popular in seventeenth- and eighteenth-century homes of the upper classes, also informed how Victorian albums were modelled.[18]

Aside from periodicals, a number of print forms resembled scrapbooks in ways that suggest mutual influence. Examples include gift books, household guides, and almanacs. Like magazines and newspapers, these commercially published texts encouraged heterogeneous consumption through their eclectic content and hybrid, multimodal aesthetics. The Grangerized or extra-illustrated book was another print form similar enough to the scrapbook to suggest potential mutual influence.[19] Popularized in the early years of the nineteenth century, extra-illustration involved reworking a published text, interleaving additional graphical materials within a book's bindings, or even remounting leaves on larger sheets to create space for more custom pictorial content. Like scrapbooks, extra-illustrated texts served as records of heterogeneous engagement with print culture.[20] Indeed, scrapbooks and extra-illustrated books categorically overlap at times. Some nineteenth-century scrapbook makers used printed codices as the basis for their albums, though this practice was more common in the United States than in Britain.[21]

In addition to commercial print media, a spectrum of personal paper media such as diaries and other types of albums had traits in common with scrapbooks and may have influenced their compilation. As broadly defined by Samantha Matthews, an album is a blank codex that simultaneously stores and displays a "unique collection of personally significant texts or objects, such as prints, letters, stamps, photographs, or printed 'scraps.'"[22] The wider tradition of album compilation in which scrapbooks participate dates back to the sixteenth century. The practice gained popularity in the nineteenth century, initially among middle-class women with increasing leisure time for and interest in domestic artistic pursuits, and later across classes, ages, and genders.[23]

Many personal media adhered to the design conventions of the commercial stationary industry that produced them en masse. Personal print media could be produced by hand, but many Victorians used commercially produced codices, which became more affordable and more popular in the second half of the nineteenth century as print technologies advanced and print culture diversified and expanded.[24] Structural features of commercial paper media, such as ruled margins, indexing systems, clips, layout guides, and pagination, shaped how album compilers curated materials. Formal, genre-specific conventions also informed individual object creation – the recounting of a day's events in a diary; the lists of signatures in an autograph book.

While structural and genre conventions are evident across the Victorian personal media housed in archives and special collections, these objects also reflect that makers regularly disregarded prefabricated features, flouted genre conventions, and physically modified codices in order to build unique models of cultural knowledge. A customized scrapbook, like any media object, offers a structured environment in which to think through the information that it mobilizes and to generate new insights.[25] To assemble a scrapbook is to design an environment that facilitates this interpretive process. Given that a model's design contributes to the meaning of the information it conveys, modelling itself is a form of creative and critical interpretation. The process of making personal print media thus combines what Jerome McGann and Lisa Samuel term "deformance," the reconstitution of a work's aesthetic form to expose new possibilities of meaning, with what de Certeau describes as "antidiscipline," the appropriation of conventional cultural representations through creative subversion.[26] Although evidence indicates that scrapbook makers appropriated representation techniques from the various print and paper media I have just reviewed, their deformation and reimagining of periodical content and techniques was particularly extensive.

Scrapbook Analysis 1: Periodicals and Scrapbook Production

At the height of scrapbooking's popularity, its practitioners heavily remediated periodical materials and adapted periodical techniques. As a result, the mid- to late-century scrapbooks that used newspaper and magazine clippings are strikingly similar to those periodicals. Because Victorian scrapbook makers drew on familiar periodical practices to model their subject matter, the objects they created offer us unique evidence of readers' print media literacy and technological imagination. Acts of critical modelling and design expand a maker's understanding of what is being modelled and of the possibilities for modelling it, as a number of digital humanities scholars have argued. When enacted by whole publics, such acts ultimately shape a culture's technological imaginary.[27] The adaptation of illustrated periodical contents and techniques into late-Victorian scrapbooks demonstrates how scrapbook makers advanced their understanding of print culture through their modelling activities.

Perhaps the most obvious way that scrapbooks adopted periodical conventions was in the use by album makers of scissors-and-paste construction, the practice of cutting materials from periodicals and pasting them into a new print context. Periodical editors often extracted and reassembled materials from other papers, a process Garvey calls "writing with scissors."[28] Editors employed scissors and paste both to save on production labour and to offer their readers highlights of the news cycle from elsewhere in the press. Scrapbook makers, meanwhile, often used this technique to archive select materials for future reference. The relationship between the scissors-and-paste practices of editors and reader-makers became reciprocal over the course of the nineteenth century, as exemplified by the origin story of *Tit-Bits*: George Newnes claimed that his first publication, founded in 1881, was inspired by his wife's long-standing practice of keeping an album of amusing periodical cuttings.[29] On the basis of this practice, Newnes conceived of a weekly collection of excerpts synthesized into a whole, an editorial undertaking not unlike the work of a scrapbook maker.[30] Whether or not it is true, the origin story of *Tit-Bits* illustrates a cultural perception that the relationship between scissors-and-paste construction in periodicals and that in scrapbooks had become circular: the miscellaneity of snippets that appeared in many periodicals was both an extension of editorial practices and an adoption of reader practices.

A scrapbook included among the papers of poet Edwin Waugh (1817–90), held by Ryland Special Collections, exemplifies some of the ways that scissors-and-paste construction was used by scrapbook makers. Developed by an unknown maker in Cheshire between 1880 and 1890,[31] this scrapbook served two functions: to save useful information for future reference and to memorialize published items pertaining to major life events. The album consists chiefly of recipe cuttings; instructions for home remedies; poetry by Waugh, published in the *Manchester Guardian*; and articles that mention Waugh. The narrative suggested by the scrapbook's materials, compiled in the years before Waugh passed away of cancer, supports the likelihood that its maker was, at the very least, someone close to Waugh who cared for him in the last years of his life. First appearing partway through the album are articles from a regional newspaper reporting on Waugh's illness. Clippings in the album increasingly focus on home remedies for illness and advice for convalescence. Without including any content written by the scrapbook maker, the album documents the changing circumstances of this person's life as a palliative caretaker. The last portion of the scrapbook displays news reportage on Waugh's passing.

Drawing on scissors-and-paste conventions, the scrapbook's maker incorporates articles, tidbits, and excerpts into an eclectic homemade magazine synthesized through organizational themes of the maker's own choosing. Like periodical editors, who often repurposed briefs and even whole articles without identifying their original source, the maker of the Waugh album does not cite their sources,[32] suggesting that provenance was not relevant to the domestic, literary, and biographical knowledge modelled through this codex.

While it does not emphasize provenance, the album does privilege the chronological sequencing of periodical publication. Aside from a loose packet of ephemera, the cuttings are assembled in the order of their publication, as indicated by dates sporadically visible in the clippings and by the unfolding narrative of Waugh's illness in newspaper articles. The passing of time, while not consistently traceable through cuttings, is also signposted by the album's handwritten pagination. The linear chronological sequence harmonizes with the progression of Waugh's illness, his death, and the ritual mourning of his community in the form of print memorials and a funeral. The album's maker breaks with periodical convention, however, in archiving print documentation of these events so that the scrapbook's readers might revisit them again and again – a reflection of the non-linear nature of personal grieving.

Other scrapbook makers used the scissors-and-paste technique to fill the pages of their codex in very different ways, to varying effects. For example, the maker of a scrapbook of uncertain provenance, part of the University of Manchester's Methodist Archives Collection, made as little effort to document the provenance of materials as Waugh scrapbook's creator made, but this compiler's lack of documentary rigour was apparently guided by personal interest. The Methodist scrapbook offers a lively exhibition of periodical images that range widely in style, reproduction method, source type, subject matter, and date of publication. The result is an unguided tour through mid-century illustrated journalism.

In contrast to the laissez-faire approach of the Methodist album's creator, scrapbook maker Rev. Frederick W. Langton made the provenance of his cuttings a central feature of his album, compiled between the 1870s and 1890s. The vicar of the Northumberland village of Ponteland from 1890 to 1934, Langton remediated periodical excerpts to develop a late-century history of art critic John Ruskin's contributions to and reception in the press. The origin of each clipping is indicated through a handwritten note or a snippet of publication masthead or running header. This context offers evidence of the central preoccupations of the scrapbook: Ruskin's visibility within the press and, in turn, his exceptional influence on Victorian culture.

The makers of the Waugh, Methodist, and Ruskin scrapbooks used the scissors-and-paste technique much as Victorian editors used it, repurposing excerpts of newspapers and magazines to populate the pages of a codex. Langton's Ruskin album also follows periodical conventions in its layout of these excerpts. Indeed, many Victorian scrapbook makers adopted the layout conventions of newspapers and magazines. Snippets of letterpress and pictures were often arranged in columns spatially regularized along the page. Clippings were often accompanied by headings and subheadings derived from periodical numbers. Many entries in Langton's scrapbook use a relatively small proportion of the page space – a rare practice among newspaper and magazine publishers – but nevertheless invoke periodical sensibilities, remediating snippets in a format akin to that of a micro-magazine page within a page. These entries sandwich short articles between cuttings with source information pasted as headers and footers, creating a tessellated effect similar to that of a page of letterpress items (figure 4.1). Such layout techniques contribute to the knowledge that Langton models through the scrapbook; intentionally mimicking journalistic media, he recreates the original print contexts of the cuttings. At the same time, he invokes the authority of print journalism for his own assemblage of these cuttings into a narrative about Ruskin and the press by performing his own familiarity with its conventions of production and circulation. Adopting periodical layout conventions was at least partly a matter of practicality: periodicals modelled tried-and-true techniques for assembling as much and as diverse an array of letterpress and pictures as possible in a manner balancing readability and economy of space. In adopting these layout conventions, scrapbook makers also ensured the accessibility of their albums. Readers could engage with each unique scrapbook using reading practices cultivated through years of consuming periodicals and other print letterpress media – for example, progressing from left to right and top to bottom, column by column; and verso to recto, page by page.

A more complex use of the visual principles of periodical layout techniques is evident in an album compiled by John Macmillan, an amateur Birmingham historian. The pages of the codex, titled "Views, Newspaper Cuttings, and Scraps, Relating to Birmingham," display balanced compositions of images and text, consistent proportions of pasted-in

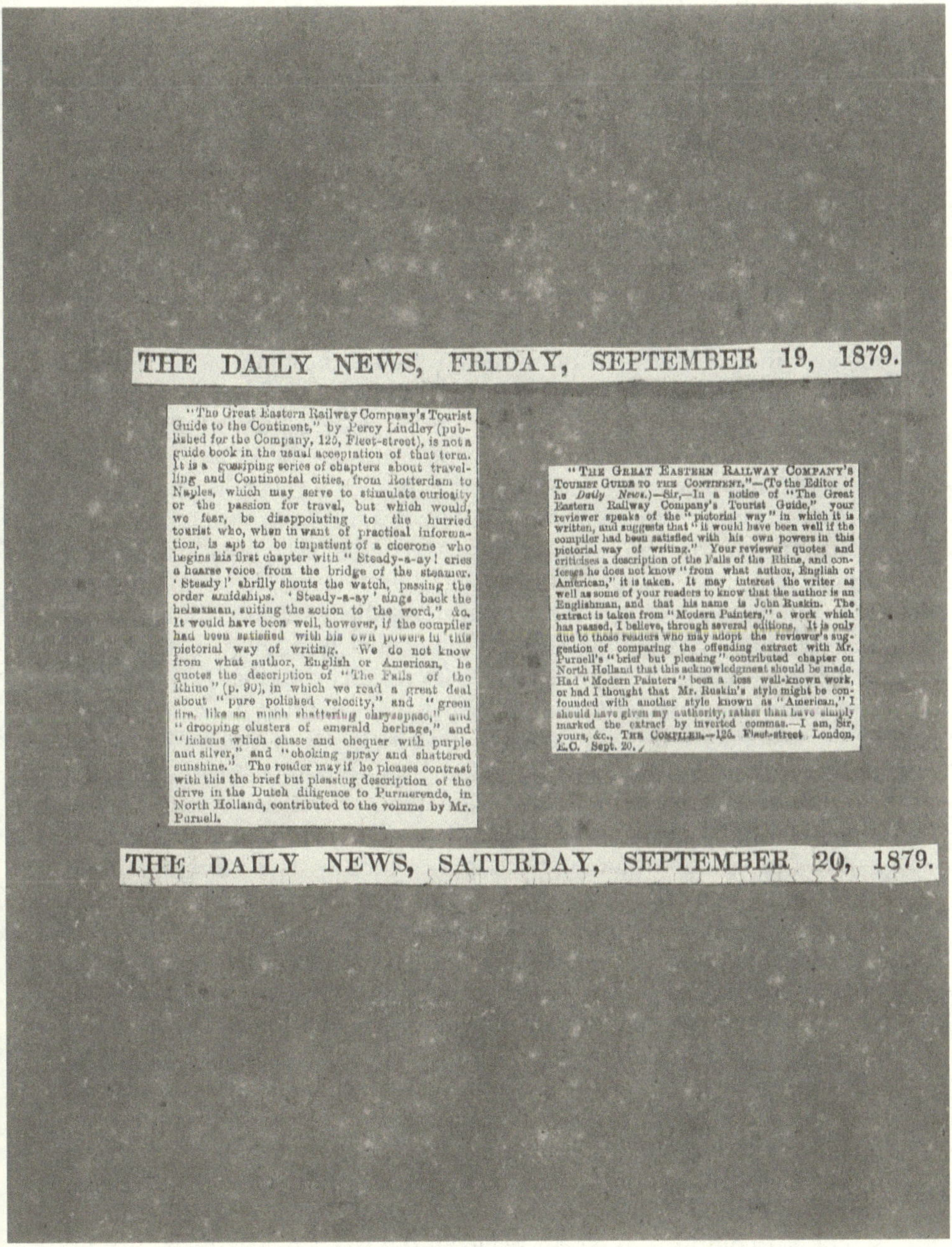

THE DAILY NEWS, FRIDAY, SEPTEMBER 19, 1879.

"The Great Eastern Railway Company's Tourist Guide to the Continent," by Percy Lindley (published for the Company, 125, Fleet-street), is not a guide book in the usual acceptation of that term. It is a gossiping series of chapters about travelling and Continental cities, from Rotterdam to Naples, which may serve to stimulate curiosity or the passion for travel, but which would, we fear, be disappointing to the hurried tourist who, when in want of practical information, is apt to be impatient of a cicerone who begins his first chapter with "Steady-a-ay! cries a hoarse voice from the bridge of the steamer. 'Steady!' shrilly shouts the watch, passing the order amidships. 'Steady-a-ay' sings back the helmsman, suiting the action to the word," &c. It would have been well, however, if the compiler had been satisfied with his own powers in this pictorial way of writing. We do not know from what author, English or American, he quotes the description of "The Falls of the Rhine" (p. 90), in which we read a great deal about "pure polished velocity," and "green fire, like so much shattering chrysopase," and "drooping clusters of emerald herbage," and "lichens which chase and chequer with purple and silver," and "choking spray and shattered sunshine." The reader may if he pleases contrast with this the brief but pleasing description of the drive in the Dutch diligence to Purmerende, in North Holland, contributed to the volume by Mr. Purnell.

"THE GREAT EASTERN RAILWAY COMPANY'S TOURIST GUIDE TO THE CONTINENT."—(To the Editor of he *Daily News*.)—Sir,—In a notice of "The Great Eastern Railway Company's Tourist Guide," your reviewer speaks of the "pictorial way" in which it is written, and suggests that "it would have been well if the compiler had been satisfied with his own powers in this pictorial way of writing." Your reviewer quotes and criticises a description of the Falls of the Rhine, and confesses he does not know "from what author, English or American," it is taken. It may interest the writer as well as some of your readers to know that the author is an Englishman, and that his name is John Ruskin. The extract is taken from "Modern Painters," a work which has passed, I believe, through several editions. It is only due to those readers who may adopt the reviewer's suggestion of comparing the offending extract with Mr. Purnell's "brief but pleasing" contributed chapter on North Holland that this acknowledgment should be made. Had "Modern Painters" been a less well-known work, or had I thought that Mr. Ruskin's style might be confounded with another style known as "American," I should have given my authority, rather than have simply marked the extract by inverted commas.—I am, Sir, yours, &c., THE COMPILER.—125. Fleet-street London, E.C. Sept. 20.

THE DAILY NEWS, SATURDAY, SEPTEMBER 20, 1879.

Figure 4.1. Excerpted page from scrapbook by Rev. Frederick W. Langton. © University of Manchester Library, ref. no. R175343.

content to blank space, and even spatial distribution of items on facing pages. In some instances Macmillan has even recreated a conventional magazine layout for an extracted periodical article through his assemblage of illustrations and text. For example, a series of pages displaying an illustrated article titled "City Libraries" opens with a conventional periodical layout: a large illustration followed by the title, a photographic image of the article's author, and the first snippet of the article's letterpress beginning with an ornamental initial (figure 4.2). On the following page, Macmillan has cut and pasted more of the article's letterpress into two columns that appear below a reproduced photograph of the subject matter (figure 4.3). The locations of the letterpress cuts suggest that, rather than reproducing the exact layout of the original article, the compiler drew on periodical media's organizational sensibilities to improvise an organization suitable to the album's page dimensions. Macmillan also adapted some of print's aesthetic flourishes – for example, repurposing a small cutting of a grocer's shop as a textual ornament below long columns of letterpress.

The design principles informing Macmillan's layouts are not the exclusive purview of periodicals. Illustrated novels, for example, also incorporated images and ornaments alongside letterpress. But Macmillan's album aligns with illustrated magazines through its hybridity of image materials and styles as well as its varied groupings of letterpress and text – all characteristics that increasingly defined illustrated magazine aesthetics over the course of the nineteenth century. The layout of Macmillan's album, like that of Langton's album, contributes to the cultural knowledge it models by signalling alignment with the mainstream periodical press. Macmillan displays expertise in illustrated periodical production that supports his credibility as a visual historian of Birmingham. The scrapbook's layout also attests to its particularly thoughtful aesthetic curation, further enhancing the album's authority.

In addition to scissors-and-paste and layout techniques, scrapbooks adapted periodical practices in their organizational logic – a central aspect of scrapbook making and the most essential means by which a compiler could impose structure on an assortment of materials.[33] As already exemplified by the Waugh album, one way that scrapbooks replicated the organizational logic of periodicals was through a sequence matching the periodical production cycle. Another approach involved formulating an organizational rubric based on how items had been materially grouped in their original contexts. For example, a scrapbook compiled in North Wales in the late nineteenth century by John Carden, a former captain of the Twentieth Regiment, Lancashire Fusiliers, assembles into hand-ruled groups a wide assortment of brief

6

INTERIOR OF SHAKSPEARE LIBRARY, BIRMINGHAM.
(Sketched by Our Own Artist.)

CITY LIBRARIES.
By WALTER POWELL, Chief Librarian of Birmingham.

Photo by Whitlock.
Mr. Walter Powell.

IT is gratifying to know that even as long ago as 1741, when "Aris's Gazette" issued its first number, Birmingham had done something for literature, and even libraries were not unknown here. In 1652 a work entitled "The Font Guarded," by the Rev. Thomas Hall, of King's Norton (whose seventeenth century library can be seen at the Reference Library, to which it was transferred in 1891), was issued for Thomas Simmons, bookseller in Birmingham. There is also a sermon in the Reference Library, entitled

Figure 4.2. Excerpted page from scrapbook "Views, Newspaper Cuttings and Scraps Relating to Birmingham," by John Macmillan, 6. Reproduced with the permission of the Library of Birmingham, ref. no. LF 85.4, acc. 302509.

7

Interior of the Reference Library.

"Honour the King," by Samuel Fisher, which was printed for Hierom Gregory, bookseller, in 1673.

The first known books to be printed in Birmingham appeared in 1717, when Mathew Unwin, whose establishment was near St. Martin's Church, issued "The Loyal Oration," by James Parkinson, chief master of the Free School of Birmingham, and "The Martyrdom of King Charles the First," a sermon by J. B. It has also now been clearly established, through the researches of our distinguished historian, Mr. R. K. Dent, that Dr. Johnson's first work, a translation of Lobo's "Abyssinia," was printed in Birmingham in 1733, though published in London in 1735.

The book is now very scarce, and realises high prices.

The activity of the town is also illustrated by the issue of a newspaper, even before the "Gazette," though only a single number dated 1733 is known of the "Birmingham Journal," issued by Thomas Warren, the friend of Dr. Johnson. There was a lending library in existence in the town in 1729, as is shown by an advertisement in a book published by Warren, the concluding paragraph of which states that "books are hired out to read, or exchanged." Beyond the advertisement, however, nothing is known of this library. William Hutton, the historian, who claimed to be the first to lend out books in Birmingham, opened a lending library about 1752, and subsequently many such libraries were established.

First Public Library.

The first public library established in Birmingham is also still in existence. It was a collection of 550 theological works bequeathed in 1733, together with an endowment of £200, by the Reverend William Higgs, first Rector of St. Philip's. It was free to all clergymen of the Church of England in the town and neighbourhood, and to all students recommended by the Rectors of St. Philip's, St. Martin's, or Sheldon. A catalogue was printed, together with a set of rules, some of which can now only be described as quaint.

Up to a comparatively short time ago this library was at St. Philip's Rectory, but it is at present stored in boxes elsewhere. There are two libraries at King Edward's School, the older one of which was founded in 1642, and is entitled to rank as one of the earliest of its kind in the country.

Dr. Priestley's Help.

In 1779 a great advance was made in library facilities in Birmingham by the establishment of the Birmingham Library, now more generally known as the Old Library. This

Figure 4.3. Excerpted page from scrapbook "Views, Newspaper Cuttings and Scraps Relating to Birmingham," by John Macmillan, 7. Reproduced with the permission of the Library of Birmingham, ref. no. LF 85.4, acc. 302509.

family notices, obituaries, and related announcements about personal and professional milestones. Carden effectively created a personalized, multi-year equivalent to the announcements section of a newspaper. His use of periodical conventions for organizing these clippings contributes to the broader theme of this scrapbook, the documentation of his diffuse social, professional, and familial networks.

The Macmillan scrapbook uses semantic associations, rather than chronology or material history, as its fundamental organizing principle, but its organization also reflects periodical conventions – specifically, illustrated journalism's practices of visual juxtaposition. When reporting on a major event or set of events, illustrated news magazines such as the *Illustrated London News* often depicted different facets of the phenomenon using a series of images and, towards the end of the nineteenth century, as new technology allowed, using different illustration types. By juxtaposing related views of the same event, the *ILN* offered readers a multifaceted news story. Macmillan similarly grouped images depicting the same subject or type of subject to offer readers multiple perspectives. For example, a large section of his scrapbook is almost exclusively devoted to images of Birmingham places of worship. A number of the city's oldest and/or most iconic churches are represented in multiple images, some drawn or printed at different historical moments. Like the illustrated periodicals, this scrapbook was sequenced to enabled readers to view its subject matter from multiple perspectives in order to understand it more comprehensively.

Macmillan's juxtapositional organization of pictures of Birmingham points to another way in which scrapbooks adopted illustrated periodical conventions, and the last that I analyse here. Many scrapbooks reflect a tacit correlation between the number of modes used to document real persons, events, organizations, and places and the authenticity of their representation. In Victorian illustrated journalism, representational fidelity involved reproducing a special artist's eyewitness account. As I discussed in chapter 1, producers of pictorial journalism claimed that it was less mediated than non-pictorial journalism because special artists recorded news events as visual phenomena.[34] Illustrated news enhanced its representational authority further by combining a range of visual and verbal modes to represent a subject more thoroughly. Scrapbooks reflect similar assumptions about the representational value of assembling a variety of images and text, including inscriptions taken first hand. For example, Carden pasted into his scrapbook a series of drawings of Lucknow, sketched two decades earlier while he was stationed there during India's First War of Independence in 1857. The drawings appear alongside newspaper excerpts commenting retrospectively on the event. Through this compilation Carden acted as his own special artist, documenting Victorian military history through both distanced accounts and first-hand observation. Similarly, a scrapbook compiled by Manchester merchant Thomas Kemp between 1890 and 1920 incorporates images and text of various types and modes to model its subject matter, the perception of feathers in popular culture. The album's materials include comics, editorials, photojournalistic accounts, illustrated news, agricultural reports, and women's fashion pages. By gleaning all kinds of verbal and visual materials from all manner of periodical media and assembling them in his codex, Kemp constructs a comprehensive overview of fashion feathers, a topic related to the family business in funereal plumes.[35]

Scrapbook Analysis 2: Imagining New Horizons for Print Design through Scrapbooks

The use by scrapbook makers of the structural conventions of newspapers and magazines attests to their familiarity with the production and organization of periodicals, as well as their understanding of how these factors shaped the information conveyed in the pages of a given media object. I have shown how scrapbook makers modelled knowledge about not only specific subject matter but also print media as such. Given that modelling and design are generative and interpretive, scrapbook making involved both the representation and the production of knowledge about its own subject matter and print media. Specifically, scrapbook makers imagined new possibilities for periodical functionality by augmenting the conventions I have already identified, such as periodical-based scissors-and-paste techniques, organization, and rubrics for fidelity, as well as introducing other practices, such as annotation. Through scrapbooks, then, Victorian readers not only exercised but also extended the horizons of their print media literacy and technological imagination.

Scissors-and-paste construction was not just the foundational mode of scrapbooking but also its defining aesthetic. In this regard, personal albums extended the heterogeneity that informed the character of popular periodical contents. Garvey observes that while periodical editors "converted clippings into text, stripping them of their material qualities … to move them back into circulation in new contexts," scrapbook makers "embraced the materiality of their cut-up papers."[36] Scrapbook makers removed items from their original contexts, but the status of these items as gathered from elsewhere remained prominent, signified by their distinctive materiality and by any information on an item's provenance that a maker included. The unique material features of each scrapbook item, which might include typeface, visual style, reproduction-based aesthetics (such as halftone granularity or linear engraving), and paper quality, set it off from the album page and other items pasted onto the page. Each piece of repurposed information retains traces of its history. In preserving not only words and images but also the pieces of paper on which these were printed, scrapbook makers "saved … the memory and evidence of where and in what form they had read an item" and made print culture itself part of the knowledge they were modelling.[37]

The anonymous Methodist scrapbook exemplifies scissors-and-paste construction as a defining medium aesthetic: the gathered nature of contents and their relationship to print culture as a whole are important to the significance of this object. The album's images and tidbits of text are endowed with additional meaning through their materially evident selection and remediation. Images and letterpress snippets exhibit a wide range of subject matter, aesthetic styles, and reproduction methods, attesting to labours of curation that spanned time and a multitude of periodicals. Evidence of curatorial labour indicates that what was saved was deemed valuable by the maker.[38] The tour of mid-century illustrated journalism offered by this scrapbook is selective, not comprehensive. At the same time, the varied nature of the scrapbook's contents demonstrates that even at its most carefully curated, a survey of the Victorian era's popular visual print culture was necessarily eclectic. Using scissors and paste as both a method and an aesthetic, the Methodist scrapbook models how Victorian readers made sense of pictorial journalism by selectively navigating through its vast, diverse materials.

Scrapbooks also extended the functionality of periodical design by devising three-dimensional uses of the codex space. As Bonnie Mak observes, the platform and the conceptual space of the page are "coextensive":[39] scrapbook makers explored the boundaries of this relationship in creative ways. Many albums include items not restricted to the flat surface of the page – for example, single-page or multi-page items could be tipped in or left loose between two pages. A cutting might be folded so that it could be pasted in a small page space and still be viewed by a reader at full size when unfolded upward, downward, or outward.

Such folding techniques evoke nineteenth-century books and ephemera that featured pop-out or fold-out images; when remediating magazine and newspaper content in a scrapbook context, however, they posit new possibilities for reader interaction with periodical media.

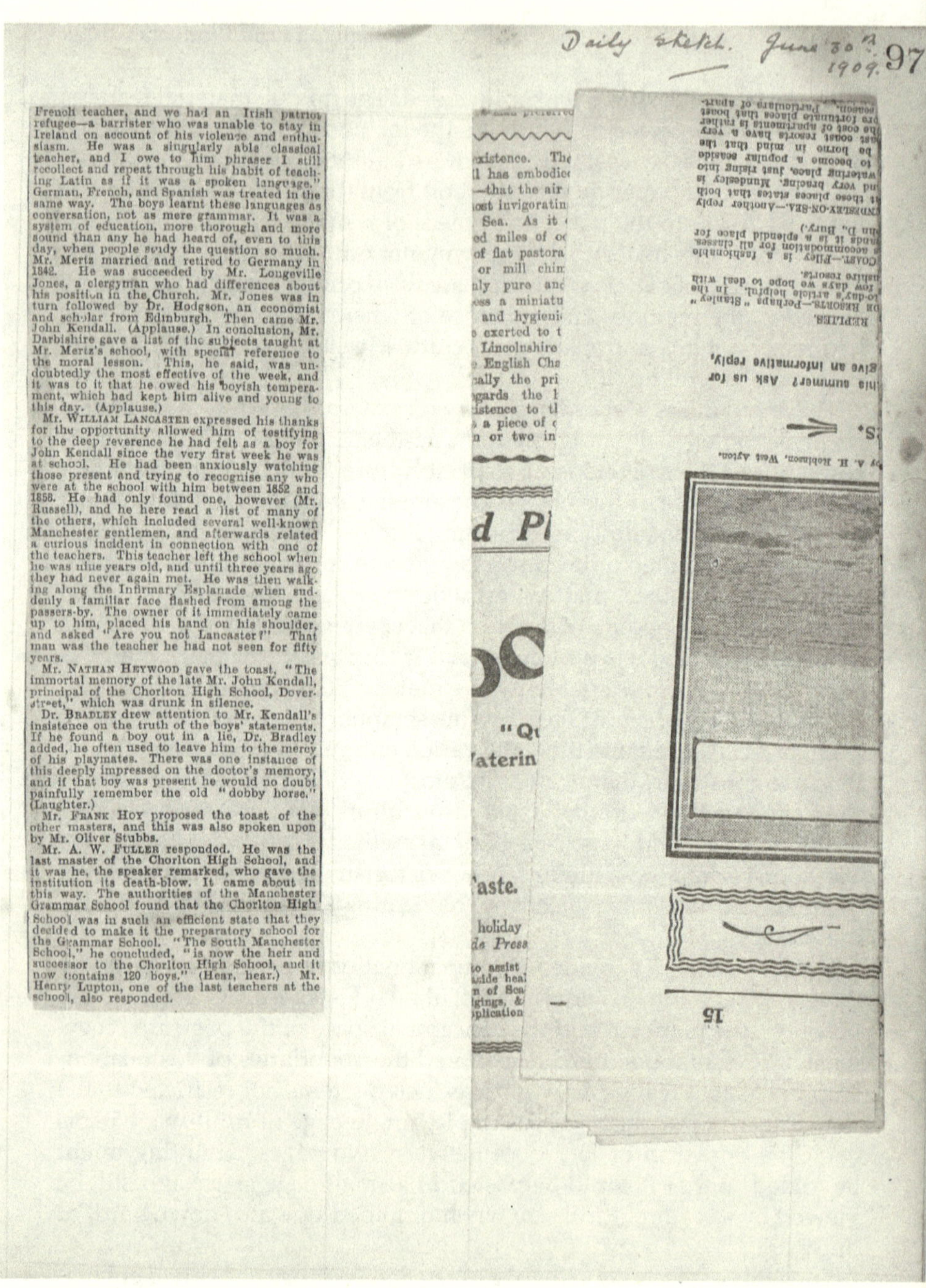

Daily Sketch. June 30th 1909.

97

French teacher, and we had an Irish patriot refugee—a barrister who was unable to stay in Ireland on account of his violence and enthusiasm. He was a singularly able classical teacher, and I owe to him phrases I still recollect and repeat through his habit of teaching Latin as if it was a spoken language." German, French, and Spanish was treated in the same way. The boys learnt these languages as conversation, not as mere grammar. It was a system of education, more thorough and more sound than any he had heard of, even to this day, when people study the question so much. Mr. Mertz married and retired to Germany in 1842. He was succeeded by Mr. Longeville Jones, a clergyman who had differences about his position in the Church. Mr. Jones was in turn followed by Dr. Hodgson, an economist and scholar from Edinburgh. Then came Mr. John Kendall. (Applause.) In conclusion, Mr. Darbishire gave a list of the subjects taught at Mr. Mertz's school, with special reference to the moral lesson. This, he said, was undoubtedly the most effective of the week, and it was to it that he owed his boyish temperament, which had kept him alive and young to this day. (Applause.)

Mr. William Lancaster expressed his thanks for the opportunity allowed him of testifying to the deep reverence he had felt as a boy for John Kendall since the very first week he was at school. He had been anxiously watching those present and trying to recognise any who were at the school with him between 1852 and 1858. He had only found one, however (Mr. Russell), and he here read a list of many of the others, which included several well-known Manchester gentlemen, and afterwards related a curious incident in connection with one of the teachers. This teacher left the school when he was nine years old, and until three years ago they had never again met. He was then walking along the Infirmary Esplanade when suddenly a familiar face flashed from among the passers-by. The owner of it immediately came up to him, placed his hand on his shoulder, and asked "Are you not Lancaster?" That man was the teacher he had not seen for fifty years.

Mr. Nathan Heywood gave the toast, "The immortal memory of the late Mr. John Kendall, principal of the Chorlton High School, Dover-street," which was drunk in silence.

Dr. Bradley drew attention to Mr. Kendall's insistence on the truth of the boys' statements. If he found a boy out in a lie, Dr. Bradley added, he often used to leave him to the mercy of his playmates. There was one instance of this deeply impressed on the doctor's memory, and if that boy was present he would no doubt painfully remember the old "dobby horse." (Laughter.)

Mr. Frank Hoy proposed the toast of the other masters, and this was also spoken upon by Mr. Oliver Stubbs.

Mr. A. W. Fuller responded. He was the last master of the Chorlton High School, and it was he, the speaker remarked, who gave the institution its death-blow. It came about in this way. The authorities of the Manchester Grammar School found that the Chorlton High School was in such an efficient state that they decided to make it the preparatory school for the Grammar School. "The South Manchester School," he concluded, "is now the heir and successor to the Chorlton High School, and it now contains 120 boys." (Hear, hear.) Mr. Henry Lupton, one of the last teachers at the school, also responded.

Figure 4.4. Excerpted page from scrapbook by Thomas Kemp. © University of Manchester Library, ref. no. R199228.

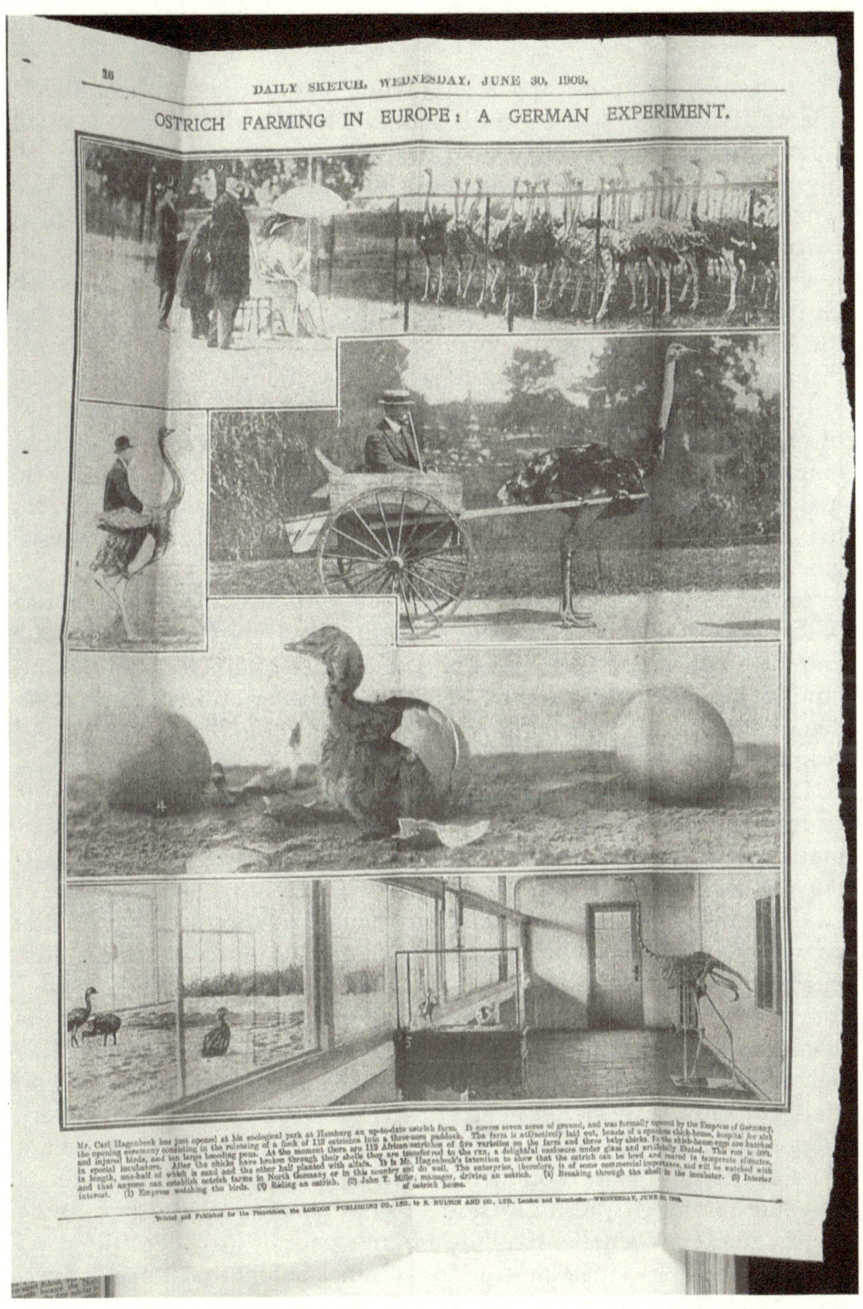

16 DAILY SKETCH, WEDNESDAY, JUNE 30, 1909.

OSTRICH FARMING IN EUROPE: A GERMAN EXPERIMENT.

Mr. Carl Hagenbeck has just opened at his zoological park at Hamburg an up-to-date ostrich farm. It covers seven acres of ground, and was formally opened by the Empress of Germany, the opening ceremony consisting in the releasing of a flock of 112 ostriches into a three-acre paddock. The farm is attractively laid out, boasts of a spacious chick-house, hospital for sick and injured birds, and ten large breeding pens. At the moment there are 113 African ostriches of five varieties on the farm and three baby chicks. In the chick-house eggs are hatched in special incubators. After the chicks have broken through their shells they are transferred to the run, a delightful enclosure under glass and artificially heated. This run is 60ft. in length, one-half of which is sand and the other half planted with alfalfa. It is Mr. Hagenbeck's intention to show that the ostrich can be bred and reared in temperate climates, and that anyone can establish ostrich farms in North Germany or in this country and do well. The enterprise, therefore, is of some commercial importance, and will be watched with interest. (1) Empress watching the birds. (2) Riding an ostrich. (3) John T. Miller, manager, driving an ostrich. (4) Breaking through the shell in the incubator. (5) Interior of ostrich house.

Printed and Published for the Proprietors, the LONDON PUBLISHING CO., LTD., by E. HULTON AND CO., LTD., London and Manchester.—WEDNESDAY, JUNE 30, 1909.

Figure 4.5. The same excerpted page from the Kemp scrapbook with the pasted-in article unfolded. © University of Manchester Library, ref. no. R199228.

For example, Kemp incorporated a whole page from the *Daily Sketch*, a large-format newspaper, in his scrapbook by folding it into a small square that a reader had to unfold multiple times to view in its entirety (figures 4.4 and 4.5). The newspaper clipping has an outsized presence when unfolded, dominating a reader's view because it is more than twice the size of each page of the album.

The spatial prominence of this image-dominated article, "Ostrich Farming in Europe: A German Experiment," attests to its importance to the album's main subject, Kemp's business in funeral plumes. Kemp's technique for incorporating the article in his album was likely devised, at least in part, for practicality's sake, but this three-dimensional use of codex space also created new possibilities for reader interaction that heightened the sense of scrapbook interpretation as the unveiling – or, in this case, unfolding – of knowledge. Such objects encouraged readers to perceive scrapbook items as three-dimensional objects and to investigate extraneous dimensions of the scrapbook's narrative.

Langton's Ruskin scrapbook presents a particularly imaginative use of three-dimensional codex space. A pamphlet, "Whistler v. Ruskin: Art and Art Critics," is tipped in as part of a series of articles about an infamous quarrel between James McNeill Whistler and Ruskin, which began with Ruskin criticizing Whistler's *Nocturne in Black and Gold* and culminated in Whistler suing Ruskin for libel.[40] In the pamphlet, dated 24 December 1878, Whistler defends his role in the lawsuit and reflects on its significance.[41] The spatial juxtaposition of the pamphlet to proximal album contents contributes to their interrelated significance. "Whistler v. Ruskin" is pasted to the page guard between a series of articles on the Whistler-Ruskin dispute. Incorporated in Langton's album, the pamphlet functions as a mini-codex; it offers momentary immersion in an otherwise unavailable perspective on the Ruskin-Whistler row, that of Whistler himself. Other items in the album that document the events of the quarrel are third-party reports and commentary by journalists and critics. In this context Whistler's pamphlet has a function analogous to a single letter in an epistolary novel. Given Langton's enthusiasm for Ruskin's oeuvre, the pamphlet's meaning may derive not from the point of view it offers but from its status as a material artefact of a sensational chapter in Ruskin's reception history. Attached to the album guard and smaller than the album's pages, "Whistler v. Ruskin" can only be viewed in juxtaposition with the content that it partly overlays, much of which effectively rebuts Whistler's point of view.

Items that makers left loose among album contents, whether intentionally or not, extended the functional dimensions of the codex space through their undetermined relationship to the rest of the scrapbook environment. Loose scrapbook items resemble periodical inserts, the promotional leaflets and advertisements included among the wrapping and content pages of a sold magazine, newspaper, or serial number. However, scrapbook inserts have a more ambiguous relationship to pasted-in content than do periodical inserts. In his scrapbook Barrow Cadbury (1867–1957), grandson of the founder of Cadbury Chocolate and eventual chairman of that company, devised a compromise between the floating status of loose inserts and the more fixed status of pasted cuttings. A glued-in leaflet offers the voyage itinerary and floor plan of a steamer that sailed from Liverpool to New York City in 1882; tucked within this documentation of Cadbury's voyage are two photographs of the steamer itself. Cadbury's design technique harmonizes the semantic and material relationship of the photographs to the leaflet without making them part of the scrapbook's fixed architecture. Perhaps for Cadbury the photographs had significance beyond archiving his travels, necessitating that they remain available to circulate beyond the context of the scrapbook. Materially, and therefore semantically, the photographs float untethered, potentially in conversation with any and all other contents in the album.

Scrapbooks exhibit an unconventional sense of time and sequencing as well as space that attests to compilers' innovative reimagining of print media. Victorian scrapbooks displaced the initial temporal status of periodical clippings, removing them from their original cycle of production, consumption, and disposal to resituate them in groups and sequences as heterogeneous as the maker's own engagement with print media.[42] Idiosyncratic sequencing informed scrapbook structure in a variety of ways, perhaps most obviously by encouraging readers to linger over items previously destined to have a short lifespan. Garvey notes that "saving clippings overcame the daily press's ephemerality and disposability"; the material status of these clippings as harvested from the larger body of disposable print matter suggests to an album's readers that they deserve an "intensive reading."[43] For example, Edwin Waugh's poems, clipped from a regional newspaper and pasted into a scrapbook, were transformed from tomorrow's rubbish to enduring artefacts – a shift that altered both the temporal status and the value of the poems from transitory to timeless. However, suspending the poems in the pages of the scrapbook draws attention to their original status as publication events at the same time that it reconfigures the timeline of those events. Garvey suggests such work effectively archives not only each publication event but also the moment when it was encountered for the first time.[44] This is borne out in the Waugh scrapbook through the compiler's inclusion of multiple copies of the same Edwin Waugh poems. Poems reprinted at different times and possibly in different periodicals were clipped and pasted into the scrapbook in different parts of the album. This repetition suggests that the compiler thought them worth saving not for their letterpress content but for their status as unique publication events, circulated among specific readerships at specific moments.

A scrapbook's sequencing is composite as well as idiosyncratic, variously adapting and augmenting the timescale of periodicals to suit the compiler's aims for the album's production and consumption.[45] A variety of design techniques contribute to the sense of composite time evident in Victorian scrapbooks. One of the most common of these techniques was non-linear revision, the removal and addition of materials by a compiler, either all at once or in multiple phases. For example, the compiler of the Methodist scrapbook added whole quires to this album at different dates over several decades. The last sections of the scrapbook to be bound in and compiled appear at the centre of the scrapbook, meaning that to navigate the album from verso to recto, left to right, is to tour excerpts of the pictorial press sequentially from the 1830s to the 1870s and then backward to the 1830s once more. The significance of items in relation to one another hinges not on their temporality but on their pictorial characteristics.

The Carden scrapbook exemplifies another model of composite time: its non-linear organization defies chronological reading, although the dates of clippings are important to their meaning. The items on the album's first two pages are dated to early 1900s; the following two pages are constituted chiefly by clippings of birth, death, marriage, and professional announcements that range from 1866 to 1894, pasted in non-sequential clusters. These are dated in handwritten notes and grouped into sections that have been ruled in black ink, creating a sense of aesthetic order in the absence of temporal order. Although the date of each clipping is carefully noted, documenting lived events in chronological sequence is not as essential to the meaning of this codex as is developing a thick documentation of connections and events in Carden's social network.

Adapting the rubric of representational fidelity espoused by illustrated journalism was another notable way that scrapbooks imagined new possibilities for print media. I have already discussed how Macmillan's use of a variety of image types and modes contributed to the authority of his representations of Birmingham. However, the scrapbook technique exemplified by this example did not simply replicate but also enhanced similar practices evident in illustrated periodicals. Scrapbook makers extended illustrated journalism's logic of pictorial fidelity to create more dynamic interpretive environments. While periodicals included a fairly diverse assortment of image types, they could not encompass as materially and temporally wide a range as scrapbooks did. The Macmillan album's pictorial items, for example, were reproduced over a period of almost a century (1830 to 1916), using methods common to inexpensive, mass periodicals, such as wood-engraving and photomechanical processes, as well as methods used for print of a higher quality and/or more limited circulation, such as etching and lithography. Macmillan repurposed these images from a variety of print media, and their paper and ink qualities range from cheap to expensive. The album's material diversity reinforces Macmillan's efforts to depict Birmingham comprehensively. Following the logic espoused by periodical journalism, Macmillan's depiction of place is authoritative because it is materially varied as well as multi-perspectival.

Kemp's scrapbook similarly includes a broader spectrum of material artefacts than a periodical could showcase, including photographs of himself in the front and back of the album, as well as an invitation to his own wedding and other mementos of his life as a husband and father. The material scraps of his own life offer traces of the lived personal experience that forms the backdrop for the project of the album, modelling cultural discourse about feathers in the fashion industry. These artefacts provide additional facets of information, adding sensory texture to the scrapbook's knowledge model.

A final way that scrapbook makers augmented print media design was through annotation. This practice drew on cultural precedents for marking up, editing, and appending materials to published print matter. However, it bore a media-specific significance. Within the context of scrapbooks, unlike other print media, annotation can take place at any point during or following a compiler's initial process of selection, curation, and design, and the end result for readers is the same. Because the album's materiality is heterogeneous from the outset, a reader cannot discern a difference between mark-up inscribed during the object's production and mark-up inserted or interjected afterwards. Although Victorian scrapbooks were inherently appropriative, then, the acts of annotation evident in their pages do not stand out as uniquely appropriative. Rather, they are perceived simply as part of the broader curatorial efforts that produced each album. And by including annotated materials in their scrapbooks, makers signalled that the comments or images inserted as annotations had archival value equal to that of other items included in the album pages.

Annotations are a significant design feature for an anonymous scrapbook devoted to documenting the women's suffrage movement in

WOMEN'S SUFFRAGE.

With reference to the woman's suffrage meeting, to be held at St. James's Hall, Piccadilly, at seven o'clock this evening, the following address has been issued:

To the Real Friends of Women.

This meeting has been called by the compromising section of the advocates of woman's suffrage to support Sir Albert Rollit's Bill. I ask you to oppose this bill, because:

1. It does not enfranchise married women. Married women cannot now vote for Town or County councils, and only those who can so vote—that is, widows and spinsters—will be enfranchised by this bill. 2. It does not enfranchise any woman lodger. As hundreds of thousands of our single working women are lodgers, the bill insults them by absolutely ignoring them. 3. It is essentially a middle-class bill, and we have had more than enough of that middle-class legislation which neglects the workers of the country. 4. It ignores the cardinal principle for which women should strive—viz., equality with men in this matter of the franchise.

As my friends know, I am totally opposed to Mr. Gladstone's attitude on this question. It is an attitude which must on every occasion be strenuously combated by the advocates of woman's suffrage. But Mr. Gladstone is right when he says: "The bill (Sir A. Rollit's) is a narrow bill, inasmuch as it excludes the entire body of married women."

On March 30 last, seven weeks after the bill was introduced, Miss Cozens, the promoter of this meeting, wrote: "At all our meetings we oppose any bills that do not include married women, and at St. James's Hall every speaker will oppose Sir A. Rollit's bill tooth and nail in his speech."

Three weeks after the bill was introduced Lady Florence Dixie, who is announced to take the chair at the meeting, wrote to me as follows: "I do hope that in discussing the vote for women question and the wage question, that women will, in the first instance, support no resolution which does not in explicit terms demand the vote on exactly the same terms as it is granted to men, thereby including the married women in its provisions. The woman who supports the suffrage to only widows and spinsters is unworthy of and unfitted to exercise the right of voting, inasmuch as she connives at the degradation and enslavement of woman in the married state. The bill of Sir A. Rollit and Mr. W. McLaren is a snare, delusion, and sham, and unworthy the support of any courageous man or woman."

In face of this condemnation of the bill these ladies and their friends now turn round on themselves and ask you to assist them to insult married women and women lodgers by supporting a bill which shuts these out from the franchise. Instead of that I appeal to you to vote for the following resolution, which will be submitted to the meeting: "That, in the opinion of this meeting of men and women, the time has arrived when all local, municipal, and parliamentary franchises should be granted to women, whether married or unmarried, on the same terms as they are granted to men, and that no bill is worthy of support which does not definitely embody this principle; and that a copy of this resolution be sent to the leaders of all political parties and to every member of both Houses of Parliament."—Faithfully yours. Herbert Burrows.

WOMAN SUFFRAGE.

THE EDITOR OF THE DAILY CHRONICLE.

19

Sir,—I shall be glad if you will allow me to ive your readers a few facts about the meeting which it is proposed to hold in St. James's Hall, Piccadilly, to-morrow (Tuesday) night, in upport of Sir A. K. Rollit's Woman Suffrage Bill.

Early in the year a committee, of which I was member, was formed to hold a demonstration in Hyde Park in favour of Woman Suffrage on the roadest possible lines. The demonstration was xed for the end of May, but in the meantime ir A. Rollit's Bill was introduced, and at my iggestion it was decided to hold a meeting in t. James's Hall on the evening before the econd reading of the Bill. The resolution which he committee decided to put to the Hyde Park emonstration and also to the St. James's Hall eeting was as follows:—

That in the opinion of this meeting of men and omen the time has arrived when all local, unicipal, and parliamentary franchises should e granted to women, whether married or unarried, on the same terms as they are granted to en, and that a copy of this resolution be sent to he leaders of all political parties, and to every Member of both Houses of Parliament.

Mrs. Annie Besant had consented to take he chair at St. James's Hall, and a numer of preliminary local meetings were held to repare for the larger one.

For some time the committee expressed no ormal opinion on Sir A. Rollit's Bill, but at all s meetings I repeatedly announced my intenion of opposing the Bill, as it fell far short of ur resolution, and from only one member of the ommittee did I meet with opposition. Suddenly, however, Miss Cozens, the secretary of the ommittee, in opposition to her previous declarations and action, advocated the support of the Bill, and thereupon, in order to give a definite expression of opinion, I moved and carried by a majority that the following words be inserted in he above resolution after the words "granted o men": "and that no Bill is worthy of support which does not definitely embody this principle." As was, perhaps, natural under the circumstances, a split occurred in the committee, and a winding-up resolution was passed, which practically included the return to the subscribers of the balance of the funds in hand. In defiance of this the minority, taking advantage of a supposed technicality in the hiring of St. James's Hall (which will probably result in future proceedings), have called to-morrow night's meeting to support Sir A. Rollit's Bill—a line of action to which not only the original resolution, but especially its addition, is

a Lie.

another

Miss Cozens, the chief promoter of to-morrow's meeting, wrote—"At *all* our meetings we oppose any Bills that do not include married women, and at St. James's Hall *every* speaker will oppose Sir A. Rollit's Bill tooth and nail in his speech." Shortly before that Lady Florence Dixie, who was announced to take the chair to-morrow, wrote to me as follows:—"I do hope that in discussing the Vote for Women question and the Wage question women will in the first instance support no resolution which does not in explicit terms demand the vote on exactly the same terms as it is granted to men, thereby including the married woman in its provisions. The woman who supports the suffrage to only widows and spinsters is unworthy of and unfitted to exercise the right of voting, inasmuch as she connives at the degradation and enslavement of woman in the married state. The Bill of Sir A. Rollit and Mr. W. M'Laren is a snare, delusion, and sham, and unworthy the support of any courageous man or woman."

Liar

I have just heard that Lady Florence Dixie is not coming to the meeting to-morrow night. She probably recognises the extreme difficulty of reconciling the above words with her presence as a supporter of the Bill.—I am, Sir, faithfully yours,

HERBERT BURROWS.

17, Avenue-road, N.W., April 25.

It's not.

Figure 4.6. Detail from scrapbook on women's suffrage, by Anonymous. © University of Manchester Library, ref. no. R152508.

England in the early 1890s. The album compiles periodical cuttings addressing the question of women's enfranchisement as well as a few related items of ephemera. Items are organized chronologically to document activism and journalistic debate about a private member's bill, proposed by Albert Rollit, to extend the franchise. Traces of the album maker's own opinions about the women's suffrage movement, particularly its internal politics, can be found in letterpress underlining and marginal commentary. An editorial letter by a member of the Women's Franchise League, written to garner support for one faction of suffrage activists over another, is marked up in red pencil. Marginal comments condemn the letter's author, Herbert Burrow: "A Lie … another … another … Departure from Truth … Liar … The cur!" (figure 4.6). The scrapbook maker does not elaborate on this criticism, perhaps simply using the space of the page to vent private frustration.

Through such annotations the album models how the women's suffrage movement functioned in the margins of mainstream cultural discourse at the time. Activism for women's rights was often figured in terms of response, talk-back, and appropriation or adaptation of the dominant narratives about women depicted in the press. The suffrage scrapbook offers an activist space to dissent in the moment as well as to contextualize and archive acts of dissent for the historical record.

Conclusion

Scrapbooks drew on periodical techniques while going above and beyond their multimodal aesthetic possibilities, extending the functions of print media to model knowledge in more richly layered ways. I have shown that scrapbook practices enabled people to model what they already knew and to generate new knowledge about both their chosen subject matter and print media's possibilities for reader engagement. Through scrapbook practices that simultaneously drew on and augmented the makers' print media literacy and technological imagining, makers could better understand the constraints and possibilities of modelling knowledge in print and the effects that these had on a reader's experience. In other words, modelling print media made scrapbook makers more aware of mediation in popular culture. Critical and creative scrapbook makers enhanced their capacity to understand how print media produced and circulated cultural knowledge. Scrapbooking also enabled makers to recognize more fully their own agency as consumers and producers of those media.

The next chapter's case study illustrates how late Victorians, as reflexive readers and producers of print media, combined this critical awareness with media production skills that were honed through activities such as scrapbooking in order to contribute to mainstream illustrated print media. Chapter 5 demonstrates that consumers could act as producers not just through interpretive poaching, as discussed in chapters 2 and 3, and itinerate material appropriation, as discussed in the present chapter, but also by widening the channels that gave them access to the dominant strategies used by periodical producers themselves for representing culture. Readers of the *Strand Magazine* drew on their media literacy and technological imagination to shape the format and content of "Curiosities," a popular pictorial feature in this pictorial monthly. Through "Curiosities," readers' practices for poaching and producing print media entered the mainstream of cultural production and helped shape the illustrated magazine's position within the new media milieu.

Chapter Five

Imagining New Media Platforms: Taking Snapshots for the *Strand*, 1896–1918

The real amateur knight of the camera scorns the taking of mere prosaic portraits of his friends and relations, and pines for higher things. Having served an apprenticeship at landscape photography, he enters with zest into the creation of bizarre and comic photos.

"Curiosities," *Strand Magazine* (1898)

The October 1898 number of the *Strand Magazine* reproduces a visual joke that is unusual even for this lively publication. The image is a reproduced photograph; the accompanying letterpress indicates that its central figure is a monk from Brittany, France (figure 5.1). The cleric, dressed in a cassock and cape, faces the viewer; he holds a wide sheet of paper or parchment at chest height, tilted to a reading angle. For the moment he is not reading the sheet but looking directly at the viewer. In fact, the monk is pulling a face: eyes squinched up, eyebrows arched sky-high, he grimaces widely and protrudes his chin. The extraordinary disproportion of his large head to his body completes the picture's comedic effect.

The image is titled "A Good Joke – Not Clerical," and the letterpress that accompanies it informs readers that its bobble-headed subject is a composite of two photographic negatives, one of the monk and one of an unnamed friend. An inspired photographer has combined the two, transforming a sacred personage into a figure of mirth. By way of explanation, the *Strand*'s editors who have reproduced this image observe that "the real amateur knight of the camera" inevitably takes to the creation of such "bizarre" images after the more conventional fields of photography, such as landscapes and portraiture, have been mastered.[1] The comment indicates that "A Good Joke," while unusual, is not completely anomalous. It embodies a set of practices through

for buildir
poses. Th
appearance
Holy Bool
lead one to
that it ha
immersed
very power
and it had
crumble
pieces."

A GOOD
NOT CLE

The real
knight
camera sc
taking o
prosaic por
his frien
relations, a
for higher
Having se
apprentices
landscape
graphy, he
with zest i
creation of
and comic

Figure 5.1. "A Good Joke – Not Clerical." Halftone illustration from "Curiosities," *Strand Magazine*, October 1898, 478.

which amateur enthusiasts experimented with photography – a kind of Victorian Photoshopping – and circulated the results.

Though generally overlooked by scholars of Victorian print, such "bizarre and comic photos" were a mainstay of the *Strand*. The magazine offered a platform for knights of the camera to exhibit their work in the form of a long-running feature titled "Curiosities."[2] Every month between August 1896 and August 1918, "Curiosities" published captioned images sent in by readers. Usually taken with portable hand cameras, which were first marketed to general publics in 1895, these were the informal, quotidian, rapidly captured images of the snapshot genre.[3] Contributors sent in photographs of exotic foreign and historical artefacts, exceptional feats and unusual events, natural anomalies, and unusual results of the photographic process itself.

"Curiosities" published its most reader-driven, innovative items between 1897 and 1903. These years happen to mark a high point of participatory New Journalism, during which popular newspapers and magazines presented an exceptional array of opportunities for readers to interact with print producers and fellow readers. These years also encompass a pivotal moment in the interaction of the illustrated magazine with the new media milieu, specifically through the medium of the snapshot photograph. Bringing these developments together, "Curiosities" offers an exceptionally extensive record of how readers leveraged their media literacy and technological imagination to appropriate print and new media practices at the same time, expressed in the form of participatory snapshot journalism.

What can the publication history of this feature teach us about readers' use of popular illustrated magazines to engage with mass new media culture? In the previous chapter, I analysed Victorian readers' tactical poaching of periodical content to produce their own multimodal print artefacts. These media were private productions; if they were circulated at all, it would be within a coterie of family and friends. Readers could also participate in mass culture, however, by submitting items for publication in popular magazines. We can gain further insight into the tactics Victorian readers used to appropriate mass culture by studying specific opportunities that periodicals offered for them to publish their own periodical content. "Curiosities" provides ample evidence of the ways in which historical readers seized on such opportunities. Like the analysis of scrapbooks in chapter 4, the investigation of the publication history of "Curiosities" in chapter 5 uncovers a dialectical relationship between the aesthetics of homemade media – in this case, curated snapshot photographs – and mass-produced print. In "Curiosities," readers used their media literacy and technological imagination to produce cultural expressions that integrated written narratives with amateur photographs.

This chapter participates in a recent movement within visual studies that uses media archaeology to analyse nineteenth-century photography. As a field, the history of photography has traditionally been separate from media history, and its primary focus has been on professional and artistic practices. Scholars have begun investigating amateur photography in relation to complex systems of nineteenth-century media and culture in order to understand more fully the "plural" history of photography.[4] As Lisa Gitelman and Geoffrey Batchen have argued, the study of photography in relation to historical media systems can shed light on both subject areas – the history of specific photographic practices and the history of media generally.[5] Recent years have seen increasing scholarly interest in the commercial, scientific, and vernacular practices that developed outside of the legitimizing boundaries of professional and artistic photography.[6] Through this recuperative work, scholars seek to understand photography's role in what Gil Pasternak describes as the "private experiences of modern everyday life and public experiences of the ordinary."[7]

In the service of developing a fuller history of photography in society, Gitelman and Batchen call for greater attention to the mobility of historical photographs across contexts and media forms.[8] In addition to contributing to the modest but growing body of periodical scholarship that focuses on the *Strand Magazine*'s non-fiction contents,[9] this chapter intervenes in the history of photography by recovering "Curiosities" as a case study in the dissemination of one photographic form, the snapshot, as it was remediated in the popular illustrated monthly. As Marc Olivier observes, many scholars and professional photographers alike have assumed that historical snapshot photography was uncritical and inartistic.[10] Snapshot photography's complex interactions with other popular media and culture prove otherwise. Nicoletta Leonardi and Simone Natale note that the 1890s were a time of transformation for photography as it shaped and was shaped by new technologies and forms of entertainment, ranging from the cinematograph to modern sports to advertising agencies.[11] The dialectic between the hand camera and the popular illustrated magazine was part of this transformation.

Intersecting these evolving media, "Curiosities" is both typical and exceptional: much popular illustrated print of this era reproduced reader photography, but no other general-interest monthly featured such contributions with such regularity over such a long period of time.

In "Curiosities" the dynamic between producer strategies and consumer tactics became a cycle in which readers used their media literacy and technological imagination to shape not only the production of print but also a new, unstable realm of popular culture, that of snapshot photography. To investigate these dynamics, I use Patrice Flichy's theoretical framework for describing technological integration.[12] In sketching the major characteristics of the process through which a new technology emerges and becomes established in a socio-cultural context, Flichy emphasizes the dynamic roles of producers and consumers and the importance of the technological imaginary. I argue that "Curiosities" became a forum for readers to contribute to the formulation of what Flichy calls the "socio-technological frame of reference" for snapshot photography. One producer of photographic technology and processes, Eastman Kodak, played a dominant role in how that frame of reference developed at the turn of the century, but "Curiosities" shows that users of snapshot technology found ways to poach Kodak's strategies. Initially "Curiosities" was conceived as conventional, editor-dominated novelty journalism, but over its twenty-two-year run this feature became a dynamic platform for readers to produce illustrated print media content in the form of snapshot photographs accompanied by written commentary. Reader-contributors became tactical producers of both "Curiosities" and the hand camera's socio-technical frame of reference, as demonstrated especially by the trick photography that was contributed regularly to the feature. In "Curiosities," then, the *Strand*'s engagement of readers' technological imagination became part of a large-scale formation of popular snapshot culture.

The Strand Magazine

Like *Pearson's Magazine*, the *Strand Magazine* printed eclectic, highly visual subject matter that appealed to a diverse but primarily middle-class audience.[13] In fact, *Pearson's* and a number of other monthly miscellanies that cropped up at the fin de siècle were modelled on the *Strand*, which was itself inspired by the format of illustrated American periodicals such as *Scribner's Magazine* and *Harper's Magazine*.[14] The second of many journals through which George Newnes established a diverse publishing empire, the *Strand* significantly influenced the modern press.[15] Its high circulation, helped along by its affordability at sixpence per monthly issue, and its unusually long print run, which extended from 1891 to 1950, made it Newnes's most successful magazine.[16]

The *Strand's* prosperity was largely due to its commercial orientation and astute sense of audience. Its affordable price was underwritten by advertisements, appearing at the beginning and end of each issue, that nearly equalled the editorial contents in volume.[17] The same New Journalism techniques evident in *Pearson's* and discussed in chapter 3, such as a personable tone, an orientation to entertainment, and readability, were pioneered in the British marketplace by the *Strand* to great success. The magazine engaged established authors and artists, such as Gordon Browne and Sidney Paget, as well as promising newcomers such as Arthur Conan Doyle, to secure a devoted regular audience.[18]

A diverse array of subject matters, including both fiction and non-fiction, enhanced the magazine's appeal to a wide readership. Scholars of Victorian periodicals and literature have often noted that the prominence of place given to fiction was essential to the *Strand*'s audience appeal and central to the magazine's character. Winnie Chan mentions that the *Strand* was promoted "primarily as a short story magazine" throughout the 1890s.[19] Journalism on news, current events, and culture topics, however, constituted a significant portion of each number, attesting to steady reader interest in non-fiction as well. In a given issue, this content might range from social commentary to popular science to celebrity gossip. Where offered, journalistic opinions were generally consistent with middle-class interests and values, although most non-fiction content had limited critical depth, containing enough specialized detail to hold interest but not enough to be challenging or controversial for an educated, general audience.

Much of the *Strand*'s amusing but superficial non-fiction content can be classified as what I term *novelty journalism*. Items in this genre appeared in every issue. Examples include "The Topsy-Turvy House at the Paris Exhibition" (1900), a report on a house constructed entirely upside-down from roof to wine cellar; and "Wonders of the West" (1902), a survey of North American novelties such as a wooden animal menagerie, a whistling choir, and long-distance hot-air-balloon sliding.[20] This genre capitalized on photomechanical technology's affordances and the magazine's highly visual layouts to create multimodal print exhibitions in which the everyday dovetailed with the fanciful.

Though its images, like its non-fiction, have received less critical attention than has its fiction, the *Strand's* rich visuality was also essential to the magazine's brand. According to its final editor, Reginald Pound, the magazine aimed to print "a picture on every page."[21] The *Strand*'s producers went so far as to create an editorial position devoted entirely to artwork, setting a new precedent among popular monthlies.[22] The magazine exhibited an exceptional array of pictures; reproduced from wood-engravings, line drawings, paintings, and photographs, the *Strand*'s illustrations showcased photomechanical image processes that were new to the popular press in the early 1890s.[23] Attentive to aesthetic impact, the *Strand*'s editors were conscientious in their pairing of letterpress genres with image types and styles.[24] In keeping with Victorian conventions, artist-drawn images consistently accompanied the *Strand*'s fiction. A wider range of image types and styles accompanied the magazine's equally diverse non-fiction, including, for example, pen-and-ink caricatures, mimetic anatomical diagrams, and documentary halftones from photographs.

Participatory Journalism and the Technological Imagination in the *Strand*

The astute sense of audience that shaped the *Strand's* diverse offerings of fiction and non-fiction text and illustration is also evident in the magazine's strategies for reader engagement. Many of these strategies can be classified as *participatory journalism*, practices that directly facilitated readers' interaction with and even contributions to magazines and newspapers. Participatory journalism emerged with the modern magazine in the late eighteenth century[25] and has remained an essential facet of Western print culture ever since. Throughout the nineteenth century, channels of participation such as the correspondence column, which published responses to periodical content and exchanges between editors and readers, fostered a sense of community and journalistic agency among periodical readers.[26]

With its emphasis on personal connectivity to readers, late-Victorian New Journalism significantly expanded the scope of participatory practices. Popular magazines augmented established channels for reader interaction, such as literary competitions, and formulated new ones, such as treasure hunts.[27] Such New Journalistic innovations in participatory journalism often leveraged recent advancements in mass print technology and portable photography; for example, during the Second Boer War, the *Illustrated London News* and other journals engraved and printed snapshots submitted by soldier-readers at the front.[28] Through these practices, periodical producers sought to strengthen readers' loyalty to specific titles and kept them invested as regular consumers of those periodicals.

George Newnes was a leading innovator of participatory New Journalism, devising exceptional schemes to foster reader interaction with his magazines. His first periodical, *Tit-Bits*, was rich in examples of participatory journalism, including advertising stunts, competitions, and correspondence features.[29] Although the *Strand* was more staid in tone than its down-market sibling,[30] the monthly sustained its share of interactive features, including puzzles, symposia, and curated reader contributions. These items often combined participatory and novelty journalism. For example, in an 1892 instalment of "The Queer Side of Things," a sporadic feature published in the magazine's first few years, the editors invited readers to send "vegetable oddities" to the *Strand* offices, promising to publish those that were "sufficiently curious."[31] Sadly, a follow-up article never appeared.

In addition to the types of interactive content already listed, the *Strand* regularly included articles about the making of the magazine, which encouraged readers' sense of membership and investment in its community, while fostering readers' print media literacy.[32] A notable example discussed in this book's introduction, "A Description of the Offices of the *Strand*" (1892), educated readers in the machines and mechanical processes involved in illustrated periodical production. Like the illustrated interviews through which the *Strand* made celebrities relatable to the average reader, "A Description" enumerates quotidian details that give vitality to the creative, editorial, and mechanical aspects of the *Strand*'s production.[33] Like other articles on the *Strand*'s production, "A Description" encourages readers to identify with the human agents involved in magazine production by individualizing these agents, bridging the conceptual gap between producer and consumer to strengthen readers' sense of affiliation with the magazine and, in turn, their brand loyalty.[34]

"Curiosities" in the *Strand*

Five years into the *Strand*'s long print run, it presented readers with a new item of novelty journalism, "Curiosities," that became a mainstay of the magazine's participatory community. Consistently appearing at the end of each number's editorial contents, this feature might seem like an afterthought of production.[35] The unchanging location of "Curiosities," however, made it easy for regular readers to find, and its long lifespan indicates that the feature filled a persistent niche in the magazine's offerings. The publication history of "Curiosities" suggests that although the feature did not initially present readers with much opportunity for engagement, it evolved to possess a unique capacity for supporting reader participation.

The first instalment of "Curiosities" appeared in August 1896 and occupied the last four pages of the *Strand*'s editorial contents (figure 5.2). The feature has no credited author or editor, and the article's text focuses

Curiosities.

ENTRANCE TO AN ARMENIAN CHURCH.

Here is a very interesting photograph, showing the entrance to an Armenian Church, situated in the Bitlis district. You will observe that the door is half-way up the wall, instead of being on the ground level. The Vali of Bitlis—a decent fellow, for a Turk — was once asked what was the reason for this architectural peculiarity. His reply was significant. "If the entrance were on the ground level, the Kurds would come in force and drive their cattle into the building. The Kurdish chiefs think there's no stable like an Armenian church." When the devout congregation have successfully negotiated the ladder, it is drawn up, and then the service proceeds without fear of rude interruption. All things considered, it must be a trifle wearying to attend service in one of these churches. There are no seats, and the congregation are detained from five to seven hours.

A WONDERFUL BOTTLE.

This is an ordinary white glass wine bottle, of European manufacture, brought from Monghyr (Ur of the Chaldees). It is without a flaw, and on the inside an Ode of Hafiz (a celebrated Persian poet of the fourteenth century) has been beautifully inscribed by a Mohammedan, whose method of executing it no one has ever been able to discover.

A BICYCLE MADE ENTIRELY OF WOOD.

A monument of patience and perseverance. It was a French peasant who constructed this cycle, using only wood for every single part. The very nails employed to fasten together the parts are of hard wood; and although Coventry might ridicule the machine, it is interesting to learn that its ingenious maker frequently rides it to the market-town some miles away.

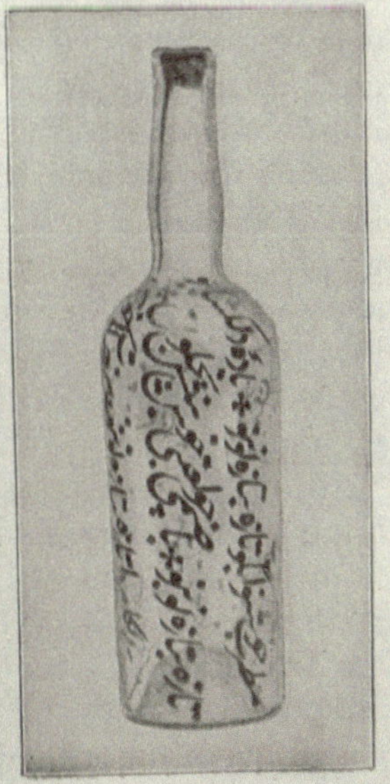

Figure 5.2. Excerpted page from "Curiosities." *Strand Magazine*, August 1896, 237.

little on the provenance of its many images. The letterpress takes the form of a series of brief notes, about five sentences in length, describing the adjacent halftone images. The subtitle over each note names the accompanying illustration's "curious item." The range of subjects in this article constitute a typical assortment for "Curiosities" in its early iterations, including "Entrance to an Armenian Church" (237); "A Bicycle Made Entirely Out of Wood" (237); "The Smallest Bank-Note in the World" (240); "The Convent Sherbanu Who Escaped from a Zenana at Amritsir" (238); and "Potato Cockatoo" (239).[36] Each of the article's fifteen items is illustrated with one or two images from photographs. The notes describe distinctive features of each visual object, detailing its original use, and, for the many foreign and historic oddities, giving some indication of origins. In keeping with the *Strand*'s New Journalistic character, the tone is conversational and playful, and the letterpress includes allusions that presuppose a readership already familiar with the *Strand*'s contents and community. For example, the note for "Dyak Darts and Quivers" quotes a passage about blow darts that had appeared in a recent novel, *The Sign of Four*, by beloved *Strand* author Arthur Conan Doyle.[37]

The article is overtly imperialistic in character. Like other novelty journalism content, "Curiosities" straddled the *Strand*'s twin realms of fiction and non-fiction, displaying oddities as strange as fiction but made all the more curious because they were real objects and events, documented as such by photography. In the early instalments of "Curiosities," as in much other novelty journalism of the *Strand*, most of these objects were foreign in origin. Their depiction reflects the *Strand*'s imperialistic use of British values as a rubric for understanding other peoples and cultures. In "Curiosities," reproduced photographs are important to this cultural work. Throughout the nineteenth and early twentieth centuries, photography was a powerful tool of cultural imperialism, fostering specific ways in which imperial subjects could see and be seen by one another.[38] While some photographic practices gave agency to the persons and cultures being photographed,[39] "Curiosities" reinscribed English hegemony by exoticizing and objectifying foreign practices that the magazine's producers deemed bizarre. Both the selection of items and their letterpress curation assume a reading community that has citizenship in the metropole, even though the *Strand* was circulated worldwide. In "Curiosities," peoples from around the globe, and especially from British colonies and dependencies, were subordinated through the article's objectification of their cultural artefacts, framed as oddities and displayed for the entertainment of British readers.

Development into a Collaborative Snapshot Forum

Although a disregard for source attribution and an imperialist orientation are prominent in the first instalment of "Curiosities," these characteristics waned during the feature's first years of publication. Their diminishing was part of the feature's evolution into an enduring keystone of the *Strand*'s participatory journalism.

By the second instalment of "Curiosities," notes began to include more information about each item's history and contributor, indicating the beginning of the feature's shift towards a participatory character. For example, readers were informed that a photograph of a stuffed elephant head had been submitted to the *Strand* offices by the naturalist "Geo. F. Butt, F. Z. S., of Wigmore Street, W.," and a photograph of a beach fort built of wet sand had been submitted by "Mrs. T. T. Ross, of Trevean, Penzance."[40] Of the feature's nine items, four are credited to named contributors. Two of these are identified as specialized scientists, but the other two do not receive a vocational distinction, suggesting to readers that the feature's contributors include amateur enthusiasts with whom they can more readily identify themselves.

The trickle of amateur contributions increased to a steady stream in subsequent numbers of the magazine. Throughout its duration "Curiosities" continued to include uncredited items procured by *Strand* editors. The amount of reader-contributed items increased markedly, however. In January 1897, "Curiosities" started actively soliciting reader submissions with a statement printed under the feature title: "We shall be glad to receive Contributions to this section, and to pay for such as are accepted."[41] This notice continued to preface each instalment of "Curiosities" until the feature disappeared in 1918. *Strand* readers evidently complied with the request, as their contributions gradually took over "Curiosities."[42]

The *Strand*'s editors likely anticipated a symbiosis between the participatory platform offered by "Curiosities" and the amateur snapshot culture when they began soliciting reader contributions. Although submissions to "Curiosities" took many forms, including curious drawings, amusing foreign handbills, and even creatively addressed envelopes, most contributions were snapshot photographs submitted with explanatory notes.

It was during the first years of "Curiosities" that amateur photography entered the popular-culture mainstream, thanks to innovations in hand-camera technology. Until the 1880s, photography had been too complex an undertaking for all but commercial professionals and "a very few avid amateurs."[43] The concept of a rapid-exposure camera that could "take a photograph, as it were, by a snap-shot" was the dream of the amateur elite.[44] By the 1880s, relatively small and light-weight detective cameras were already available from several manufacturers, but these were too finicky for most amateurs to produce "presentable images."[45] In the late 1880s and early 1890s the Eastman Kodak Company modified existing mechanisms and processes to develop light, portable cameras and equipment that were easy to manufacture and use.[46]

In 1895 Eastman Kodak launched the Pocket Kodak, the first amateur snapshot camera and the breakthrough product that marked Eastman Kodak's ascendance to the top of the amateur photography market. The Pocket Kodak and the other early folding cameras appealed primarily to an upper-middle tier of amateur photographers who could afford to invest a modest sum of time and money on personal photography. Kodak's smaller and more affordable successor, the Folding Pocket camera, expanded this demographic, becoming the first folding camera to catch on with a wide consumer market.[47] The Brownie camera, which was smaller and cheaper still, entered the market in 1900. Through this succession of cameras and photographic equipment, Kodak catered to multiple amateur demographics, ranging from serious to casual non-professional photographers.[48] The most novice-friendly cameras required simply that a user press a button to take each exposure and then send the whole apparatus to a local photographer or factory to have the film developed and a new film roll loaded.[49] This revolutionized photography's position within popular culture, including print culture.

"Curiosities" provided a wide point of access through which any reader with a camera and an eye for an interesting shot could become a paid, credited photographer for the *Strand*.[50] Some of the *Strand*'s other non-fiction content included images from amateur photographs – for example, a 1900 article on steam-boiler explosions is illustrated with photographs by the chief engineer of the Manchester Steam Users' Association.[51] But such contributions required the perspective and expertise of an industry insider. Thanks to the new hand-camera technology, amateur enthusiasts could document and publish private and local phenomena in "Curiosities" without specific training and expertise.

Although it is not clear whether a formal agreement positioned the *Strand* within Kodak's system of vertical integration, "Curiosities" synergistically linked the entrepreneurial and populist mandates of George Newnes and George Eastman, the American founder of Eastman Kodak. Many social and technological agents contributed to vernacular photography's expansion, but histories of snapshot technology and culture consistently place Eastman at the centre of this industry's transformation.[52] Like Newnes, Eastman mobilized a populist history, an altruistic purpose, and a corpus of promotional materials to forge a strong brand identity throughout the products of his company. Both men directly oversaw the day-to-day operations of their companies and cultivated public personas as paternalistic leaders of the communities that formed around their products. Eastman recognized the cultural authority of print, insisting on writing the copy for Kodak's numerous advertisements and brochures in its early years in order to shape hand-camera discourse as much as possible.[53] Similarly, Newnes understood the potential of photographic-image technology for illustrated journalism, as demonstrated by the cutting-edge illustrations of the *Strand*. Indeed, the proximity of "Curiosities" to the *Strand*'s advertising pages brought it into dialogue with the full-page and half-page Kodak advertisements that often appeared in the magazine.[54]

"Curiosities" boosted a sense of loyalty and community among two overlapping groups, Kodak users and *Strand* readers, by linking participatory cultural expression to mass consumption. The feature particularly appealed to the middle echelon of amateur photographers who had leisure time and money to snap images of novel subject matter and to tinker with photographic processes. Evidence from the *Strand*'s "Curiosities" suggests that many of these amateurs used folding Kodak cameras, which gave users options to manipulate the shot. Some enthusiasts apparently developed their own film, although others may very well have used simple box cameras and left film development to Kodak's professionals.[55] Many of the notes that appear alongside "Curiosities" items identify the images as Kodak-produced snapshots. For example, an 1898 snapshot, depicting a man on a balcony, "was taken with a Kodak camera from another balcony high above."[56] The note for another image, appearing in 1900, informs readers that the photograph was taken with a Kodak camera suspended on the ceiling.[57]

"Curiosities" opened a channel for promoting both the Kodak and the *Strand* brands, but it also had cultural functions shaped by neither Newnes nor Eastman. In fact, many reader contributions to "Curiosities" rejected Eastman's vision for the emerging field of snapshot photography. As amateur photographers became its primary reader-contributors, "Curiosities" became a participatory feature framed by the ordinary amateur's perspective. As I have shown, editors initially devised "Curiosities" as a miscellaneous exhibit of local and exotic artefacts accompanied by brief commentary. Over time, readers superseded editors to fashion "Curiosities" into an exhibit of snapshots that were diverse and novel but that largely derived meaning from their status relative to a community-centred forum. In other words, reader-contributors tactically appropriated Kodak's strategies for amateur photography (elements of what Flichy would characterize as the hand camera's *frame of functioning*) and incorporated the resulting snapshots into multimodal print (its *frame of use*).[58] In the forum of "Curiosities," reader-contributors used the technological imagination to create multimodal print expressions that functioned not as private mementos of personal experience, as Kodak intended, but as cultural knowledge shared within the *Strand* community.

"Curiosities" as a Participatory Forum

The May 1901 instalment of "Curiosities" illustrates how the types of individuals who contributed to the feature, and the subject matter of their contributions, changed over its first few years of publication (figure 5.3). Feature editors and elite collectors were displaced by the middle-class British and North American consumers who dominated both the hand-camera market and the *Strand*'s readership. Instead of showcasing anthropological and zoological artefacts that one might find in a museum, the feature exhibited unusual objects and events that emerged from quotidian middle-class life.

Of the May 1901 instalment's nineteen curious items, only one has no contributor information and was therefore likely included by the editors. Two other items are credited to anonymous individuals, one of whom is a soldier in an unnamed war (which readers would identify as the Second Boer War, then in progress in South Africa) who submitted a New Year's card fashioned from painted khaki. Aside from the soldier's contribution, all other submissions reproduced are from photographs.

"Curiosities" typically included submitters' names and addresses when given, making it possible to profile this instalment's spectrum of contributors in more detail. Less than half of the signed items (eight of nineteen) came from within the United Kingdom. Of the remaining items with named contributors, five came from America, one from Canada, one from Australia, and one from Spain. The latter appears to have been contributed by a British or anglophone citizen ("Mr. W. L. Smith, of the Eastern Telegraph Co."), rather than a Spanish national.[59] This range indicates that "Curiosities" became more international in scope as it became more participatory, although the feature's commentary suggests that contributors continued to take for granted a white, Western, anglophone audience.

By the date on which this instalment of "Curiosities" was published, the spectrum of contributors had also expanded to include women and even children. Items evidently submitted by children were relatively rare, as most contributors did not list their age, but in 1901, one to two

*Curiosities.**

[*We shall be glad to receive Contributions to this section, and to pay for such as are accepted.*]

A PLUCKY FEAT.

Mr. Douglas N. Willis sends a remarkable snap-shot taken at the Python Mine, Kamloops, B.C. The photo. represents a friend of the sender suspended by his knees on a rope swung 50ft. above the ground between two fir trees. One of the trees was stripped by the men for a flag pole, to be used during the Boer War and in celebration of British successes. The photograph was taken directly from below, and is eloquent testimony to the nerve of Mr. Willis's young friend.

MAMMOTH MIMOSA THORNS.

Mr. McTaggart Cowan, of 53, Ashton Terrace, Glasgow, sends a photograph which illustrates in a remarkable manner one of the many hardships that meet Mr. Thomas Atkins in his struggles with the enemy. The photo. represents the gigantic thorns of the mimosa bush, which of course is plentiful in South Africa. The sizes are, reading from top to bottom, 4¼in., 6¼in., 6½in., 5¾in. Surely bushes covered with thorns as large as penholders would be sufficient to disorganize the most efficient cavalry! It is curious to note *en passant* that the pods of these mimosa bushes supply a large quantity of tannin, and the fruit, having been found highly serviceable in America for cattle feeding, was officially recommended, in 1877, for cultivation in South Africa for like purposes.

A LIGHT-FINGERED CLOCK.

Mr. H. D. Gasteen, of 66, The Common, Woolwich, in sending the next photo. writes: "I inclose a photo. of a funny occurrence which happened not long ago. Someone carelessly left an opened letter against the dial of the clock shown in my photograph. As the minute hand went round it got between the sheets and gently lifted its strange burden in the manner shown. I just arrived in time to photograph it."

Figure 5.3. Excerpted page from "Curiosities." *Strand Magazine*, May 1901, 595.

named contributors to each instalment, roughly 5 per cent of the total, had women's names. This percentage is small but notable, given that women's contributions to the first instalments of "Curiosities" were exceedingly rare. The increased diversity of contributor locale, age, and sex reflects the demographic variety within the *Strand* community, as well as the appeal of amateur photography to the technological imaginations of various types of persons within that community.

Most items in the May 1901 iteration of "Curiosities" are connected geographically and temporally with the reader-contributors themselves, refuting the imperialist preoccupation with exotic anomalies that was evident in early instalments of "Curiosities" and the *Strand*'s other novelty journalism. As "Curiosities" became increasingly reader driven, the feature focused more on phenomena that contributors could document in their own neighbourhoods. Serendipity and an eye for the novelties of one's day-to-day life became more important criteria for participating in "Curiosities" than access to exclusive foreign locales and rare archaeological artefacts. Of the nineteen items, two document contemporary novelties that would have been foreign to most British, colonial, or American readers of the *Strand*. The local items submitted to "Curiosities" record unusual events, such as a gas explosion, as well as peculiar feats and creations, such as a home-made "wind carriage."[60] One item, "A Literary Bird," cleverly references the *Strand Magazine* itself: an image from Hamilton, New York, depicts a nest into which an oriole has woven a piece of the *Strand*'s cover. The contributor playfully notes that the bird "showed excellent taste" in choosing its materials.[61]

If the changing contributor demographics and subject matter of "Curiosities" offer two ways to index the feature's transition to a more fully participatory forum, the changing authorship of "Curiosities" item notes between 1901 and 1902 offers a third way to track this shift. Although the feature facilitated participation from its inception, contributors initially had limited agency to shape how their images were framed by titles and letterpress. Until the end of 1897, every note was written by the *Strand*'s editorial staff, giving the feature a consistent tone despite its diverse content. *Strand* editor(s) sometimes referred to the letters that contributors had submitted along with their images, paraphrasing or quoting a sentence verbatim to provide detailed information about a subject or the circumstances of its documentation. For example, the note for an item titled "A Tree Tied in a Knot," from February 1898, reports: "Mr. Colquhoun writes, 'I have a tree in my garden which has tied itself into a knot in its growth; the knot is more than 12in. in circumference.'" But such contributor commentary is always framed by editorial intervention. The editors supplement Colquhoun's statement with their own speculation: "No doubt some years ago this branch, at that time a mere twig, got twisted or knotted … and was never afterwards disturbed."[62] Such commentary supersedes contributor input, ensuring that editorial curation dominates the text of the feature as a whole.

Between 1901 and 1902 the proportion of quoted material in each note increased until almost every note was a direct statement by an item's contributor (still framed as such by quotation marks). An absence of grammatical or spelling mistakes suggests that the *Strand*'s editors still silently intervened, correcting any typographical errors. The editors continued occasionally to write a note about a reader-contributed item, in some cases because the contributor included no explanatory letter (as stated by the editors). However, most of the letterpress and images in "Curiosities" appear to be the work of reader-contributors by 1902, marking the feature's shift to fully participatory journalism in both the visual and the textual materials.

This shift to reader-authored notes underscores that, although an invisible editorial selection process determined the monthly assortment exhibited in "Curiosities," reader-contributors made the feature their own, superseding the editorial *we* with individualized voices in conversation with one another. The witticisms, declarations, and exhortations of individual contributors were printed at the *Strand* offices, along with reproductions of their snapshots, and circulated among the *Strand*'s international readership. The ability to curate both their images and the accompanying text translated to increased editorial agency for "Curiosities" contributors. Readers tactically appropriated the multimodal potential of "Curiosities" to exhibit their accomplishments, share images of personal interest, and, as the remainder of this chapter will relate, exchange ideas on photography itself.

Eastman Kodak and the Culture of Snapshot Photography

The Eastman Kodak Company influenced heavily how hand cameras and snapshot photographs were used by publics, and its role in snapshot culture is evident in "Curiosities." Just as reader-contributors tactically appropriated the form and content of this feature, however, they appropriated Kodak's prescriptions for producing and circulating snapshot photography. "Curiosities" illuminates alternative practices and values that were part of turn-of-the-century snapshot culture: in some ways, reader contributions to "Curiosities" adhered to Kodak's guidelines for hand-camera use; in other ways, the novelty items and notes that readers contributed to the feature clearly deviated from these rules.

Flichy's theorization of the process through which a new technology integrates with a culture illuminates how "Curiosities" operated as an interface at the border between the intended functions of the hand camera and its heterogeneous use by real individuals and groups. In Flichy's terms, "Curiosities" contributed to amateur photography's developing "socio-technical frame of reference," the field shared by various actors collaborating in a technological activity – in this case, snapshot photography.[63] According to Flichy, the actions of various agents, particularly technology designers and users, shape the place that a new technology comes to occupy in a culture. In this dynamic process, agents interact as strategists and tacticians within two subframes that constitute the larger socio-technical frame of reference: the frame of functioning, which encompasses technological activities and knowledge, and the frame of use, which encompasses a technology's social significance.[64] According to Flichy, these two frames interact through a feedback loop that involve strategies and tactics, in Michel de Certeau's sense.[65] In the context of snapshot photography history, the hand camera's producers acted as strategists by designing this technology to be used in a specific set of ways, for a specific set of purposes. The camera's users, as well as other agents who interacted with the technology after it had been shaped by strategists, became tacticians by poaching the camera's intended functionality, using it for their own purposes.[66]

The hand camera's frame of functioning was shaped largely by Eastman Kodak's designers and producers.[67] As indicated by its first slogan, "You press the button – We do the rest," Kodak designed a frame of functioning that sharply constrained user input. It prioritized simplicity of manufacture and use for all its cameras, from the middle- and upper-tier folding cameras that offered a user many setting options, to the low-end box cameras, such as the Brownie, which offered few to no options for adjustment.[68] Whether an amateur photographer used a foolproof, point-and-shoot box camera or a slightly more complex folding camera, Kodak's "complete system" of equipment and resources for snapping and developing photographs made advanced technical knowledge unnecessary to photographers. In short, Kodak took care of every aspect of photography except for selecting a subject and taking a picture.[69]

Kodak distributed user manuals and guidebooks to educate novice photographers on the hand camera's frame of functioning. It strategically provided only enough information, however, to persuade readers of Kodak's technological superiority and to instruct them on intended product uses.[70] Even more detailed Kodak literature, such as the personal portrait guide "At Home with the Kodak" (1915) and the periodical *Kodakery: A Magazine for Amateur Photographers*, focuses chiefly on the steps involved in taking, but not developing, photographs. These publications offered minimal explanation of the film-development process, although they always included at least one promotional item about Kodak's film-development services. Even when Kodak introduced a mobile film-development tank, the company shed little light on the chemical development process for hand-camera users. Kodak streamlined the steps of development so that a tank's user could simply mix the appropriate ratio of premade powders and water and follow the instructions.[71]

Kodak's highly determined frame of functioning limited user agency, grooming consumers to depend on Kodak's supplies and services rather than invest the additional time and money required to use more elite photographic equipment or devise homemade methods. Strategies to foster user dependency were important to Kodak's success: most of the company's profits came from developing film, which was a periodic expenditure for most consumers, rather than from selling cameras, which required a one-time purchase.[72] In its promotional literature Kodak presented its constrained frame of functioning as a public service: thanks to Kodak, individuals who lacked the technical knowledge, financial resources, and leisure time of the elite amateurs could enjoy the freedom "to take pictures of the things that they themselves [were] interested in."[73] This rhetoric reinforced Kodak's efforts to cultivate an image of benevolence.[74]

Flichy describes a technology's interface as the "point of articulation between the frame of functioning and the frame of use."[75] Here, the agents involved in the two frames indirectly negotiate with one another. Kodak's user manuals and other promotional ephemera were part of the company's efforts to shape the publics' engagement with this interface and, in so doing, to determine snapshot photography's frame of functioning as well as its frame of use. Kodak held amateur photography competitions, seminars, and exhibitions and published literature and promotional ephemera, all of which contributed to a homogeneous narrative of snapshot photography's place in popular culture and individual lives. According to Kodak, snapshot photography's purpose was to document special occasions and happy times for the sake of recording memories. The "true witchery of Kodakery," the company claimed, was "in the recording not only of the unusual and the picturing of our travels, but even more in its portrayal of the every-day, common places at home."[76] While professional photography was often as carefully planned and staged as a public performance, amateur snapshot photography could – and should, according to Kodak – be spontaneous and personal. Snapshot photography was also democratically progressive, according to the Kodak ethos, providing all people with means to create their own visual archives.[77]

By disregarding technical and artistic expertise, Kodak's version of democratic photography was naïvely simplistic, presenting a "child-like" perception of experience and its documentation in snapshots.[78] Even the autonomy of the idealized Kodak Girl, the company's fictional brand ambassador, was limited: as Nancy West indicates, her ever-youthful appearance reinforced her amateur status.[79] Kodak thus encouraged a narrow range of user participation. Although its appeal rested largely on giving consumers agency as producers of cultural expressions, Kodak limited this agency by discouraging media literacy and technological awareness.

Reimagining Snapshot Production and Use in "Curiosities"

Eastman Kodak made every effort to determine how hand-camera technology fit into the cultural landscape, but the frame of use was still necessarily the domain of the individual snap-shooters who integrated photography into their everyday lives. "Curiosities" presents an opportunity to examine how hand-camera users – particularly middle-tier, folding-camera amateurs – responded to Kodak's strategies. Although "Curiosities" was not part of Kodak's initial frame of functioning and therefore not part of the initial interface, it became a secondary interface enabling amateur photographers to use participatory journalism to adapt and subvert the frames of functioning and use formulated by Kodak. According to Flichy, agents draw on the technological imagination to develop strategies and tactics for a technology's functioning and use.[80] The *Strand*'s use of participatory journalism to engage readers' technological imagination made "Curiosities" an interface through which the hand camera's frames of functioning and use interacted.

Some of the feature's photographs follow Kodak's prescriptions by using snapshot photography to archive memorable experiences. For example, an item from October 1902, "Capturing an Octopus," depicts a cephalopod that the photographer and a friend "overpowered and secured" just off the coast of Australia. The contributor, A.S. Faulkner, notes that "no one here had ever seen such a huge octopus before." Indeed, the impulse to record the moment was shared; Faulkner observes that many "photographers availed themselves of the opportunity to secure prints of this unique catch."[81] The reproduced photograph in "A Fortunate Little Lady," from the same instalment of "Curiosities," functions as an archive of an archive. In the image a crowd of dolls surrounds a young girl's face. The child, Miss B. Priest, explains in her note that the forty dolls visible in the image represent only half of her large collection. The reproduced photograph archives both the collection and the collector, whose youth renders her appearance and her keenness for collecting toys subject to change over time.[82]

Virtually all the snapshots reproduced in "Curiosities" exhibit a sense of play that draws in part on the feature's general tone of amusement but also on Kodak's prescriptions for the snapshot camera's frame of use. As West observes, Kodak "inject[ed] play into the experience of photography."[83] This playfulness augmented the heady combination of the fanciful and the real with which all the "Curiosities" items were imbued. The 1899 item titled "A Good Jump" exemplifies the playfulness of snapshot photography: the image depicts a group of young women, linked arm in arm, at the midpoint of a collective hop (figure 5.4). Suspended in midair, their feet tucked behind them, the girls express a sense of play through their kinetic posture and their gleeful facial expressions. Like many snapshot subjects appearing in the reader contributions to "Curiosities," they look directly at the camera, acknowledging the performative nature of their activity and inviting the image's viewers to join the game, if only in spirit. Socio-cultural context adds to the image's ludic appeal: the women's emphatically physical humour and direct engagement with the camera's gaze contradicted Victorian expectations for female propriety, particularly in a group portrait.[84]

Reader-contributors drew on Kodak's principles of spontaneity, informality, and playfulness, but they also created their own photographic techniques and sensibilities. Collectively, their contributions to "Curiosities" articulated a shared value system separate from Kodak's model. *Strand*'s reader-contributors appropriated snapshots as components of multimodal cultural expressions. From subverting snapshot subject matter to manipulating film development, contributors employed tactics at multiple levels of production to create innovative journalism. In turn, Kodak eventually refashioned and incorporated this innovative tactic as part of the stabilized frame of use for hand cameras and amateur photography.

Building homemade snapshot cameras was one way that "Curiosities" contributors appropriated amateur photography, altogether avoiding Kodak's model of vertical consumer integration. In the note for a relatively unremarkable image of a house from 1899, the contributor relates that her thirteen-year-old son took this snapshot with a pinhole-camera "apparatus" that he made using an old cigar box.[85] Another item from the following year documents amateur "telephotography," the practice of photographing a distant object. A brief but specific description of the contributor's homemade telescopic camera accompanies two photographs that he produced using the device, district." Whilst going the rounds, certain lady customers have been in the habit of giving the horse bread. Preceding his master, and arriving at the houses of these good friends, he draws his float up on to the pavement, and then knocks at the door by raising the knocker with his mouth, and then letting it drop again. This he continues to do till the door is opened, when he receives his well-earned reward.

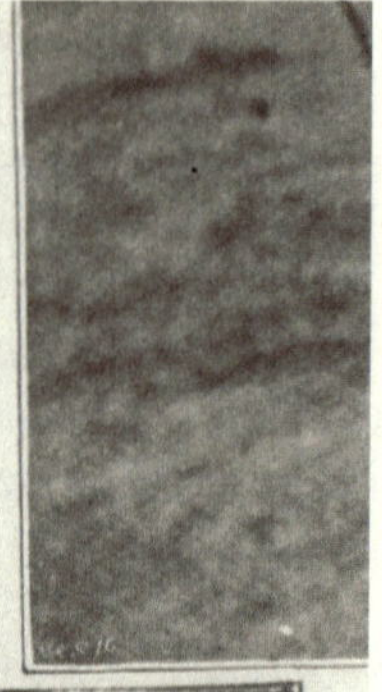

A GOOD JUMP.

Here we have a group of merry-faced schoolgirls indulging in a jump arm-in-arm together, and the snap-shot gives us a very vivid idea of the

* Copyright, 1899, by George Newnes, Li

Figure 5.4. Lilian Noble, "A Good Jump." Halftone illustration from "Curiosities," *Strand Magazine*, January 1899, 117.

offering a kind of blueprint for others who might want to make similar apparatuses.[86] A third item, from 1903, documents a "top-hat camera," pictured in a photograph, which uses a lens and a glass-plate negative and has a stand comprising a stool and a walking stick.[87] Through these homemade technologies, "Curiosities" contributors took control of snapshot camera design, resituating and individualizing this process outside the frame of use formulated largely by Kodak.

Reader-contributors to "Curiosities" also reimagined snapshot photography's functions by putting their work into conversation with other editorial content in the *Strand*, blurring the distinction between snap-shooting, professional photojournalism, and fictional storytelling. For example, a reader contribution from 1901 directly links snapshot photography to the Sherlock Holmes stories that were a mainstay of the magazine. The photograph depicts the Lower Reichenbach Falls "not long after the time when Dr. Conan Doyle ... ended the life of his hero." In other words, the image was taken in 1891 or shortly thereafter, the year that Holmes supposedly fell to his death in the Reichenbach Falls as related in "The Final Problem" (1893). The contributor, George Mason, says, "I thought your readers might be interested in seeing a photo. [*sic*] of the place where [Sherlock Holmes's] body is stated to have been recovered."[88] Mason playfully conflates the imagined with the real, using "Curiosities" to include the *Strand* community in his Swiss holiday.

Other items in "Curiosities" make less direct references to the *Strand*'s detective fiction but similarly draw on its precepts to imagine creative uses for snapshot photography. These items use text and image to create multimodal mystery narratives in which the snapshots provide evidence for uncovering a truth. A small mobile camera lends itself easily to secret surveillance – indeed, the Pocket Kodak's immediate predecessor was known as the detective camera because it was relatively easy to hide, if not to operate.[89] However, Kodak literature posited snapshot documentation as a means of archiving memories, not collecting evidence. Nonetheless, Conan Doyle's Sherlock Holmes stories and other detective fiction in the *Strand* demonstrated that photographs could be appropriated as evidence in either a professional or an amateur investigation. For example, in Conan Doyle's first Sherlock Holmes story, "A Scandal in Bohemia," published in the *Strand* in 1891, the case centres on recovering photographic evidence. While the King of Bohemia initially prizes this photograph as a token of his affection for an American opera singer, Irene Adler, it becomes even more valuable as proof of their dalliance that could be used for blackmail. For readers familiar with such fiction, the use of snapshot photography for surveillance offered an obvious avenue of exploration. "Conclusive Evidence," a "Curiosities" item from October 1898, depicts a boy dressed in work clothes and sound asleep on a bench. In the item's note the contributor, Fred Common, writes that the boy, his employee, was supposed to be dusting at the time: "You can judge his amazement and chagrin when I showed him this photograph."[90] Invoking the print conventions and literary imagination of illustrated detective fiction, Common combines candid snapshot evidence with a textual narrative that explains what the image proves.

As has been suggested by the ways in which contributors sought to engage one another with their submissions to "Curiosities," the community orientation of the *Strand* created a range of opportunities for reimagining snapshot photography's production and use. Some contributors' notes reference the magazine's offices, perhaps drawing on "A Description of the Offices of the *Strand*" or their own visits to the firm, which Newnes kept open to the public. One contribution from 1901 uses an image of the *Strand* offices in place of text to address an envelope. In this case the envelope itself is the curious item.[91] Other notes specifically address the community of "Curiosities" readers and editors through comments such as, "I am sure [this photo] is quite unique, even amongst the interesting collection that has been appearing for some time in the Strand Magazine."[92]

In keeping with Victorian journalism's self-referential tendency, contributors often engaged with the "Curiosities" community by referencing previous items or contributors. For example, in the note for an item titled "Helping Atlas," contributor Frank H. Williams supposes that a photograph of himself "turning head-over-heels for the amusement of a few friends" is "a fitting companion to 'A Candidate for Apoplexy,'" an image that appeared in a previous number of the *Strand*.[93] Direct and indirect references to other participants in "Curiosities" fostered a sense of community and idea exchange within the broader network of *Strand* producers and consumers. They also added a unique dimension to the participatory agency of the *Strand*'s readership. The amateur photographers who submitted to "Curiosities" asserted their individuality by not only contributing unique images but also contextualizing the images in their own words and positioning them in relation to other contents of the feature and the magazine broadly.

These assertions of individual identity and creativity were tactical in that they repositioned periodical readers as unique persons with unique responses to printed matter. They were also tactical in that they personalized the typically generalized protocols of vernacular photography. Batchen notes that snapshots tend to be "predictable, conservative, and repetitive in both form and content."[94] Similarly, Catherine Zuromskis observes that most snapshot photographers are not creating individual records so much as simply "going through the motion of a prescriptive cultural ritual."[95] "Curiosities" contributors, while engaging with a set of cultural conventions developed within the feature's snapshot community, insisted on presenting their photographs as the result of highly individual processes.

For female contributors to "Curiosities," exercising participatory agency had particular socio-political connotations. As previous examples suggest, a relatively significant portion of the feature's items were contributed by and/or depicted women. Women readers engaged in participatory journalism throughout the nineteenth century, and they constituted a substantial portion of the *Strand* community, but they were often marginalized in journalistic discourse that privileged male readerships.[96] "Curiosities" made individual women's participation in both periodical production and snapshot culture highly visible. A large section of the hand-camera market was women; indeed, Kodak's use of the Kodak Girl in its promotional literature reflects its efforts to target female consumers.[97] In her self-reliance and energetic engagement with the world, this figure represented the autonomy that a modern woman could exercise as a snapshot photographer, using her camera to document experiences for personal satisfaction.

Although the discourses of both professional and amateur photography were dominated by men, and male contributors to "Curiosities" outnumbered women, the feature's consistent inclusion of items by women increased their visibility as participants in snapshot culture. Although these women resembled the Kodak Girl in some ways, they tacitly undermined Kodak's gendered narrative of snapshot cultural participation. A number of female contributors to "Curiosities" fit the Kodak Girl's profile in that they were apparently unmarried (or would have been perceived as such, given their use of the prefix *Miss*), and they used their cameras to document adventures out and about in the world, rather than domestic scenes. The female subjects of "Curiosities" items such as "A Good Jump" (figure 5.4) and "A New Style in Photography" (figure 5.5) also resemble the Kodak Girl in their youthful exuberance and willingness to actively engage with the camera's gaze. Many of the women who participated in the *Strand*'s snapshot journalism, however, were media innovators whose technological experiments exceeded the narrow uses of photography modelled by the Kodak Girl – for example, E.F. Fox's "A Photographic Curiosity," an unorthodox image taken from under an old church bell tower (figure 5.6). "Curiosities" offered women an opportunity not only to become more visible participants in the *Strand* community but also to produce subversive, multimodal cultural expressions that shaped the hand camera's frame of reference. "Curiosities" showcased women's contributions to the magazine that were far more innovative than the Kodak Girl's personal mementos.

Expanding the Horizons of Print and the Snapshot through Trick Photography

Trick photography – that is, snapshots that made photography itself the curiosity on display – offered an exceptional array of opportunities for "Curiosities" contributors to tactically appropriate amateur photographic culture by devising their own methods and values. Walter

bottom of the cocoanut represents the making of curry. There were only three of these cocoanuts made—two were shown at the Paris Exhibition, and the other is in my possession." Photo. by Powls and Mays, Birmingham.

A NEW STYLE IN PHOTOGRAPHY.

Minneapolis has the honour of inventing a new method of photographic grouping. The contributor of this example, with the modesty of genius, desires to withhold his name. He says: "These are a group of Minneapolis's fairest girls. They were taken while they were all lying on the floor with their heads together, and the Kodak suspended from the ceiling."

Figure 5.5. "A New Style in Photography." Halftone illustration from "Curiosities," *Strand Magazine*, August 1899, 240.

Benjamin posits that photography frees the hand of the artist or documentarian so that representation and reproduction become "a matter of the eye's perception only."[98] While Benjamin uses this premise as a springboard to the analysis of film, his insight offers a rationale for the consistent interest in submitting and viewing trick photographs in "Curiosities." Thanks to the hand camera's automation, amateur photographers could focus on other aspects of production that might offer opportunities for creativity, such as the angle and timing of a shot and the development process. Unlike other types of "Curiosities" items, such as local attractions and unusual feats, trick-photography items were almost entirely the purview of reader-contributors. Indeed, they constituted the only new category of subject matter to emerge in "Curiosities" as readers became the feature's dominant contributors. Amateur photographers produced trick photographs in various intentional and unintentional ways, ranging from the creative positioning of subject matter to unusual chemical reactions, exposures, and post-production touch-ups.

The first instance of photography itself as curiosity appeared in March 1897, when two English aeronauts took snapshots of London from a hot-air balloon.[99] Although this item drew attention to the photographic process in interesting circumstances, the results had been produced by skilled semi-professionals. The first instance of *amateur* trick photography appeared later that year, when E.F. Fox contributed her snapshot of the view from below a church tower (figure 5.6). The note for her photograph, written by the editors, explains how she stood inside the bottom of the tower and held the camera lens upwards to obtain this "curious perspective."[100] The image compels reader interest by subverting expectations about snapshot aesthetics that were based on Kodak's ideals. Far from representing a clearly defined, well-lit, and evenly proportioned object,[101] the image is indecipherable without the accompanying letterpress: defamiliarization, rather than mimetic documentation, is precisely the point of Fox's creative photography.

A second amateur trick photograph appeared in "Curiosities" two months later, in November 1897. Like Fox's item, it is an optical oddity, but unlike the church tower snapshot, this photograph's curiosity was created unintentionally. In a portrait that the contributor, E.H. Horton, took of his sister, the profile of a "curious, impish-looking little woman" appears to the right of the sitter's chair.[102] In December 1897 an item titled "Astonishing Photographic Freak" includes a photograph in which a horse seems to be missing one leg. The item's note quotes the contributor's letter, in which he describes this unusual development as an unexplained "mystery."[103] By including such comments, the feature's editors encouraged readers to attend to the wonders wrought by photographic mediation of the world. Although Kodak's rhetoric indicates that photography represents real phenomena with straightforward fidelity, these images highlight the curious gaps that appear as reality is remediated in snapshots.

These examples illustrate how "Curiosities" contributors subverted conventional photographic values by exploring how snapshots simultaneously offered immediate and mediating records of lived

Figure 5.6. E.F. Fox, "A Photographic Curiosity." Halftone illustration from "Curiosities," *Strand Magazine*, September 1897, 359.

phenomena. As Miles Orvell points out, the Victorians embraced an aesthetic of "artificial realism" in photography: it seemed both to depict reality with perfect mimesis and to offer a "vehicle for fantasy and illusion."[104] The snapshot discourse articulated by Kodak extended this contradictory sensibility. Kodak presented photographs as offering virtually unmediated access to lived experiences while emphasizing that photography curated a specific version of those experiences.

The tension between immediacy and mediation is an inevitable result of the unique materiality of photographs and derivative print media. The physicality of a photograph, particularly in non-aesthetic genres such as snap-shooting, testifies to the past existence of the real phenomenon it has recorded, offering what Roland Barthes describes as a "certificate of presence" for its subject matter.[105] Zuromskis terms this, with material specificity, the "indexical nature" of photography – its status as "a physical trace of its subject."[106] Precisely because of its indexical nature, photography is often regarded as more accurate than other media.[107] Snapshot photography is often considered particularly accurate because it is supposedly more spontaneous and less crafted than other types of photography. At the same time, snapshots – and photographs in general – are often heavily managed by their producers. Indeed, Kodak literature silently sustains this contradiction, presenting Kodak snapshots as authentic records of lived experience while encouraging consumers to adhere to specific guidelines for taking, developing, and circulating photographs.

Much of the trick photography reproduced in "Curiosities" seized on this tension and explored it to various effect. In this way, "Curiosities" contributors enhanced their photographic media literacy and technological imagination. The trick photographers of "Curiosities" embraced snapshots as both indexical and immediate, on the one hand, and as managed and mediated, on the other hand, in a manner unparalleled in mainstream vernacular photography at this time. Each trick photograph of "Curiosities" offers proof not of a physical object in a specific moment in time but of a unique instance of shooting and developing a picture. In contrast to the values advocated by Kodak and central to the way amateur photography was conventionally viewed, the purpose of the trick photographs in "Curiosities" was not to memorialize personal events. Rather, the trick snapshots were souvenirs of the photographic process itself.

Between 1898 and 1903, at least one item of amateur trick photography appeared in every "Curiosities" feature. This subset of "Curiosities" snapshots could comprise almost half of an instalment's items. Trick photography items included those snapped from unusual perspectives, such as the view of a man from one storey directly above him,[108] or from his feet in dramatically foreshortened perspective.[109] Several items depict an urban landscape as viewed from high above (for example, "Looking Down from Blackpool Tower").[110] Some images showcase the manipulation of the photographic process through post-production editing – for example, "A Good Joke – Not Clerical" (figure 5.1) – or through carefully timed exposure of the negative – for example, "Studying Virgil," in which a young man appears to be reading studiously upside down while flipping over a gate on one hand.[111]

Each of these "Curiosities" contributions draws attention to the acts of taking, developing, and looking at photographs. It is telling that nearly all trick-photography items include some explanation of the process that produced them; contributors could not resist encouraging readers directly to reimagine the photographic process and its outputs. For example, the anonymous male contributor of "A New Style in Photography," explains that the snapshot was taken "while [the young women] were all lying on the floor with their heads together, and the Kodak suspended on the ceiling" (figure 5.5).[112] By revealing his technique, the contributor enables readers to reconstruct the production history of this image.

Creating their photographic and print productions in collaboration, contributors of trick photography to "Curiosities" offer the fullest evidence of how this feature's reader-contributors engaged in what photography historian Lynn Berger calls "peer production."[113] Berger has documented such knowledge sharing and collective invention found in the articles and correspondence pages of specialized amateur photography periodicals in the 1850s and 1860s. Peer production was no longer a feature of the photography trade press by the end of the century because firms such as Kodak had gained control over many patents and processes.[114] However, "Curiosities" demonstrates that the new practices of snapshot photography also generated enthusiasm for more itinerant collaborative forums. In the context of popular magazines, peer production was supported by the participatory New Journalistic ethos. Just as "A Description of the Offices of the *Strand*" educated the *Strand* community about the periodical's production process, "Curiosities" contributors drew attention to the possibilities at play in the intersection of new media use and print culture production. In doing so, they fostered the technological imagination of other readers.

Although trick photography remained outside the use guidelines espoused by Kodak, contributors gradually established their own conventions for it within the forum of the peer production offered by "Curiosities." Some contributors took pride in reproducing or adapting techniques that had already appeared in "Curiosities" – as illustrated by the multiple snapshots taken from below in tall, narrow structures, beginning with Fox's church tower photograph. Almost every variety of trick photography appeared multiple times during the publishing history of "Curiosities," each one submitted by a different contributor. Other contributors were similar in their insistence on being unprecedented, implying the value of amateur innovation in a competitive community. For example, the contributor of an item titled "An All-Night Photograph" surmises that he is probably the first amateur photographer to take his own portrait "whilst asleep."[115] Both the recurrence of tactics and the consistent efforts to improve on them attest to the patterns of use that an international community of "Curiosities" contributors established over time.

"Curiosities," 1904–18

In the first few years of the twentieth century, the range of subject matter and item format in "Curiosities" crystallized into a set of conventions from which contributors seldom deviated for the rest of the feature's print run. This may have been due, in part, to the *Strand*'s relative cultural stagnancy in this period. As Jonathan Cranfield has argued, the magazine adapted little to changing cultural perspectives and the new media milieu after 1903.[116] However, the stabilization of snapshot photography's socio-technical frame of reference may have been the most direct factor in the entrenchment of "Curiosities." Kodak's shrewd business strategies, including marketing campaigns and patenting initiatives, maintained the company's central position in this frame. Kodak's name became synonymous with amateur photography, and its version of snapshot culture did not include subversive processes such as trick photography.

After 1911, "Curiosities" shrank in size and began to share page space with a puzzles section, suggesting that the feature's importance to the *Strand*'s participatory journalism had declined. The feature continued to print multimodal items curated by contributors, and oddities selected by *Strand* editors, but these were joined by crosswords, riddles, and other items that, although they invited reader interaction, did not foster community production. By 1913, "Curiosities" had dwindled to two sides of a single page, which it shared with assorted puzzles. The feature made its last appearance in August 1918, and the *Strand* offered no explanation for its demise.

Many of the imaginative photographic methods that "Curiosities" contributors devised did not become part of the technology's stabilized socio-technical frame of reference. Nevertheless, "Curiosities" presents an important record of the ways in which print media literacy and the technological imagination of periodical readers contributed to an early chapter in the history of vernacular snapshot photography. As a case study, "Curiosities" is also significant because it contributed to a relationship between popular illustrated periodicals and reader-contributed photographs that became essential to the snapshot's role in popular culture. Specialized photography periodicals had featured forums for knowledge exchange beginning several decades before "Curiosities," and they played an important role in photography culture well into the twentieth century. For example, the *Amateur Photographer* printed the images of competition winners and the correspondence of readers soliciting and offering answers to photographic dilemmas.[117] However, these journals had a consistently narrower readership than did the *Strand*. Although the *Amateur Photographer*'s full title identifies it as a "popular journal," the technical specificity of its subject matter indicates a readership of relatively advanced photographers. Journals such as the *Amateur Photographer* were careful to distinguish their contributors and readers from the lower tiers of amateur snap-shooters.[118] As a forum for amateur photographers of all demographics to exchange ideas and share their creations, "Curiosities" became the *Strand* community's fin-de-siècle analogue to the specialized photography publications. Indeed, many periodicals would follow the *Strand* in becoming sites for exploring snapshot photography's cultural roles. For example, in 1906, the *Pall Mall Magazine* inaugurated its own amateur photographer competitions, publishing the winning images in its pages.[119]

Eventually Kodak launched its own journal, *Kodakery*, in 1913, and the more elite journals, such as the *Amateur Photographer*, began including articles on hand cameras.[120] By this time the socio-technical frame of reference for vernacular photography had begun to stabilize; the role of snapshots in popular culture altered little over the following decades.[121]

Conclusion

Kodakery's emergence signals that the use of periodicals as a forum for amateur snap-shooters had become part of vernacular photography's stabilizing frame of reference. This evidence indicates that the Victorian technological imagination on display in "Curiosities" influenced how users consumed and produced cultural expressions in the new media milieu. Although the trick photographers of "Curiosities" rejected the homogeneous aesthetic values of mainstream snapshot culture, they nonetheless embraced an aesthetic of mechanical remediation. Their chosen photographic input was parsed and rendered by mechanical processes, producing a perspective on reality that combined reflective human and automated-machine interpretation. In this way, the trick snapshots bear an unlikely resemblance to both the mid-Victorian composite photography of Henry Peach Robinson and Oscar Rejlander and the twentieth-century experimental photography of modernist surrealists such as Man Ray. All three artists produced aesthetically innovative photographs that attest to a shared preoccupation with how the mechanical technologies of communication and expression shape the perception of reality. The surrealists explicitly framed their work as the decoupling of photography and representational accuracy in order to study perception itself, but the creative photographic experiments of the previous century suggest an ongoing discourse about representation and mediation in the industrial age.

The Victorian cultural reception of photography, including the uptake of snapshot photography to produce "Curiosities," demonstrates that this communication technology helped pave the way for modernist thought, by, as Kate Flint puts it, "allowing us to notice, appreciate, and interrogate the ordinary" in a new way.[122] In other words, photography augmented popular media literacy and drew popular attention to mediation. However, as "Curiosities" illustrates, it often did so in conversation with other print media that people had long been viewing with the aid of their media literacy and technological imagination, particularly the magazines. As I will elaborate in the conclusion, Victorian print media literacy and the technological imagination offer important contributions to a debate about representational fidelity and the politics of media participation that began well before the nineteenth century and continues today. These concepts are essential to understanding the genealogy of twentieth- and twenty-first-century mass-media engagement. They also serve as tools for historicizing the politics and possibilities of digital culture.

Conclusion

Victorian Media Literacies and the Genealogy of the Present

Illustrated print journalism evolved in step with major technological changes during the Victorian era. Incorporating the latest reproduction methods to become a unique medium in its own right, the popular illustrated magazine managed to embody both the old and the new in the early years of the twentieth century. Even as non-print media began reshaping the landscape of popular culture, the continued success of pictorial journalism seemed, to many, to be inevitable. But as the long history of human communication attests, no media practice is invulnerable.

In an 1899 essay for the *Contemporary Review* titled "Illustrated Journalism: Its Past and Its Future," Clement Shorter, editor of the *Illustrated London News*, appraises the innovations and triumphs of pictorial news. The article's title notwithstanding, Shorter directs his gaze chiefly to the past, rather than the future. Not until the article's final section, after offering a post-mortem of the wood-engraved images that had all but disappeared from the major illustrated journals by the late 1890s, does Shorter venture into speculation about the future of illustrated journalism. Unfortunately, his preoccupation with print's expansion during the previous century hindered his ability to imagine the media landscape of the next hundred years. While he rightly doubts that the public will ever tire of images reproduced from photographs, Shorter also maintains that images reproduced from artwork will remain essential to journalism, declaring that "the future of the black-and-white artist who illustrates current topics is absolutely assured."[1] He reasons that some aspects of "life, and particularly of public life, cannot be depicted by the camera." Though Shorter elaborates little, he tacitly distinguishes photographers as a separate class from that of "genuine" artists capable of representing affectively complex sites, such as weddings and funerals.[2]

Shorter takes for granted the continued cultural centrality of not just the special artist but also pictorial print journalism as a whole. He boasts that the illustrated magazine has become so indomitable that the most "we can all of us wish for it" is that this medium maintain the high standards set by the founders of the *ILN* and the *Graphic* as it sails into the twentieth century.[3] In effect, Shorter deems the illustrated magazine too big to fail.

Contrary to Shorter's forecast, images reproduced from artwork became rare in pictorial news reporting of the twentieth and twenty-first centuries, although they continued to appear, to some extent, in more specialized periodicals. Today artist-drawn images are seldom used for documentary purposes; the aesthetic sensibilities of photography and film dominate the visual expression of lived events. Significantly, illustrated print journalism lost its position at the forefront of popular culture as other media technologies, including radio, television, and online digital platforms, transformed how visual and verbal expressions of news and culture were circulated. Magazines became more niche – or, rather, specialized journals remained visible in the media landscape while general interest news and miscellany magazines all but disappeared. In this climate, the major late-Victorian pictorial weeklies and monthlies eventually folded. The *Graphic* ceased publication in 1932; *Pearson's Magazine* ended its run in 1939. After decades of gradual decline, the *Strand* ceased publication in 1950. Although the *ILN* had a longer lifespan, its publication schedule slowed increasingly from the 1980s onward; after publishing only two issues per year for almost ten years, the magazine went out of print in 2003.

Illustrated print journalism was gradually sidelined in the media ecosystems of the twentieth- and twenty-first centuries, but popular late-Victorian magazines have continued to collide with newer forms and genres, from modernist art to Instagram, in surprising ways. As Jussi Parikka explains, media cultures are "sedimented and layered, a fold of time and materiality."[4] This book's case studies reveal sites of inter-media folding where Victorian print forms are embedded in the strata. By fostering media literacy and creating space for dynamic reader engagement, turn-of-the-century pictorial magazines contributed to later media cultures. To conclude this book, I will briefly consider what that history can teach us about new media production, reception, and criticism broadly, and then I will gesture to some of the specific ways in which the Victorian legacy of digital media continues to shape user engagement.

Victorian New Media, Representational Fidelity, and Mass Literacy

The reception history of late-Victorian magazines as new media was inscribed with a pattern of ambivalence that has long structured how critics talk about media change, from Wordsworth and Ruskin's criticism of "dumb Art" in pictorial journalism to Marxist critical assessment of machine-age spectacles to digital media theorists' rhetoric of "ethereal" remediation.[5] New media are often thought to be epistemologically unstable, even dangerous. Reflecting specifically on visual new media, W.J.T. Mitchell relates: "The deeply ambivalent relationship between human beings and the images they create seems to flare up into crisis at moments of technical innovation, when a new medium makes possible new kinds of images, often more lifelike and persuasive than ever before, and seemingly more volatile and virulent, as if images were dangerous microbes that could infect the minds of consumers."[6]

As a category of expression, images have been inscribed and stored by humans using countless media types over thousands of years. In the context of the industrial age, though, Mitchell's comments apply equally to a wide range of primary expressive phenomena: images still and moving; sound; and combinations of images, sound, and/or written words in dynamic environments. The new media that thrust these phenomena into uncertain cultural status included, in turn, nineteenth-century illustrated print; fin-de-siècle mechanized media; twentieth-century broadcasting media; and the digital media of our own time.

The perception of industrial and post-industrial media as unstable is the result of a failure to assess new media on their own terms, rather than in relation to established formats. This perennial tendency among critics of media and culture is a defining feature of a debate about representational fidelity and the politics of media engagement that began well before the nineteenth century and continues today. The Victorian-specific interplay between positions in this debate has been a latent theme of the case studies through which I have studied publishers' strategies and readers' tactics in the new media milieu of the fin de siècle.

Threading concurrently through the discourse that surrounded every new medium as it became part of the Victorian cultural landscape were two conflicting viewpoints: first, that the new medium offered a more accurate expression of reality than more established forms did because it less heavily mediated its subject matter; and, second, that the medium offered a less accurate expression of reality because, in its immediacy, it flattened or oversimplified its subject matter. The first viewpoint was espoused chiefly by cultural producers who used new media to engage readers and audiences; the second was often voiced by social and cultural critics.

The reception of pictorial journalism exemplifies this tension. As discussed in chapter 1, the illustrated news weekly proclaimed its own capacity to offer superior representational fidelity. Images, as Mitchell observes, are often perceived as having "an aura of self-evidence," a "sensuous presence" that "can lend them an easy credibility."[7] Throughout the nineteenth century, producers of the *ILN* strategically capitalized on this conception of visual veracity to promote their pictorial medium. Continuing the tradition in "Illustrated Journalism: Its Past and Its Future," Shorter concedes that interpreting pictorial journalism's "resplendent" depictions involves less imagination than interpreting a sparer expression does. He considers this "sacrifice," however, akin to no longer having to speculate on the meaning of inscriptions because one has learned to actually read them – in other words, it is no sacrifice at all.[8]

Shorter's overview of developments in illustrated journalism attests to the way in which his industry escalated its rhetoric of fidelity as it adopted new image-reproduction methods. For example, although Shorter feels that the camera was unable to depict some aspects of public life, he unequivocally declares that photographic images convey "incidents of the hour" with "intense reality."[9] Using such terms, periodical producers framed the outputs of photomechanical processes as less mediated – and therefore even more faithful to reality – because fewer steps and fewer human agents were involved in producing them.

While producers championed the supposed immediacy of illustrated magazines as evidence of their veracity, naysayers seized on the same quality as proof of pictorial journalism's inferiority. Throughout the nineteenth century, conservative social and cultural critics took up this supposition of mass image immediacy to argue that illustrated magazines made their subject matter *too* accessible, pandering to the semi-literate working classes. For example, as I mentioned in chapter 1, William Wordsworth condemned pictorial journalism, along with illustrated books, as "a backward movement" that appealed to a reading public that deteriorated intellectually as it expanded.[10] Accepting the precept that images were less mediated than script was, critics such as Wordsworth thought that the illustrated press lowered the bar for reader engagement by oversimplifying cultural expression. Established visual forms, such as painting, were not subject to similar criticism, although their roles in popular culture were certainly discussed in other ways. In his *Ariadne Florentina* lectures later in the century (1872–4), John Ruskin echoed Wordsworth's view, contrasting mass print images with paintings and fine art engravings to argue that the former could only convey degraded culture through their inferior aesthetic capacity. In this lecture series, Ruskin argued that modern mass engravings prioritized the wrong aesthetic values to simplify production and maximize viewer impact – in his words, to catch "the last gleams in the glued eyes of the daily more bestial mob."[11] He contended that the popularity of mass pictorial print had been "ruinous" to British society's engagement with art and culture.[12] According to Ruskin, audiences who only took in such inferior visual media were unable to cultivate the "subtle attention" necessary to interpret more sophisticated visual forms.[13]

In their assessments of new media, Wordsworth and Ruskin, like many critics of popular culture generally and illustrated print specifically, were influenced by class bias. Both authors believed that a decline in British taste was due to the tandem increase of mass image reproduction and cultural engagement by persons "railroad born and bred" – in other words, members of the working and lower-middle classes who lacked the sensibilities and literacy to engage with the right kinds of cultural expression in the right way.[14] Maintaining a hierarchy of cultural expressions was essential to how Wordsworth and Ruskin distanced their own contributions to Victorian journalism (in, for example, the *Friend* magazine and the *Nineteenth Century* magazine, respectively) from the scourge of media change and the masses who embraced it. Wordsworth and Ruskin shared this disconnect with fellow writer Wilkie Collins, who presumed in his 1858 essay "The Unknown Public" that the readers of cheap sensation fiction were a mysterious demographic distinct from readers of *Household Words* magazine.[15] Raymond Williams slyly observed that "the mass is other people"; this was certainly true for Wordsworth, Ruskin, and Collins.[16]

Popular illustrated journalism boasted wider audiences than Wordsworth, Ruskin, and Collins were willing to recognize. As this book has discussed, the circulation history of pictorial magazines attests to readerships concentrated in the middle classes but hailing from all socio-economic ranks. Indeed, new pictorial media were perceived by critics as threatening because they created opportunities for members of all classes to not merely consume but also contribute to the production of cultural expressions that were circulated across the social hierarchy. In doing so, the magazines introduced unpredictable elements into the social fabric.

Critics such as Wordsworth and Ruskin underestimated participants of popular culture partly because of class bias and partly because they insisted on understanding new print media in relation to established forms such as (unillustrated) poetry and painting. Thus positioned, they were slow to recognize the development of new illustrated periodical formats into distinctive media in their own right, particularly in the last decades of the nineteenth century.[17] Popular journalism was developed for and by the masses in response to the changing priorities of a nation in the industrial age. Illustrated magazines, in particular, responded to and fostered new expectations for representational fidelity that reflected fast-paced, mechanized, industrial modernity. Comparing the magazines to established letterpress formats and fine art, many cultural critics failed to see the dynamic terms of reader engagement that were made possible by the multimodal aesthetics of editorial news content, commercial advertisements, genres such as population journalism, and features such as "Curiosities." As I have shown throughout this book, each of these sites hosted the interaction of periodical producers and consumers. Such exchanges enabled readers to exercise complex interpretive processes and produce cultural expressions of their own, for both personal use and the popular press.

Mediation and Modernity

If and when Victorian cultural producers, critics, and consumers engaged with new media on their own terms, they were in a position to formulate a third viewpoint on the debate about media fidelity and engagement. As I have suggested throughout this book, in such circumstances, persons were equipped to recognize that the new technologies and processes of expression did not mediate reality *less*, only *differently*. This was essential to the popularity of illustrated magazines: the ways in which they newly mediated cultural knowledge brought pleasure and meaning to the interpretive process. John Guillory observes that a characteristic of modern society is that we create new media for their own sake, rather than out of a social need to communicate, because engaging with mediated expression gives people pleasure.[18] This pleasure is evident in the proliferation of print media at the end of the nineteenth century, as well as the abundance of ways in which readers poached and remediated print content. Mass print's mechanized mediation of expression was also, in and of itself, meaningful to readers, resonating strongly with the public's own sense of reality in the industrial age. Using the aesthetic registers afforded by their unique characteristics, the magazines both formulated and instantiated the conditions of modern life. As Victorian readers could understand through their print media literacy and technological imagination, illustrated magazines and other new media encapsulated the zeitgeist through expressions that were rapidly automated, mass-mechanized simulacra.

Consciousness of the relationship between mechanized mediation and modern reality was one of the many ways in which Victorian print culture not only shaped mass culture sensibilities but also laid the groundwork for modernist art and criticism. Particularly towards the end of the century, Victorian art and criticism reflected a modernist preoccupation with how form conditions interpretation – for example, in James McNeill Whistler's *Nocturne in Black and Gold* (1875) and Walter Crane's *Line and Form* (1900). The relationship between industrialism, new media, and modernism is well known to scholars of Victorian and modernist culture, but less familiar is modernism's lineage in Victorian popular journalism.[19] The awareness of mediation that participants of popular culture developed during the nineteenth century was essential to modernist theorizations of and experiments with form and medium. Seeds of modernist sensibilities are evident in some of this book's case studies. For example, some of the contributions to "Curiosities" in the *Strand* discussed in chapter 5 embrace an aesthetics of mechanization that involves decontextualizing photographic subject matter by manipulating the production process. The uncanny effects that resulted from this manipulation resonate with the later surrealist photography of Man Ray. Although Victorian illustrated journalism enhanced reading publics' awareness of media and mediation, modernist artists such as Ray brought these subjects to the foreground by explorating the relationship between technological processes, form, and perception.

The legacy that illustrated magazines left to modernism has not always been apparent to cultural historians because the myopia that made Wordsworth and Ruskin impervious to the cross-class influence of mass print also informed how artists and theorists distinguished the modernist movement from past and present mass media and culture. Mass-media discourse of the twentieth century, like that of the late Victorian period, continued to reflect both a perception of new media as offering more immediate access to reality and a conflicting awareness of mediation as essential to cultural expression. It was the notion of new media as immediate that many twentieth-century thinkers seized on to characterize the terms of mass media and culture engagement, even as the modernist movement manifested a growing cultural awareness of form and mediation. Marxist theorists such as Guy Debord, Max Horkheimer, and Theodor Adorno effectively adopted the perspective of Wordsworth and Ruskin by characterizing the audiences of cinematic and broadcasting media as passive. Comparing new media to old ones and seeing that new ones did not offer the kinds of engagement afforded by established media, they assumed a lack. Rather than focusing on class and an inferior popular culture, however, as Wordsworth and Ruskin had done, Horkheimer and Adorno focused on the culture industry and homogeneous mass culture. They argued that industrial mechanization led to the separation of production and consumption in the eyes of the Victorian public, encouraging passive acceptance of capitalism's terms of distribution and consumption and, in turn, passive engagement with the media of the mass "culture industry."[20]

The turn-of-the-century history of mass-media literacy that this book has recuperated indicates that twentieth-century modernist and mass cultures constitute two different but parallel avenues for exploring an increasing awareness of the media and mediation shared across classes. As nineteenth-century popular culture developed into twentieth-century mass culture, tactical practices of periodical consumption and production contributed to the active, heterogeneous terms of media engagement. As readers, mass-culture participants attended to the influence of production history on a periodical's affordances. As viewers, listeners, and users, they could similarly attend to the influence of production history on the affordances of other mass media – and use the knowledge they gained from this process to appropriate mass cultural representations. For example, in the age of broadcasting, Western publics built their own radios.[21] Producer strategies for conditioning user engagement continued to capitalize on the sense of immediacy that new media afford; responding-user tactics continued to leverage media literacy and the technological imagination.

New Media Discourse in the Digital Age

Awareness of how mediation conditioned reader, audience, and user engagement with new media – and, indeed, with all media – increased during the twentieth century. As broadcasting and digital communication technologies emerged, assumptions about new media immediacy persisted. At the same time, many popular-culture audiences and critics, including in the new field of media studies, continued to pay attention to different forms of mediation and the intricate dialectic between technology, society, and culture.

The same three perspectives on the representational fidelity of new media that I identified as being at work in nineteenth-century culture have carried over into twenty-first-century discourse about digital media. We continue to conceptualize popular media as less mediating, to the detriment or betterment of society, and, at the same time, as differently mediating. The assumption of new media immediacy underlies a contemporary interest in computational *disintermediation* – the myth that innovation is synonymous with reducing an operation's intermediary agents. J. David Bolter and Richard Grusin argue that the media of our digital age attest to a socio-cultural desire for disintermediation: we strive to develop new media that will disappear from our view as they relay content.[22] While this tenet holds theoretical appeal, as Liz Losh points out, in practice it often involves displacing, not eliminating, mediative labour, effectively making this labour less visible.[23] One corrective approach is offered by the field of media archaeology, which emphasizes the study of media's physical particularities. While this knowledge domain has uncovered generative insights, however, its arguments can lean towards technological determinism, suggesting that rather than disappearing into the ether, media contain us all too concretely. Emerging critical work resists the more extreme forms of discourse on new media engagement by zooming in on historical case studies, profiling the interaction of historical persons and groups with specific media artefacts. For example, Susan Zieger uses affect theory to assess how people individually and collectively interact with print ephemera.[24] Losh recovers invisible forms of intermedial labour, enacted by women, that were involved in mid-twentieth-century computational innovation.[25]

My investigation of Victorian print media literacy contributes to this work. Losh's essay highlights that pairing specific case studies with a long view of media change can equip scholars to undermine identity-based biases (including those of class, race, gender, sexuality, and ability) that continue to underwrite how media engagement is often characterized. To understand the role of new media in society we must also understand the meta-conversation about media consumption itself, subject as it is to marked turns. Just as importantly, we need to place our understanding of media literacy within historical contexts. For example, the *New York Times* has recently reinvigorated a cultural conversation on children's exposure to digital media, which would benefit from an approach along the lines of the present study. As recently as 2016, American educators and parents were concerned that children from socio-economically marginalized backgrounds would not have the same digital media literacies, and in turn the same opportunities, as privileged peers who used digital media technologies from an early age.[26] In 2018 the *New York Times* reported that this had given way to a concern that the same underprivileged children were too uncritically reliant on digital media technologies, while children from affluent backgrounds benefited from carefully limited exposure to these devices.[27] Situated within a centuries-long genealogy that implicates media literacies in the agency of the citizen-subject, this disparity can be recognized as less epochal in and of itself, but more significant as an expression of the ongoing struggle of marginalized subjects for cultural and political power.

Media Literacy, User Agency, and Digital Victorianisms

As digital media have a physical make-up more minutely complex than that of print and mechanical media, their literacy requires different capacities, some of which are possessed by few popular-culture participants. Digital processes of information inscription, storage, and transmission happen at a scale and pace that defy unaided human cognition. Users have more agency in terms of content production; the distinction between using and making blurs in the digital environments of, for example, social media, which run on user-created and curated content. However, users have less agency in terms of critical interpretation. The complex materiality of digital hardware and the programming architecture of software are such that few users understand digital media production on a level comparable to that of Victorian readers' familiarity with the simpler processes of print production. Digital journalism seldom regales us with accounts of its own material production history; these would describe servers and domains, code and graphical user interfaces, content management systems, and search engine optimization – features seemingly of little interest to most twenty-first-century reading publics. In the digital age how concretely do we understand our own perception of modern media as offering both immediate and mediated cultural knowledge? Is it easier now to lose sight of how it is precisely that media mediate? Literacy is a matter deserving careful consideration because, at any given historical moment, it is an essential factor in how people understand cultural representations and their own agency as critics and poachers.

The politics of media engagement that I have outlined in this book's case studies can help answer these questions because the digital media landscape retains many characteristics of its Victorian heritage. Digital media that adapt the aesthetic strategies of Victorian print media similarly condition user agency and reiterate Victorian cultural values. Two examples that connect to this book's case studies, digital population journalism and pictorial social media, illustrate how Victorian aesthetic strategies continue to shape user engagement.

Digital Population Graphics

In chapter 3, I demonstrate that line-block population graphics encouraged readers to understand persons as statistical units within a delineated socio-biological population, and photorealistic graphics encouraged readers to view persons as units of mass mechanized popular culture. Similarly, the quantitative population graphics expressed in digital form posit individual persons as binarized units of data.

Biopolitics have evolved in the era of big data, but the ideological tenets outlined by Michel Foucault remain the foundation for the way in which statistical knowledge is taken up by the state and integrated into popular representations of bodies and behaviours, including population journalism.[28] Twenty-first-century population journalism uses many of the aesthetic strategies developed in late-Victorian illustrated magazines, including visualizations designed to inform and entertain. Where articles in this genre draw on data analytics, they often engage readers' technological imagination through use of state-of-the-art visualizations, such as relational network graphs, that are capable of depicting incredibly detailed information. Like the characteristics of the Victorian examples studied in chapter 3, the materiality and aesthetics of such visualizations buttress journalistic credibility. Big-data visualizations invoke authority through a sense of total comprehensiveness. Dynamic, detailed visualizations can display every single datum; this high precision of visual information suggests high accuracy of data analysis. Given the biopolitical paradigm within which population data analysis and reporting continues to operate, such detail encourages viewers to treat the argument conveyed by a given data graphic as a comprehensive account of persons or groups as population subjects.

While data analytics do not rely on the Victorian statistical methods that require calculating averages, they involve normalization in the cultural sense that first emerged in the nineteenth century: unique individuals and groups are abstracted and reduced to uniform units. Although their capacity to render detail may make digital population visualizations seem comprehensive, their production, like that of their print predecessors, involves a series of steps that flatten information about real persons. Data are simplified to fit a series of fields, often with controlled vocabularies, and then aggregated, graphed, and visualized through a series of formulas and programs. Such streamlining is an inevitable aspect of statistical inquiry: no technique of statistical modelling is perfect in the sense of total comprehensiveness.[29] The programming involved in visualizing statistical data computationally adds another layer of interpretation. Like the processes of drawing a data graphic in pen and ink or compositing it from several photographs, generating a visualization digitally requires series of choices about the assignment of colours, shapes, sizes, and other aesthetic characteristics to statistical variables. In the resulting graphic, individual persons and groups are typically displayed as uniform units so that readers can focus on specific variables, such as behaviours or characteristics, that are key to the image's intended meaning. Abstraction of information about persons also takes place on the material level; through every step of statistical analysis and visualization that takes place in a computer environment, data are necessarily processed by the machine as strings of binary code – either yes or no, this or that.

Many statisticians and programmers are well aware of these limitations, but general publics presented with big-data visualizations are not necessarily equipped to recognize them. The majority of digital population journalism's readers are literate in neither the statistical processes and mathematical formulas involved in gathering and processing the data, nor the programs used to visualize the results. Digital population journalism encourages users to engage with their media literacy and technological imagination just enough for affective impact. Most users will attribute cultural authority to this genre through its use of state-of-the-art visualizations depicting intricately detailed information. In this sense, big-data visualizations parallel the state-of-the-art photorealist data graphics of the late nineteenth century, such as "The Mathematics of Marriage." However, the audiences for these digital graphics have a more limited understanding of the production history behind what they are looking at. In turn, they have less agency to critique its biopolitical messaging.

General publics encounter data visualizations more frequently than did our Victorian predecessors but have limited knowledge of the complex statistical processes involved in developing these graphics in a digital environment.[30] They also have limited agency to interpret most population journalism because its many stages of production, from statistical analysis to visualization programming to journalistic argumentation, remain opaque. As a result, reader-users are less equipped than Victorian audiences to appropriate population graphics critically. Where it deploys a rhetoric of big-data comprehensiveness, illustrated population journalism strengthens the mandate of biopolitics by limiting the critical agency of its subjects.

New Journalism and Visual Social Media Forums

Pictorial social media display a Victorian legacy in their use of participatory New Journalism strategies. To suit these techniques to digital contexts, social media have refashioned some particulars of these strategies without compromising their overall purpose: fostering active audience engagement to turn a profit. Although consumer sales might seem the most obvious way for media producers to gain capital, this profit model has consistently been less successful than one relying on advertising revenue. In the nineteenth century it was not until advertising restrictions were lifted that the periodical marketplace became highly lucrative. *Strand* founder George Newnes became head of Britain's first journalism empire by cultivating large, stable audiences for the advertisements that bookended each number of his magazines. Similarly, most digital start-up companies profit chiefly not from user purchases within an app but from third-party advertisements and access to user data. Both New Journalist editors and app developers have been most successful when they have cultivated strategies for continuous, dynamic community engagement among users. In both contexts, producers use aesthetic strategies designed to keep consumer engagement within boundaries that suit their capitalist interests, but consumers can respond with appropriative tactics that extend their agency.

A comparison of "Curiosities" and the snapshot-based app Instagram illustrates how New Journalism strategies, including aesthetic ones, continue to shape the agency of participants in popular culture. Both platforms have fostered the community-driven creation of multimodal media that capitalize on a sense of novelty derived from recent technological advancements – of hand cameras, in the case of "Curiosities," and cell-phone cameras, in the case of Instagram. In each case, consumer-contributors have used their media literacy and technological imagination to devise innovative and provocative cultural expressions that combine text and image. Over the publication history of "Curiosities," the aesthetic strategies of producers retreated to the background as reader contributions took over the feature. However, the magazine still retained some degree of control: an invisible editorial process continued to filter the contents printed in each instalment. Similarly, Instagram users produce the snapshots and videos that constitute the app's content, but algorithms unseen to users determine which content is displayed on their devices. "Curiosities" contributed to the dynamic community engagement that made the *Strand* desirable to advertisers; Instagram user activity enables the app to profit through targeted advertising and third-party data sharing.

Viewing Instagram through the lens of "Curiosities" clarifies how the digital app has changed in recent years, shifting from an experimental participatory forum to an increasingly staid marketplace of spectacular capitalism. "Curiosities" was most robustly participatory in the years when hand cameras rose in popularity among the working and middle classes and snapshot photography was a new, exploratory form of cultural expression. I suggest at the end of chapter 5 that "Curiosities" stalled and then withered away as snapshot culture stabilized and *Strand* readers lost their enthusiasm for participating in itinerant snapshot journalism. Instagram's rise coincided with a similar moment in new media technology. The app gained popularity during a period when smartphone technology, including capabilities for taking and displaying digital photographs, rapidly increased in both quality and affordability. But the evolutionary trajectory of Instagram has departed from that of "Curiosities" in its mature phase. "Curiosities" stagnated and dwindled as the hand camera's novelty faded, but Instagram has continued to evolve in new directions as smartphone technology has plateaued and cell-phone photography has stabilized.[31]

In fact, Instagram's developers are leveraging the predictability of its content – the very characteristic that portended the decline of "Curiosities" – to ensure its commercial success. Beginning in 2013, Instagram has introduced changes to design, functionality, and content curation – in other words, changes to its strategies for representing culture and fostering user engagement.[32] Some of these strategies have yielded new possibilities for content creation; for example, the "Stories" feature, introduced in 2016, enables users to add visual effects and overlay text on photographs and videos, as well as to broadcast themselves live. However, Instagram's commercial evolution ultimately constrains user navigation and fosters homogeneity: users are incentivized to create more content, but content that adheres to specific conventions. A major driver of this trend is the app's use of algorithms to determine which posts and stories are displayed for a user and which accounts the user is encouraged to follow. Since 2016, Instagram has controlled algorithmically the sequence and display of its content.[33] Criteria assessed by the algorithm include popularity (initially calculated in "likes," now expressed as "hearts") and the user's engagement with an account's previous posts. Users cannot adjust or turn off this algorithm; in fact, they cannot access it at all, meaning their literacy of and agency within Instagram are constrained.

Drawing on the history of "Curiosities," we might interpret this use of algorithmic curation as an aesthetic strategy: it shapes what content users can most readily engage, and it also shapes the content that users themselves produce. The algorithmic news feed incentivizes the creation of content that maximizes approval metrics, encouraging users to replicate the successful techniques used by others, and ultimately fostering aesthetic sameness among user-consumers. Paid advertisements also adopt these techniques in order to harmonize with other content in a user's feed and invoke cultural authority. The result is an endless train of similar visual brand narratives offered up for user consumption.[34]

Instagram has curbed the interpretive agency of users to such an extent that it has lost the dynamic vitality germinated through itinerant innovation and play. Unbeknownst to most users, the increasing homogeneity of user-created content is a significant benefit to the app's developers. It simplifies the profit pipeline that involves conducting market research, profiling users based on their demographic information and online behaviours, sharing demographic information with third-party advertisers, and displaying personalized advertisements based on that profiling.[35] In other words, homogeneity of user content makes the commercial activities at the core of the app's profit model easier to conduct.[36]

Instagram's popularity demonstrates that general publics continue to seek opportunities to act simultaneously as cultural consumers and producers. The aesthetics and functionality of this platform show that Victorian media strategies, such as techniques enabling community participation and individual content curation, continue to play a role in how users can engage with and appropriate cultural expressions. Contrasting the history of Instagram with that of "Curiosities" highlights that although cultural participants continue to make meaning by learning to produce expressions for themselves, producers of social media are increasingly leveraging characteristics unique to digital technologies to constrain user activity in the interests of profit.

This book's case studies have shown a clear correlation between media literacy, technological imagination, and the agency of media audiences: in our current cultural moment, popular media literacy seems to be declining – and with it our capacity to imagine new uses for media and new subversions of cultural representation. This need not be interpreted as the demise of individual agency in the realm of cultural production. I observed previously that critics of new media often fail to engage with them on their own terms, understanding them only in relation to more established forms of cultural expression. Similarly, to understand digital media literacy only in relation to historical literacies of previous media would be to disregard the unique possibilities presented by the specific socio-cultural, technological, and material contexts of digital media. Engaging with and imagining new forms of mediation continues to bring pleasure to participants of popular culture. I posit that although they may be more or less defining of a given milieu, media literacy and the technological imagination will remain essential to media engagement that is creative, critical, and diverse. Mass-media users will continue to poach meaning, taking especial pleasure in devising their own remediations, just as readers and audiences always have. It remains to be seen whether popular-culture participants of the twenty-first century will cultivate the media literacies that will enable them also to critique and reshape the contours of our shared cultural knowledge.

Notes

Introduction

1 Lisa Gitelman, *Always Already New: Media, History, and the Data of Culture* (Cambridge, MA: MIT Press, 2006), 7.
2 Used in this sense, "mass culture" denotes popular culture on a large scale, broadly describing the tastes and values of the majority. See Raymond Williams, *Culture and Society, 1780–1950* (London: Pelican Books, 1963), 289.
3 Richard Altick, *The English Common Reader: A Social History of the Mass Reading Public, 1800–1900*, 2nd ed. (Columbus: Ohio State University Press, 1998), 364.
4 Robert Scholes and Clifford Wulfman, *Modernism in the Magazines: An Introduction* (New Haven, CT: Yale University Press, 2010), 27.
5 Graham Law, *Indexes to Fiction in the "London Illustrated News" (1842) and "The Graphic" (1869–1901)* (Queensland, Australia: University of Queensland, 2001), vi.
6 E. Foley O'Connor, "*Pearson's Magazine*," in *Dictionary of Nineteenth-Century Journalism*, ed. Laurel Brake and Marysa Demoor (London: British Library, 2009), C19: Nineteenth Century Index, http://c19index.chadwyck.co.uk.
7 Altick, *English Common Reader*, 171.
8 Kate Jackson, *George Newnes and the New Journalism in Britain, 1880–1910* (Aldershot, UK: Ashgate, 2001), 266.
9 Laurel Brake and Marysa Demoor, *The Lure of Illustration in the Nineteenth Century: Picture and Press* (Basingstoke, UK: Palgrave Macmillan, 2009), 12.
10 Jerome McGann, *Radiant Textuality: Literature after the World Wide Web* (Basingstoke, UK: Palgrave Macmillan, 2001), 62.
11 Joseph Pennell, "The Making of Illustration: The Art of the Last Fifty Years," *Illustrated London News Summer Number*, 14 May 1892, 584, Illustrated

London News Historical Archive (hereafter referred to as ILNHA), https://www.gale.com/c/illustrated-london-news-historical-archive.

12 E.H. Lacon Watson, *Hints to Young Authors* (London: G. Richards, 1902), 84.

13 Clement Shorter, "Illustrated Journalism: Its Past and Its Future," *Contemporary Review* 75 (1899), ProQuest British Periodicals.

14 T.R. Nevett, "Advertising," in *Victorian Periodicals and Society*, ed. J. Don Vann and Rosemary T. VanArsdel (University of Toronto Press, 1994), 223.

15 Gerry Beegan, *The Mass Image: A Social History of Photomechanical Reproduction in Victorian London* (Basingstoke, UK: Palgrave Macmillan, 2008), 27, 48.

16 Scholes and Wulfman, *Modernism in the Magazines*, 28.

17 J. Matthew Huculak, "Reading Forensically: Modernist Paper, Newfoundland, and Transatlantic Materiality," *Journal of Modernist Periodical Studies* 6, no. 2 (2015): 162, https://muse.jhu.edu.

18 Scholes and Wulfman, *Modernism in the Magazines*, 28.

19 James Thorpe, *English Illustration: The Nineties* (London: Hacker Art Books, 1975), 10.

20 Kristin St. John and Linda Zimmerman, "Print Processes," in *Dime Novels and Penny Dreadfuls* (Stanford, CA: Stanford University, 1997), www.stanford.edu.

21 Bamber Gascoigne, *How to Identify Prints*, 2nd ed. (London: Thames & Hudson, 2004), section 33.g.

22 Ibid., sections 33.f–33.g.

23 Beegan, *Mass Image*, 8.

24 St. John and Zimmerman, "Print Processes."

25 Beegan, *Mass Image*, 77.

26 For statistics on the increase of photograph-based graphics in the popular illustrated press, see chapter 1.

27 Brian Maidment, *Reading Popular Prints, 1790–1870*, 2nd ed. (Manchester, UK: Manchester University Press, 2001), 145.

28 George Eliot, *Adam Bede* (Boston: Estes & Lauriat, 1893), 243, https://archive.org; Mary Elizabeth Braddon, *Lady Audley's Secret*, ed. Natalie M. Houston (Peterborough, ON: Broadview Press, 2003), 329.

29 Lynne Warren, "'Women in Conference': Reading the Correspondence Columns in *Woman*, 1890–1910," in *Nineteenth-Century Media and the Construction of Identities*, ed. Laurel Blake, Bill Bell, and David Finkelstein (Basingstoke, UK: Palgrave Macmillan, 2000), 123–4; Hilary Fraser, Stephanie Green, and Judith Johnston, *Gender and the Victorian Periodical* (Cambridge: Cambridge University Press, 2003), 48.

30 Paul Fyfe, "A Great Exhibition of Printing: *The Illustrated London News* Supplement Sheet (1851)," in *Cahiers victoriens et édouardiens* 84 (2016), para. 1, https://journals.openedition.org.

31 Ibid., para. 2–3.
32 "The Commercial History of a *Penny Magazine*," in the *Penny Magazine*, September 1833, 383.
33 Ibid., November 1833, 469.
34 *Punch; or, the London Charivari*, a satirical magazine, was Britain's first illustrated weekly, having gone to print one year before the *ILN*.
35 T.F. Henderson, "Chatto, William Andrew (1799–1864)," rev. M. Clare Loughlin-Chow, in *Oxford Dictionary of National Biography*, ed. H.C.G. Matthew and Brian Harrison (Oxford: Oxford University Press, 2004), http://www.oxforddnb.com.
36 William Chatto, "The Practice of Wood-Engraving," *Illustrated London News*, 6 July 1844, 425.
37 Peter Sinnema, *Dynamics of the Pictured Page: Representing the Nation in the "Illustrated London News"* (Aldershot, UK: Ashgate, 1998), 22.
38 Jackson and Chatto were part of the same community of journalistic engravers. Jackson apprenticed under his brother John Jackson, who had trained with the famous engraver Thomas Bewick and co-authored the *Treatise on Wood-Engraving* with Chatto. (According to their respective introductions to the *Treatise*, John Jackson initiated the book and enlisted Chatto to write the text so that he could focus on developing its copious illustrations.) Mason Jackson went on to publish a revised version of this series, titled *The Pictorial Press: Its Origins and Progress*, in 1885. The book, like the series, privileges the *ILN* as the top pictorial news journal.
39 Mason Jackson, "Illustrated News: A Sketch of the Rise and Progress of Pictorial Journalism," *Illustrated London News*, 16 August 1879, 158, ILNHA.
40 Ibid., 30 August 1879, 206.
41 "A Description of the Offices of the Strand Magazine," *Strand Magazine* 4 (December 1892): 595.
42 Ibid., 596–7.
43 Beegan, *Mass Image*, 2.
44 Roger Taylor, "Some Notes on Photographic Exhibitions in Britain, 1839–1865," in *Photographic Exhibitions in Britain 1839–1865: Records from Victorian Exhibition Catalogues* (2002), http://peib.dmu.ac.uk.
45 For example, Clement Shorter gives a brief summary of line-engraving and halftone processes in "Illustrated Journalism: Its Past and Present," *Contemporary Review*, 1899. Magazines such as the *Journal for the Society of the Arts* and the *Academy* discussed photomechanical technologies as depicted in and used by specialized publications under review. For example, see "Mr. Strang's Etchings," *Academy*, 19 May 1906, 482–3. The forty-seventh annual exhibition of the Royal Photographic Society, held in 1902, included "Samples of Photomechanical Printing for

Advertising and Other Purposes by Patented Machinery on Rotograph Paper," exhibited by the Rotary Photographic Company. See "The Rotary Photographic Company Ltd," in *Illustrated Catalogue of the Forty-Seventh Annual Exhibition of the Royal Photographic Society of Great Britain* (1902), 39. Exhibitions of the Royal Photographic Society, 1870–1915: Catalogue Records for the Annual Exhibitions, https://erps.dmu.ac.uk.

46 For example, in 1901 the Society of the Arts held a series of lectures on the photography used for illustration and printing, and in 1905 the Victoria and Albert Museum hosted an exhibition of process engraving. See "Notices," *Journal of the Society of the Arts* 2555 (8 November 1901), 846, and *Catalogue of the Loan Exhibition of Process Engraving: Held at the Victoria and Albert Museum* (London: Wyman & Sons, 1905).

47 Friedrich Kittler, *Discourse Networks, 1800–1900* (Stanford, CA: Stanford University Press, 1990), 225; Kittler, *Gramophone, Film, Typewriter* (Stanford, CA: Stanford University Press, 1999), 83.

48 John Guillory, "Genesis of the Media Concept," *Critical Inquiry* 36, no. 2 (2010): 347; Matthew Kirschenbaum, *Mechanisms: New Media and the Forensic Imagination* (Cambridge, MA: MIT Press, 2012), 15, 250.

49 One recent example of note is Andrew Burkett's *Romantic Mediations*, which investigates Romantic treatments of mediation in relation to nineteenth- and twentieth-century technologies such as photography, phonography, film, and virtuality (Albany: State University of New York Press, 2016).

50 On new materialism in print history scholarship, see Jonathan Senchyne's "Vibrant Material Textuality: New Materialism, Book History, and Archive in Paper," *Studies in Romanticism* 57, no. 1 (2018): 67–85. Notable applications of media theory to Victorian periodicals can be found in James Mussell's *The Nineteenth-Century Press in the Digital Age* (London: Palgrave Macmillan, 2012); Julia Thomas's *Nineteenth-Century Illustration and the Digital* (London: Palgrave Macmillan, 2016); and Lorraine Janzen Kooistra's "Charting Rocks in the Golden Stream: Or, Why Textual Ornaments Matter to Periodical Studies," *Victorian Periodicals Review* 49, no. 3 (2016).

51 For a detailed introduction to media archaeology, see Jussi Parikka, *What Is Media Archaeology?* (Cambridge: Polity, 2012).

52 Perhaps the most influential adaptation of media archaeology in book and periodical history is Bonnie Mak's *How the Page Matters*, which excavates the material history of the page as an interface of Western cultural expression to show how the modes and practices of past media remain embedded in present ones (Toronto: University of Toronto Press, 2011). Similarly, in "Great Exhibition of Printing," Fyfe shows how the exhibition supplement sheet is both an artefact of the *ILN*'s aesthetic and

technological priorities and an embodiment of the unstable status of new industrial print media. Andrea Korda draws on media archaeology to investigate the mutually influential production histories of paintings and news images participating in social realism; see *Printing and Painting the News in Victorian London: The Graphic and Social Realism, 1869–1891* (Abingdon, UK: Routledge, 2015), 22. For other examples from Victorian periodical studies specifically, see Fyfe, "An Archaeology of Victorian Newspapers," *Victorian Periodicals Review* 49, no. 4 (2016); Melissa Score, "Interred in Printing House Vaults: Pianotype Composing Machines of the 1840s," *Victorian Periodicals Review* 49, no. 4 (2016); Shannon Smith, "Technologies of Production," in *Routledge Handbook to Nineteenth-Century British Periodicals and Newspapers*, ed. Andrew King, Alexis Easley, and John Morton(Abingdon, UK: Routledge, 2016); Thomas Smits, "Making the News National: Using Digitized Newspapers to Study the Distribution of the Queen's Speech by W. H. Smith & Son, 1846–1858," *Victorian Periodicals Review* 49, no. 4 (2016).

53 McGann, *Radiant Textuality*, 138–9.

54 For a detailed analysis of attention's importance to human engagement with media, see N. Katherine Hayles, *How We Think: Digital Media and Contemporary Technogenesis* (Chicago: University of Chicago Press, 2012).

55 McGann, *Radiant Textuality*, 152.

56 Michel de Certeau, *The Practice of Everyday Life* (Berkeley: University of California Press, 1988).

57 Benedict Anderson, *Imagined Communities: Reflections on the Origins and Spread of Nationalism*, rev. ed. (New York: Verso, 2006).

58 For example, Tamara Ketabgian studies the contemporary notions of humanness that emerged from the "close mingling and identification" of people and machines in the nineteenth-century "industrial imaginary" and its literatures, in *The Lives of Machines: The Industrial Imaginary in Victorian Literature and Culture* (Ann Arbor: University of Michigan Press, 2011), 1–2. In periodical studies specifically, Michèle Martin and Christopher Bodnar use the technological imagination concept to analyse innovative techniques that the press developed to circulate illustrated news during the 1870–1 siege of Paris; see "The Illustrated Press under Siege: Technological Imagination in the Paris Siege, 1870–1871," *Urban History* 36, no. 1 (2009), 73. Elizabeth Meadows and Jay Clayton study the "generative" technological imaginary through which social exchange is mapped onto techno-material infrastructure in canonical works of Victorian fiction; see "'You've Got Mail': Technologies of Communication in Victorian Literature," in *Oxford Handbook of Victorian Literary Culture*, ed. Juliet John (Oxford: Oxford University Press, 2016).

59 Beegan, *Mass Image*, 1.

60 Beegan argues that the aesthetics of photomechanical images, and particularly halftone images, contributed to a separation of production and consumption in the British social imaginary (*Mass Image*, 15). The case studies of *Making Pictorial Print*, particularly in chapters 4 and 5, take my argument in the opposite direction.

61 Max Horkheimer and Theodor Adorno, "The Culture Industry: Enlightenment as Mass Deception," in *Dialectics of Enlightenment*, ed. Gunzelin Schmid Nuerr, trans. Edmund Jephcott (Stanford, CA: Stanford University Press, 2002), 95; Guy Debord, "The Commodity as Spectacle," in *The Society of the Spectacle* (New York: Zone Books, 1994), 119.

62 Bernard Stiegler, "Memory," in *Critical Terms for Media Studies*, ed. W.J.T. Mitchell and Mark B.N. Hansen (Chicago: University of Chicago Press, 2010), 177.

63 André Gaudreault and Phillippe Marion, "A Medium Is Always Born Twice …," *Early Popular Visual Culture* 3, no. 1 (2005): 3, https://www.tandfonline.com.

64 Hayles, *How We Think*, 12.

65 Michel Foucault, *Security, Territory, Population: Lectures at the Collège de France, 1977–78*, trans. Graham Burchell, ed. Michel Sellenart (London: Palgrave Macmillan, 2007), 477.

66 Patrice Flichy, *Understanding Technological Innovation: A Socio-Technical Approach*, trans. Liz Carey-Libbrecht (Cheltenham, UK: Edward Elgar, 2007), 81.

1. The *Illustrated London News*, Popular Illustrated Journalism, and the New Media Landscape, 1885–1907

1 G.K. Chesterton wrote "Our Note Book" each week from September 1905, when he took it over from journalist and playwright Louis Frederic Austin, until his death in June 1936. See Julia Stapleton, "The *Illustrated London News* and Our Note Book" (Gale Cengage, 2011), 1–2, ILNHA, https://www.gale.com.

2 G.K. Chesterton, "Our Note Book," *Illustrated London News*, 5 January 1907, 4, ILNHA.

3 Brain Maidment, "*Illustrated London News* (1842–1989)," in *Dictionary of Nineteenth-Century Journalism*, ed. Brake and Demoor (2009).

4 "Our Address," *Illustrated London News*, 14 May 1842, 1, ILNHA.

5 Kittler, *Gramophone, Film, Typewriter*, 83. To be fair, Kittler is not the only media scholar to conflate books and periodicals, perhaps because, as Sean Latham contends, periodicals so successfully "masquerade as books"; Sean Latham, "Affordance and Emergence: Magazine as New Media," Modern Languages Association Annual Convention, Boston, 4 January

2013. For example, Adriaan Van der Weel characterizes the media system of the pre-digital era as "The Order of the Book"; *Changing Our Textual Minds: Toward a Digital Order of Knowledge* (Manchester, UK: Manchester University Press, 2011), 2. George Landow considers the difference between the Victorian book and its "close relations" to be one of degree, rather than kind; *Hypertext 3.0: Critical Theory and New Media in an Age of Globalization*, 3rd ed. (Baltimore, MD: Johns Hopkins University Press, 2006), 11.

6 See Latham, "Affordance and Emergence"; Laurel Brake, *Print in Transition, 1850–1910: Studies in Media and Book History* (Basingstoke, UK: Palgrave Macmillan, 2000); Anne Ardis, "Toward a Theory of Periodical Studies," Modern Languages Association Annual Convention, Boston, 4 January 2013.

7 Richard Altick, *The English Common Reader: A Social History of the Mass Reading Public, 1800–1900*, 2nd ed. (Columbus: Ohio State University Press, 1998), 344; Patrick Collier, "Imperial/Modernist Forms in the *Illustrated London News*," *Modernism/modernity* 19, no. 3 (2012): 488, https://muse.jhu.edu; Peter Sinnema, *Dynamics of the Pictured Page: Representing the Nation in the "Illustrated London News"* (Aldershot, UK: Ashgate, 1998), 15.

8 André Gaudreault and Phillippe Marion, "A Medium Is Always Born Twice …," *Early Popular Visual Culture* 3, no. 1 (2005): 3,https://www.tandfonline.com.

9 Ibid., 12.

10 Ibid.

11 Ibid.; André Gaudreault and Philippe Marion, "The Double-Birth Model Tested against Photography," in *Photography and Other Media in the Nineteenth Century*, ed. Nicolette Leonardi and Simone Natale (University Park: Penn State University Press, 2019), 192.

12 Gaudreault and Marion, "Double-Birth Model," 201.

13 Gaudreault and Marion, "A Medium," 5; "Double-Birth Model," 194.

14 Gaudreault and Marion, "A Medium," 12.

15 "Our Address."

16 Mason Jackson, *The Pictorial Press: Its Origin and Progress* (London: Hurst & Blackett, 1885), 4, https://catalog.hathitrust.org.

17 Gaudreault and Marion, "A Medium," 3.

18 "*Illustrated London News*, The," in *Waterloo Directory of English Newspapers and Periodicals, 1800–1900*, ed. John S. North, series 2, www.victorianperiodicals.com/series2.

19 Gaudreault and Marion, "A Medium," 12.

20 Developments in print technology finally made possible the publication of a daily illustrated paper in 1890, when the *Daily Graphic*

launched. See Andrew King, "*Daily Graphic* (1890–1926)," in *Dictionary of Nineteenth-Century Journalism*, ed. Brake and Demoor (2009).

21 Mason Jackson, *Pictorial Press*, 328.

22 Andrea Korda, *Printing and Painting the News in Victorian London: "The Graphic" and Social Realism, 1869–1891* (Abingdon, UK: Routledge, 2015), 22.

23 Korda, *Printing and Painting*, 21; Julia Thomas, *Nineteenth-Century Illustration and the Digital* (London: Palgrave Macmillan, 2016), 3–4; Thomas Richards, *The Commodity Culture of Victorian England: Advertising and Spectacle, 1851–1914* (Stanford, CA: Stanford University Press, 1991), 24.

24 In the poem, Wordsworth criticizes illustrated journalism as "a backward movement" in which poor "prose and verse" enlist "dumb Art" to pander to the tastes of "this once-intellectual Land" – in other words, to appeal to the sensibilities of readers who lack an advanced education. See William Wordsworth, "Illustrated Books and Newspapers," in *Victorian Literature: An Anthology*, ed. Victor Shea and William Whitla (Hoboken, NJ: Wiley Blackwell, 2014), 40.

25 "Our Address."

26 The *ILN*'s marital metaphor participates in British print culture's long-standing approach to gendering image as feminine and text as masculine, as Lorraine Janzen Kooistra and others have documented. See Kooistra, *The Artist as Critic: Bitextuality in Fin-de-Siècle Illustrated Books* (Aldershot, UK: Scolar, 1995).

27 Gaudreault and Marion, "A Medium," 12.

28 After the magazine's initial year, in which the first number was printed in May, samples are taken from early January to ensure consistent representativeness: this season was usually free of holidays and major social events, so January numbers are less likely to include special news features that often skewed the ratio of letterpress to images by including more pictures. Where possible, sample percentages include advertisement pages, some of which are chiefly textual and some of which are chiefly visual. My rationale for this choice is that the advertisements conveyed as much cultural information as did the editorial contents. Unfortunately advertisement pages are not consistently included across all available bound volumes of the *ILN*. However, I have found that this inconsistency does not detract from the general pattern evident in the statistics.

29 Paul Fyfe and Qian Ge, "Image Analytics and the Nineteenth-Century Illustrated Newspaper," *Journal of Cultural Analytics*, 25 October 2018, https://culturalanalytics.org.

30 "Our Illustrations: Crisis in the Transvaal," *Illustrated London News*, 9 September 1899, 358–9, ILNHA.

31 For example, it was in a special issue of the *Graphic* that the first mass-print halftone image appeared in 1884. See Fyfe and Ge, "Image Analytics."

32 The "Coronation Record Number" was released to coincide with the original coronation date, 9 June 1902, but illness delayed the king's actual coronation, so that the number preceded the actual event by two months.
33 "Coronation and Procession," supplement, *Illustrated London News*, 14 August 1902, 1, ILNHA.
34 Ibid., 3.
35 Ibid., 21.
36 Ibid., 3, 4, 9.
37 "Coronation and Procession," supplement, *Illustrated London News*, 14 August 1902, ILNHA.
38 In fact, the *Coronation Record Number* that the page's letterpress describes is much like the *Coronation and Procession* number in format but is longer, at eighty-one pages, and is slightly *less* pictorial in character because its contents include several letterpress pages of coronation history.
39 Samuel Begg, "The New Cabinet Minister," *Illustrated London News*, 13 August 190), 549, ILNHA.
40 "The World's News in Brief," *Illustrated London News*, 13 April 1907, 550.
41 Graham Law, *Indexes to Fiction in the "Illustrated London News" (1842) and the "Graphic" (1869–1901)* (Queensland, Australia: University of Queensland, 2001), 5.
42 F.H. Townsend, "The Planters," *Illustrated London News*, 25 September 1895, 414, ILNHA.
43 Shan F. Ballock, "The Planters," 416, ILNHA.
44 "Great Novelists' Suggestions for Stories without Words," *Illustrated London News Christmas Number*, 26 November 1906, 20, ILNHA.
45 Ibid., 29.
46 Walter Wood, ibid.
47 "Great Novelists' Suggestions for Stories without Words," *Illustrated London News Christmas Number*, 26 November 1906, 20, ILNHA.
48 Gaudreault and Marion, "A Medium," 13.
49 Ibid., 3–5.
50 Tom Gretton, "Richard Catton Woodville (1856–1927) at the *Illustrated London News*," *Victorian Periodicals Review* 48, no. 1 (2015): 89, https://muse.jhu.edu.
51 Ibid., 90.
52 Ibid., 89.
53 Beegan, *Mass Image*, 162.
54 Michèle and Christopher Bodnar, "The Illustrated Press under Siege: Technological Imagination in the Paris Siege, 1870–1871," Urban History 36, no. 1 (2009): 78, http://www.jstor.org.
55 Lorraine Janzen Kooistra, "Illustration," in *Journalism and the Periodical Press in Nineteenth-Century Britain*, ed. Joanne Shattock (Cambridge: Cambridge University Press, 2017), 118.

56 Gerry Beegan, "Carl Hentschel (1864–1930)," Yellow Nineties 2.0 (website), ed. Lorraine Janzen Kooistra (Toronto: Ryerson University Centre for Digital Humanities), http://1890s.ca/hentschel_bio.

57 Kooistra, "Illustration," 119.

58 Beegan, *Mass Image*, 9.

59 Gaudreault and Marion, "A Medium," 3.

60 Kittler, *Gramophone, Film, Typewriter*, 143.

61 Geoffrey Winthrop-Young and Michael Wutz, "Translators' Introduction: Friedrich Kittler and Media Discourse Analysis," in Kittler, *Gramophone, Film, Typewriter*, xxiv; John Guillory, "Genesis of the Media Concept," *Critical Inquiry* 36, no. 2 (2010): 321.

62 Kittler, *Gramophone, Film, Typewriter*, 3.

63 Guillory, "Genesis of the Media Concept," 347.

64 Ibid.

65 *Oxford English Dictionary*, 3rd ed. (Oxford: Oxford University Press, 2001), s.v. "medium, *n.* and *adj.*," www.oed.com.

66 Henry Bradley, "Medium," in *A New English Dictionary on Historical Principles: Founded Mainly on the Materials Collected by the Philological Society*, vol. 6, ed. James A.H. Murray (Oxford: Oxford University Press, 1908), 299, Internet Archive, http://archive.org.

67 Guillory, "Genesis of the Media Concept," 348.

68 Jack Zipes, introduction to *Victorian Fairy Tales: The Revolt of the Fairies and Elves*, ed. Jack Zipes (Abingdon, UK: Taylor & Francis, 1987), xviii.

69 "Fairy Stories by Photography: Grimm Illustrated," *Illustrated London News Christmas Number*, 25 November 1907, 24, ILNHA.

70 Gaudreault and Marion, "A Medium," 13.

71 Lorraine Janzen Kooistra, "The Politics of Ornament: Remediation in/and *The Evergreen*," in "English Studies in Canada," supplement, *Magazines and/as Media: The Aesthetics and Politics of Serial Form* 41, no. 1 (2015): 108; Korda, *Printing and Painting*, 22.

72 "Fairy Stories," 20. The photographer credited for every image, Bassano, also advertised in regular numbers of the *ILN* in 1907, although not in the Christmas number in which "Fairy Stories" appears. See "Bassano Limited," *Illustrated London News*, 5 January 1907, 2, ILNHA.

73 Derry E. Voysey, "Realism and Sentimentality in Victorian Fairy Tale Illustrations," The Victorian Web, ed. George Landow (25 December 2015), www.victorianweb.org.

74 David Evans, "Photomontage," in *Grove Art Online* (Oxford: Oxford University Press, 1996), Oxford Art Online, https://oxfordartonline.com. As Elizabeth Siegel has discussed, photocollage was a widespread practice of Victorian scrapbooking that combined the domestic arts of painting and album-making with the new medium of photography. When

it was first practised in the mid-nineteenth century, photocollage was chiefly the purview of upper-class women, but by the end of the century it had disseminated across mass culture, appearing "on everything from postcards to advertisements and newspapers." See Siegel, *Playing with Pictures: The Art of Victorian Photocollage* (Chicago: Art Institute of Chicago and Yale University Press, 2009), 13.

75 Daniel Wojcik, "Spirits, Apparitions, and Traditions of Supernatural Photography," *Visual Resources* 25, nos. 1–2 (2009): 111,https://www.tandfonline.com.

76 Ibid., 114.

77 Jordan Bear, *Disillusioned: Victorian Photography and the Discerning Subject* (University Park: Pennsylvania State University Press, 2015), 32.

78 Ibid., 43, 6.

79 Siegel, *Playing with Pictures*, 37.

80 For example, Valli, the model for Rapunzel in "Fairy Stories," appeared in a production of Cinderella in 1896. The first theatrical role of Gladys Cooper, the model for Rapunzel's prince in "Fairy Stories," was in the musical comedy *Bluebell in Fairyland* in 1905. See "Death of Miss Valli Valli," *Times*, 5 November 1927, 10, Times Digital Archive, https://www.gale.com; "Dame Gladys Cooper," *Times*, 18 November 1971, 17, Times Digital Archive. Three of the four models for "Fairy Stories" – Gladys Archbutt, Gladys Cooper, and Ethel Oliver – were Gaiety Girls, chorus girls in the musical comedies shown at the Gaiety Theatre. This theatre's productions often featured fairy-tale motifs and characters. Images of some of the "Fairy Stories" models also circulated in another intermedial context on cigarette cards; for example, Gladys Archbutt appears on a cigarette card, dressed in a peasant costume reminiscent of fairy- and folk-tale motifs. See "Miss Gladys Archbutt," in New York Public Library Digital Collections, https://digitalcollections.nypl.org.

81 Jon Burrows, "Penny Pleasures: Film Exhibition in London during the Nickelodeon Era, 1906–1914," *Film History* 16, no. 1 (2004): 63, 72.

82 Jack Zipes, *Happily Ever After: Fairy Tales, Children, and the Culture Industry* (London: Routledge, 1997), 2–3.

83 David Reed, *The Popular Magazine in Britain and the United States, 1880–1960* (London: British Library, 1997), 131.

84 Mike Ashley, *The Age of Storytellers: British Popular Fiction Magazines, 1880–1950* (London: British Library and Oak Knoll Press, 2006), 198.

85 Ibid., 1.

86 Illustrated magazine fiction's narrative and pictorial techniques set precedents for the comic books that would attain mass popularity as magazine fiction waned after the First World War, although the comic book is a unique genre in its own right.

87 Beth Palmer, "Prose," in *Routledge Handbook to Nineteenth-Century British Periodicals and Newspapers*, ed. Andrew King, Alexis Easley, and John Morton (London: Routledge, 2016), 142–3.
88 Cheryl Alexander Malcolm and David Malcolm, "The British and Irish Short Story to 1945," in *Companion to the British and Irish Short Story*, ed. Cheryl Alexander Malcolm and David Malcolm (Hoboken, NJ: John Wiley & Sons, 2009), 9–10.
89 Another major factor was the tandem decline of the three-volume novel and the circulating library system.
90 Ashley, *Age of Storytellers*, 12.

2. Imagining Consumer Culture: Reading Advertisements in the *Illustrated London News* and the *Graphic*, 1885–1906

1 Diana Hindley and Geoffrey Hindley, *Advertising in Victorian England, 1837–1901* (London: Wayland, 1972), 10–14.
2 Laurel Brake, *Print in Transition, 1850–1910: Studies in Media and Book History* (Basingstoke, UK: Palgrave Macmillan, 2000), 27.
3 Priti Joshi, "Audience Participation: Advertisements, Readers, and Anglo-Indian Newspapers," *Victorian Periodicals Review* 49, no. 2 (2016): 249–77.
4 Beegan, *Mass Image*, 17; Patrick Collier, "Imperial/Modernist Forms in the *Illustrated London News*," *Modernism/Modernity* 19, no. 3 (2012): 487; Hilary Fraser, Stephanie Green, and Judith Johnston, *Gender and the Victorian Periodical* (Cambridge: Cambridge University Press, 2003), 187.
5 Robert Scholes and Clifford Wulfman, *Modernism in the Magazines: An Introduction* (New Haven, CT: Yale University Press, 2010), 142.
6 I focus on two major weekly magazines for both pragmatic and contextual reasons. Although advertising increased in aesthetic sophistication and scale in all illustrated periodicals, it is easier to study primary materials from the weeklies than from the monthlies. By the end of the nineteenth century, advertising sections shared space with editorial content in the weeklies but remained mostly cordoned off in the front and back sections of monthlies. Twentieth-century archivists usually discarded as many commercial paratexts as possible without removing editorial content; this included wrappers and advertising pages. Archivists also favoured preserving the bound volumes of monthlies, which typically included fewer advertisements than did the first issues.
7 Michel de Certeau, *The Practice of Everyday Life* (Berkeley: University of California Press, 1988), xix.
8 Katherine Hayles, *How We Think: Digital Media and Contemporary Technogenesis* (Chicago: University of Chicago Press, 2012), 12.

9 Ibid., 62.

10 James Mussell, *The Nineteenth-Century Press in the Digital Age* (London: Palgrave Macmillan, 2012), 2.

11 Henry Sampson, *A History of Advertising from the Earliest Times* (London: Chatto & Windus, 1874), 65–9, Google Books.

12 Andrew King, "Advertisements," in *Dictionary of Nineteenth-Century Journalism*, ed. Brake and Demoor (2009); T.R. Nevett, "Advertising," in *Victorian Periodicals and Society*, ed. J. Don Vann and Rosemary T. VanArsdel (Toronto: University of Toronto Press, 1994), 223.

13 King, "Advertisements"; Andrew King, "Advertising in the *Illustrated London News*" (Gale Cengage, 2011), ILNHA, https://www.gale.com; Lori Anne Loeb, *Consuming Angels: Advertising and Victorian Women* (Oxford: Oxford University Press, 1994), 5.

14 Thomas Richards notes that consumer culture took aesthetic cues from Victorian spectacles such as the Great Exhibition and the queen's golden and diamond jubilees, which associated prestige with the display of material abundance. See Richards, *The Commodity Culture of Victorian England: Advertising and Spectacle, 1851–1914* (Stanford, CA: Stanford University Press, 1991), 14.

15 See the introduction for a more detailed account of these developments.

16 Richards, *Commodity Culture*, 10.

17 Nevett, "Advertising," 223.

18 An aggressive advertiser such as Louis Velveteen could buy multiple spaces in the same column, or even across columns, so that a reader might encounter several advertisements for the same product on a single page.

19 J.C. Eno, "Eno's Fruit Salt," *Graphic* 25 (22 April 1882), 411.

20 Tom Gretton, "Culture and Anarchy in the Advertising Pages of Illustrated Weekly Magazines c. 1875–c. 1900: Forms, Icons, Typematter," Journalliteratur Aesthetics and Mediality Lecture Series, Marburg, Germany, 9 May 2017.

21 T.R. Nevett traces these innovations to the 1880s and 1890s ("Advertising," 223), but they are evident in working-class magazines from the 1870s onward (Loeb, *Consuming Angels*, 5). As Andrew King points out, downmarket periodicals were the first to publish illustrated advertisements because mid-Victorian advertisers held that visual messaging would be most appealing to working-class audiences ("Advertising in the *ILN*," 1). Indeed, single full-page advertisements appeared in working-class periodicals from the mid-nineteenth-century onward. In contrast, full-page advertisements did not appear in middle-class periodicals until 1875, when the *ILN* permitted Pulvermacher's Galvanic Chain Bands and Belts to place the first

full-page advertisement (Hindley and Hindley, *Advertising in Victorian England*, 66).

22 De Certeau, *Practice of Everyday Life*, xix.

23 Matei Calinescu, *Five Faces of Modernity: Modernism, Avant-Garde, Decadence, Kitsch, Postmodernism*, 2nd ed. (Durham, NC: Duke University Press, 1987), 235–6.

24 Richards, *Commodity Culture*, 88.

25 Calinescu, *Five Faces of Modernity*, 236; John Glaves-Smith and Ian Chilvers, "Kitsch," in *Dictionary of Modern and Contemporary Art*, 3rd ed. (Oxford: Oxford University Press, 2015), Oxford Reference Online, https://oxfordreference.com.

26 For example, as Anne McClintock documents in *Imperial Leather*, the domestic kitsch used by late-Victorian soap advertisers such as Pears and Monkey Brand also frequently had imperialist overtones. As a commodity fetish, McClintock argues, soap transformed imperial progress into a domestic spectacle to be consumed by British and colonial subjects (*Imperial Leather: Race, Gender, Sexuality in the Colonial Contest* (London: Routledge, 1995), 231.

27 Pears, "Pears' Soap," *Graphic* 49 (24 January 1891): 120.

28 Although this strategy became a familiar one in the late nineteenth century, the purchase and adaptation of artistic images by advertisers was a contentious point in a larger debate about whether artists ought to market their work for mass tastes. On artworks as advertisements see Andrea Korda, "The Streets as Art Galleries: Hubert Herkomer, William Powell Frith, and the Artistic Advertisement," *Nineteenth-Century Art Worldwide* 11, no. 1 (2012), www.19thc-artworldwide.org. On Victorian perceptions of art market economics see Julie Codell, "The Art Press and the Art Market," in *The Rise of the Modern Art Market in London, 1850–1939*, ed. Pamela M. Fletcher and Anne Helmreich (Manchester, UK: Manchester University Press, 2011), 128–50.

29 Richards, *Commodity Culture*, 90.

30 Marah Gubar, *Artful Dodgers: Reconceiving the Golden Age of Children's Literature* (Oxford: Oxford University Press, 2009), 4; Korda, "Streets as Art Galleries."

31 Miles Orvell, *The Real Thing: Imitation and Authenticity in American Culture, 1880–1940*, anniversary ed. (Chapel Hill: University of North Carolina Press, 2014), 33–4.

32 In terms of common usage, *mélange* is virtually equivalent to *bricolage*, a term more widely used in literary and cultural studies to describe cultural assemblages. While bricolage has currency within Victorian studies, however, it has theoretical associations that I do not wish to invoke here; namely, in Victorian studies and elsewhere (including de Certeau's

work), bricolage often refers to practices that are appropriative and otherwise tactical, rather than strategic, in nature.

33 Beegan, *Mass Image*, 9.

34 Savory and Moore, "Peptonized Cocoa and Milk," *Graphic* 73 (27 January 1906): 120.

35 Siegel, *Playing with Pictures: The Art of Victorian Photocollage* (Chicago: Art Institute of Chicago and Yale University Press, 2009), 13.

36 Mussell, *Nineteenth-Century Press*, 24.

37 De Certeau, *Practice of Everyday Life*, xix.

38 Ibid., 31.

39 Ibid., xix.

40 Ibid., 29.

41 Olive Schreiner, *The Story of an African Farm* (London: Penguin, 1983), 174.

42 Katie Day Good, "From Scrapbook to Facebook: A History of Personal Media Assemblage and Archives," *New Media and Society* 15, no. 4 (2012): 559, https://journals.sagepub.com.

43 Maria Damkjaer, *Time, Domesticity and Print Culture in Nineteenth-Century Britain* (Basingstoke, UK: Palgrave Macmillan, 2016), 148.

44 Alexis Easley, "The Resistant Consumer: Scrapbooking and Satire at the Fin de Siècle," *Nineteenth Century Studies* 30 (2018): 90, https://www.jstor.org.

45 Ibid., 100.

46 De Certeau, *Practice of Everyday Life*, 165.

47 Ibid., xiv.

48 Gretton, "Culture and Anarchy."

49 Ibid.

50 Hayles, *How We Think*, 91.

51 "Home and Foreign News," *Illustrated London News*, 13 January 1894, 39, ILNHA.

52 Beegan, *Mass Image*, 22.

53 For an example of typical *ILN* coverage of South Africa at this time see "The Trouble in the Transvaal," supplement, *Illustrated London News*, 11 January 1896, 1–4, ILNHA.

54 Filomena [Florence Fenwick Miller], "Ladies' Pages," *Illustrated London News*, 29 March 1902, 468, ILNHA.

55 H.C. Shelly, "Mr. Rhodes' Home near Cape Town: Groote Shuur," *Illustrated London News*, 29 March 1902, 458, ILNHA.

56 "General Sir George White, Commanding at Ladysmith," *Illustrated London News*, 21 October 1899, 568, ILNHA; "The Late Admiral Colomb," *Illustrated London News*, 21 October 1899, 568, ILNHA.

57 Kenneth O. Morgan, "The Boer War and the Media (1899–1902)," *Twentieth Century British History* 13, no. 1 (2002): 3–5, https://academic.oup.com.

3. Imagining Subjectivity: Reading Data Visualizations in *Pearson's Magazine*, 1896–1902

1 T.D. Denham, "The Mathematics of Marriage," *Pearson's Magazine* 5 (1898): 396.

2 My definition of data visualization draws on Johanna Drucker's *Graphesis*. See *Graphesis: Visual Forms of Knowledge Production* (Cambridge, MA: Harvard University Press, 2014), 8. Quantitative data visualizations are related to but distinct from qualitative information graphics, as Edward Tufte has noted. See his *Visual Display of Quantitative Information*, 2nd ed. (Cheshire, CT: Graphics Press, 2001), 9. They also differ from diagrams, which offer visual and spatial analogues for physical objects, and from the non-graphic information displays that Ryan Cordell has dubbed "information journalism," such as number tables. See Cordell, "'Many Facts in Small Compass': Information Literature in C19 Newspapers," 9 January 2015, ryancordell.org.

3 Michel Foucault, *Security, Territory, Population: Lectures at the Collège de France, 1977–78*, trans. Graham Burchell, ed. Michel Sellenart (Basingstoke, UK: Palgrave Macmillan, 2007), 477.

4 Drucker, *Graphesis*, 70; Michael Friendly, "A Brief History of Data Visualization," in *Handbook of Data Visualization*, ed. Chun-houh Chen, Wolfgang Karl Härdle, and Antony Unwin, vol. 3 (Berlin: Springer-Verlag, 2008); Tufte, *Visual Display*, 36–47.

5 Friendly, "A Brief History," 27.

6 It bears mentioning that there is growing interest in this historical subject outside the domain of the strictly academic. Most notably, journalist Scott Klein has studied key examples of infographic use in nineteenth-century American newspapers. See Klein, "The Forgotten Origins of News Infographics," in the *History of Information Graphics* by Sandra Rendgen (Cologne, Germany: Taschen, 2019), 431–54.

7 Klaus Hentschel, *Visual Cultures in Science and Technology: A Comparative History* (Oxford: Oxford University Press, 2014).

8 Katharine Anderson, *Predicting the Weather: Victorians and the Science of Meteorology* (Chicago: Chicago University Press, 2005), 201–8.

9 James Thompson, "Printed Statistics and the Public Sphere," in *Statistics and the Public Sphere: Numbers and the People in Modern Britain, c. 1800–2000*, ed. Tom Crook and Glen O'Hara (Abingdon, UK: Routledge, 2011).

10 The closest model to the medium-focused approach that I take to data graphics in print journalism may be found in Murray Dick's analysis of the information graphics printed in the 1950s *Daily Express*. Combining content analysis and structural semiotic analysis, Dick is less concerned than I am with medium in the sense of material aesthetics, but he is

mindful of the printed periodical's role, as a medium, in how readers interpreted infographics. See Dick, "Just Fancy That: An Analysis of Infographic Propaganda in *The Daily Express*, 1956–1959," *Journalism Studies* 16, no. 2 (2015): 152–74, https://www.tandfonline.com.

11 Drucker, *Graphesis*, 91.
12 Foucault, *Security, Territory, Population*, 16.
13 Libby Schweber, *Disciplining Statistics: Demography and Vital Statistics in France and England, 1830–1885* (Durham, NC: Duke University Press, 2006), 23.
14 Simon Szreter, *Health and Wealth: Studies in History and Policy* (Rochester, NY: University of Rochester Press, 2005), 26.
15 Notable examples include Sally Ledger's *The New Woman: Fiction and Feminism at the Fin de Siècle* (Manchester, UK: Manchester University Press, 1997) and Ann McClintock's *Imperial Leather*. These works examine how fin-de-siècle discourses of race, gender, sexuality, and class medicalized and biologized subaltern subjects. An exception to the trend I observe is found in Elizabeth Carolyn Miller's *Slow Print: Literary Radicalism and Late Victorian Print Culture* (Redwood City, CA: Stanford University Press, 2013), which uses a more holistic approach, combining biopolitical discourse analysis with material analysis of textual artefacts to examine sex censorship in radical Victorian print.
16 Guy Debord, "The Commodity as Spectacle," in *The Society of the Spectacle* (New York: Zone Books, 1994), 27.
17 Drucker, *Graphesis*, 65–88; Friendly, "Brief History," 21.
18 Drucker, *Graphesis*, 69.
19 Friendly, "Brief History," 23.
20 Thompson, "Printed Statistics," 127. One notable example is the jubilee volume of the *Journal of the Statistical Society of London* (June 1885). Several articles on the use of graphics and illustration are included in the number, which reflects on the recent progress of statistics as a field.
21 Drucker, *Graphesis*, 68–9.
22 Although statistical visualizations were relatively infrequent in the popular press until late in the century, there was another technique, similar in function, on which journalists relied often throughout the century to make data more tangible to readers. This was the use of descriptive verbal analogies that encouraged readers to transform statistics into mental images. For example, one year into publication, in 1845, the *Illustrated London News* boasted of its success to date by stating that the paper used to print a week's number, if cut into one-inch strips, would "reach round the Earth, a distance of about 24,000 miles." See "The Post Office Van Calling at the Office of the *Illustrated London News*," *Illustrated London News*, 18 January 1845, 48. Such analogies were often used to make large

quantities more concrete. Population journalism enhanced this practice by representing analogues pictorially instead of verbally.

23 Indeed, the Census of England and Wales was a statistical initiative particularly familiar to non-scientific publics, as its mandate implicated every British subject, and its data featured in public discourse on many biopolitical topics.

24 Weather journalism was the only staple genre to present visualized statistical data regularly to general readerships. Cartographic maps displaying Great Britain's weather patterns accompanied the data tables and verbal summaries of the *Times* weather report from 1875 onward; line charts summarizing changes in temperature and barometric readings were printed in the *Graphic* from 1876.

25 Another key domain of popular data visualization at the turn of the century was electoral data mapping, as Thompson discusses in his "Printed Statistics."

26 George B. Waldron, "The World's Bill of Fare," *Pearson's Magazine* 6 (1898): 666; J. Holt Schooling, "Is the Length of Life Increasing?," *Pearson's Magazine* 4 (1897): 30; Chauncey McGovern, "Anglo Saxons: Sovereigns of the Modern World," *Pearson's Magazine* 12 (1901): 383.

27 J. Holt Schooling, "The Modern Mercury," *Strand Magazine* 15 (1896): 334.

28 Waldron, "The World's Bill of Fare," 666.

29 "Our Overseas Trade," *Daily Graphic*, 8 January 1908, 3.

30 E. Foley O'Connor, "Pearson's Magazine," in *Dictionary of Nineteenth-Century Journalism*, ed. Brake and Demoor (2009).

31 Marie Alexis Easley, "Pearson, Cyril Arthur (1866–1921)," in *Dictionary of Nineteenth-Century Journalism*.

32 Within the field of nineteenth-century periodical studies, *Pearson's* receives mention in survey works, such as James Thorpe's seminal *English Illustrations: The Nineties*, as well as reference sources, such as the *Dictionary of Nineteenth-Century Journalism* and the *Waterloo Dictionary of English Newspapers and Periodicals, 1800–1900*. See James Thorpe, *English Illustration: the Nineties* (London: Hacker Art Books, 1975), 178; and O'Connor, "Pearson's Magazine." Aside from these brief studies, Victorian scholars tend to regard *Pearson's* only as a publication vehicle for work by major fin-de-siècle authors such as Arthur Conan Doyle, Rudyard Kipling, E. Nesbit, and H.G. Wells. Two exceptions are Judith R. Walkowitz's account of photojournalism in *Pearson's* and Andrew Shail's study of interacting text and images in Wells's *War of the Worlds* and in M. Griffith's "An Electric Eye," both published in *Pearson's* in 1896. See Judith R. Walkowitz, "The Indian Woman, the Flower Girl, and the Jew: Photojournalism in Edwardian London," *Victorian Studies* 42, no. 1 (1998): 3–46; Andrew Shail, "M. Griffith 1896. An electric eye. *Pearson's Magazine*

2, no. 12 (December): 749–56," in *Early Popular Visual Culture* 10, no. 2 (2012): 187–96.

33 O'Connor, "Pearson's Magazine."

34 Ibid.

35 Mike Ashley, *The Age of Storytellers: British Popular Fiction Magazines, 1880–1950* (London: British Library and Oak Knoll Press, 2006), 163.

36 O'Connor, "Pearson's Magazine."

37 J. Brand, "Is Suicide a Sign of Civilization?," *Pearson's Magazine* 2 (1896): 666.

38 Ibid.

39 Ibid., 669.

40 Theodore M. Porter, *The Rise of Statistical Thinking' 1820–1900* (Princeton, NJ: Princeton University Press, 1986), 6; Schweber, *Disciplining Statistics*, 4; Mary Poovey, *A History of the Modern Fact: Problems of Knowledge in the Sciences of Wealth and Society* (Chicago: Chicago University Press, 1998), xii–xv. While prevalent, this special epistemological status was contested in various contexts over the eighteen and nineteenth centuries, as Poovey documents. Politicians and social thinkers embraced it as a tenet of vital statistics, although Schweber, among others, reports some dissent among practising statisticians (*Disciplining Statistics*, 22).

41 Szreter, *Health and Wealth*, 23.

42 A member of the Royal Statistical Society, Schooling published on economic and statistical matters for both elite and popular audiences. His output included the *British Trade Book*, an overview of British commerce that he updated and published every three years from 1902 until at least 1911; economic journalism for newspapers and magazines, including the *Morning Post*, the *Nineteenth Century*, the *Monthly Review*, and the *National Review*; and fiction in the *English Illustrated Magazine*, *Sketch*, and others. See "Schooling, John Holt," *Who Was Who Online* (Oxford: Oxford University Press, 2007), www.ukwhoswho.com. No other journalist contributed so substantially to popularizing statistics in late-Victorian magazines. Indeed, Schooling's role in population journalism did not go unnoticed in the press. The article "Statistics Gone Mad," discussed later in this chapter, bears the subtitle "With Apologies to the Statistical Society and Mr. Holt Schooling." See J.G. Grant, "Statistics Gone Mad," *Harmsworth Magazine* 1 (1899): 609.

43 J. Holt Schooling, "The Lion's Share," *Pearson's Magazine* 3 (1896): 612.

44 Schooling, "Land versus Sea," *Pearson's Magazine* 4 (1897): 525–6.

45 Given that most of Schooling's population journalism uses abstract visualization, it is probably not a coincidence that *Pearson's* departed from this type of graphic at the same time that a cohort of other journalists largely displaced Schooling as contributors to this genre. Unfortunately,

I have not been able to locate evidence about the circumstances of these editorial decisions.

46 T.D. Denham, "The Mathematics of Marriage," *Pearson's Magazine* 5 (1898): 396–7.

47 Ibid.

48 Graham Mooney, "Still Births and the Measurement of Infant Mortality Rates," *Local Population Studies* 53 (1994): 42.

49 Denham, "Mathematics of Marriage," 396–7.

50 Ibid., 398–9.

51 Ibid., 397.

52 Thompson, "Printed Statistics," 125.

53 Michael G. Mulhall, *Dictionary of Statistics* (London: George Routledge & Sons, 1884). See John Aldrich's discussion of this and other visualization techniques in "Tales of Two Societies: London and Paris, 1860–1940," *Journal Electronique d'Histoire des Probabilités et de la Statistique* 6, no.1 (2010): 34–44.

54 Tufte, *Visual Display*, 59.

55 Ibid., 55, 61.

56 Ibid., 108.

57 William Playfair, *The Commercial and Political Atlas, Which Represents at a Single View, by Means of Copper Plate Charts, the Most Important Public Accounts of Revenues, Expenditures, Debts, and Commerce of England* (London: John Stockdale, 1787), 3–4.

58 Tufte, *Visual Display*, 51.

59 Drucker, *Graphesis*, 9.

60 Ibid., 107, 113. Tufte's principles for data visualization simultaneously uphold that there is an objective truth that data visualization should transparently reveal, and, contrarily, that visualization necessarily involves making choices to present an argument. I disagree with Tufte's position and take for granted here that the steps involved in gathering, analysing, and visualizing data are all interpretive. In other words, data visualization does not simply reveal a truth embedded in the data but highlights a pattern perceived by the data analyst. That pattern is not the only one that might be perceived in the data.

61 Some of the journalists who wrote *Pearson's* population-data articles between 1898 and 1902 had backgrounds in mathematics, economics, and social science (for example, Simon Newcomb and George B. Waldron, who published on mathematics and geometry). However, most authors wrote more widely on miscellaneous popular topics, ranging from acrobatics to the future of telegraphy.

62 Lauren Klein, "Visualization as Argument," 2014, lklein.com.

63 See chapter 1 for a detailed explanation of the aesthetic and cultural significance of halftone images in the 1890s.

64 Beegan, *Mass Image*, 13.
65 Ibid., 72.
66 A search of C19: The Nineteenth Century Index, which documents a fairly comprehensive range of periodical titles, reveals that no other articles published under this name appeared between 1890 and 1910.
67 Grant, "Statistics Gone Mad," 610.
68 Michel Foucault, *An Introduction*, trans. Robert Hurley, vol. 1, *History of Sexuality* (London: Vintage, 1990), 141.

4. Imagining Print Production: Making Scrapbook Media, c. 1830–1918

1 Walter Benjamin, "Unpacking My Library," in *Illuminations: Essays and Reflections*, ed. Hannah Arendt, trans. Harry Zohn (New York: Schocken Books, 1968), 61.
2 Ibid., 66.
3 Susan Tucker, Katherine Ott, and Patricia P. Butler, "An Introduction to the History of Scrapbooks," in *The Scrapbook in American Life*, ed. Susan Tucker, Katherine Ott, and Patricia P. Butler (Philadelphia, PA: Temple University Press, 2006), 22.
4 Ellen Gruber Garvey, *Writing with Scissors: American Scrapbooks from the Civil War to the Harlem Renaissance* (Oxford: Oxford University Press, 2012), 10; Tucker, Ott, and Butler, "An Introduction," 7.
5 Luisa Calè and Patrizia Di Bello, "Introduction: Verbal and Visual Interactions in Nineteenth-Century Print Culture," *19: Interdisciplinary Studies in the Long Nineteenth Century* 5 (2007), https://19.bbk.ac.uk; Maria Damkjaer, *Time, Domesticity and Print Culture in Nineteenth-Century Britain* (London: Palgrave Macmillan, 2016), 148.
6 Alexis Easley, "Scrapbooks and Women's Leisure Reading Practices, 1825–60," *Nineteenth Century Gender Studies* 15, no. 2 (2019): para. 3, www.ncgsjournal.com.
7 Tucker, Ott, and Butler, "An Introduction," 17.
8 Garvey, *Writing with Scissors*, 22.
9 Damkjaer, *Time, Domesticity and Print Culture*, 165; Alexis Easley, "The Resistant Consumer: Scrapbooking and Satire at the Fin de Siècle," *Nineteenth Century Studies* 30 (2018): 89–111,https://www.jstor.org. In another essay on this subject Easley focuses particularly on one type of scrapbook content, poetry, to understand how Victorian women used scrapbooking to "imbue their leisure time with meaning" ("Scrapbooks and Women's Leisure," para. 1). Claire Farago, Brian Caldwell, Hannah Dunn, Alicia McKim, Sarah Price, Christina Putnam, Louis Schmidt, Tamar Scoggin, Dan Staylor, and D.J. Dupancic study scrapbooks as spaces of both imagination and embodiment, material manifestations of

"time past and time passed" (Farago et al., "'Scraps as It Were': Binding Memories," *Journal of Victorian Culture* 10, no. 1 (2005): 116,https://www.tandfonline.com. Jillian Hess investigates how Victorian scholar James Orchard Halliwell used scrapbooks to compile a "concrete" archive of original and facsimile source material for the works of Shakespeare; see "The Scholar's Scrapbook: Reading Shakespeare in the Nineteenth Century," *Book History* 21 (2018): 215.

10 Damkjaer, *Time, Domesticity and Print Culture*, 148.

11 Tucker, Ott, and Butler, "An Introduction," 9.

12 Alan Galey and Stan Ruecker, "How a Prototype Argues," *Literary and Linguistic Computing* 25, no. 4 (2010): 405, https://academic.oup.com.

13 I focus particularly on selected items from the Methodist Archives and Research Centre and John Rylands Special Collections at the University of Manchester; the Harry Page Scrapbook Collection at Manchester Metropolitan University; and the Antiquarian Collections and Research of John Macmillan, as well as the Records of the Cadbury Trusts, at the Library of Birmingham. The skew of the collections' demographics is indicative more of biases in historical archiving practices than of patterns among scrapbooking enthusiasts. The collections studied include fewer scrapbooks by women and working-class persons than would be proportionally representative of the era because archivists traditionally prioritized the personal papers of socio-economically privileged men.

14 For the purposes of this chapter, I attribute only one maker per album because I have no evidence to the contrary, but some of these albums may have been co-produced, given that collaborative scrapbooking among family and friends was a common activity. See Garvey, *Writing with Scissors*, 48–9.

15 Damkjaer, *Time, Domesticity and Print Culture*, 148.

16 De Certeau, *Practice of Everyday Life*, 165. See chapter 2 for a detailed explanation of poaching and its relevance to the way in which Victorian readers engaged with illustrated periodicals.

17 Damkjaer, *Time, Domesticity and Print Culture*, 152.

18 Jennifer Lei Jenkins, "Cut and Paste: Repurposing Texts from Commonplace Books to Facebook," *Journal of Popular Culture* 48, no. 6 (2015): 1374, https://onlinelibrary.wiley.com.

19 Tucker, Ott, and Butler, "An Introduction," 7.

20 Luisa Calè, "Dickens Extra-Illustrated: Heads and Scenes in Monthly Parts (The Case of Nicholas Nickleby)," *Yearbook of English Studies* 40 (2001): 8, www.jstor.org.

21 Garvey, *Writing with Scissors*, 49.

22 Samantha Matthews, "Album," *Victorian Review* 34, no. 1 (2008): 13, doi:10.1353/vcr.2008.0005.

23 Jane Rutherston, "Victorian Album Structures," *Paper Conservator* 23, no. 1 (1999): 14, https://www.tandfonlin.com.

24 Ibid., 15.

25 Johanna Drucker, *SpecLab: Digital Aesthetics and Projects in Speculative Computing* (Chicago: University of Chicago Press, 2009), 15–16.

26 Jerome McGann and Lisa Samuels, "Deformance and Interpretation," *New Literary History* 30, no. 1 (1999): 33; de Certeau, *Practice of Everyday Life*, xv.

27 Anne Burdick, Johanna Drucker, Peter Lunenfield, Todd Presner, and Jeffrey Schnapp, *Digital_Humanities* (Cambridge, MA: MIT Press, 2012), 13.

28 Garvey, *Writing with Scissors*, 25.

29 "Table Talk," *Literary World*, 19 July 1895, 52, Google Books, https://books.google.ca.

30 Kate Jackson, "The *Tit-Bits* Phenomenon: George Newnes, New Journalism and the Periodical Texts," *Victorian Periodicals Review* 30, no. 3 (1997): 206, www.jstor.org.

31 According to historians, Waugh separated permanently from his legal spouse in the 1850s. In an introduction to a volume of Waugh's work, his friend George Milner states that he lived alone and was cared for by a nurse until he passed away from cancer of the tongue in 1890. See George Milner, "Editor's Introduction," in *Lancashire Sketches*, by Edwin Waugh, ed. George Milner (Manchester, UK: John Haywood, 1884), ix–xlii. The labour involved in curating the scrapbook's materials suggests a compiler who was more invested in Waugh's reception history than a domestic servant or nurse would be. Other potential traces of the scrapbook maker appear in the form of a pharmacist's note addressed to a Mrs. Waugh, perhaps a relative, and two unlabelled photographs of a middle-aged woman, both tucked into the scrapbook in a loose insert of papers.

32 Garvey, *Writing with Scissors*, 29.

33 Damkjaer, *Time, Domesticity and Print Culture*, 155; Garvey, *Writing with Scissors*, 21.

34 Whether visual representation *actually* involves less remediation and therefore greater accuracy than verbal representation does was a perennial debate that began well before the Victorian period and continues today. However, as discussed in chapter 1, illustrated journalism claimed to attain greater fidelity to reality than non-illustrated journalism could achieve.

35 Black ostrich feathers were used in a number of ways as part of the material pomp of these processions – for example, in hearse coverings, as plumes for the horses that pulled the hearse, and by a member of

the procession termed the "feather-man," who carried a tray of waving plumes. See Pat Jalland, *Death in the Victorian Family* (Oxford: Oxford University Press, 1996), 195. Kemp's family business is not detailed in his album, but an 1882 number of the *Manchester City News* briefly mentions James Kemp, father of Thomas, as an "Ostrich feather and Funereal plumes Manufacturer." See "Notes and Queries," *City News Notes and Queries: Reprinted from the Manchester City News* 4 (1882): 275.

36 Garvey, *Writing with Scissors*, 25.
37 Ibid, 28.
38 Ibid., 7.
39 Bonnie Mak, *How the Page Matters* (Toronto: University of Toronto Press, 2011), 4.
40 Nicholas Frankel, "On the Whistler-Ruskin Trial, 1878" in *BRANCH: Britain, Representation and Nineteenth-Century History*, ed. Dino Franco Felluga, www.branchcollective.org.
41 Ibid.
42 Damkjaer, *Time, Domesticity and Print Culture*, 148–9.
43 Garvey, *Writing with Scissors*, 36.
44 Ibid., 28.
45 Damkjaer, *Time, Domesticity and Print Culture*, 154.

5. Imagining New Media Platforms: Taking Snapshots for the *Strand*, 1896–1918

1 "A Good Joke – Not Clerical," Curiosities, *Strand Magazine* 16 (October 1898): 478.
2 Scholars studying the *Strand* in depth have consistently sidelined this feature. In the introduction to her *Index to the "Strand Magazine,"* Geraldine Beare mentions "Curiosities" in passing, but the feature does not make it into the index itself. See Beare, *Index to the "Strand Magazine": 1891–1950* (Westport, CT: Greenwood Press, 1982), xx. In his scholarship on Arthur Conan Doyle and the *Strand*, Jonathan Cranfield briefly cites "Curiosities" only as an example of the *Strand*'s prominent visuals, but otherwise gives little attention to this feature and other items of "useless information" in the magazine's contents. See Jonathan Cranfield, "Arthur Conan Doyle, H.G. Wells and the *Strand Magazine*'s Long 1901: From Baskerville to the Moon," *English Literature in Transition, 1880–1920* 56, no. 1 (2013): 27n9, muse.jhu.edu; Jonathan Cranfield, *Twentieth-Century Victorian: Arthur Conan Doyle and the Strand Magazine, 1891–1930* (Edinburgh: Edinburgh University Press, 2016), 2. Kate Jackson reaffirms *Strand* editor Reginald Pound's view that "Curiosities" was merely a legacy of the *Tit-Bits* editorial style. See Kate Jackson,

George Newnes and the New Journalism in Britain, 1880–1910 (Aldershot, UK: Ashgate, 2001), 94.

3 Catherine Zuromskis, *Snapshot Photography: The Lives of Images* (Cambridge, MA: MIT Press, 2013), 8.

4 André Gaudreault and Philippe Marion, "The Double-Birth Model Tested against Photography," in *Photography and Other Media in the Nineteenth Century*, ed. Nicoletta Leonardi and Simone Natale (University Park: Penn State University Press, 2019), 194.

5 Lisa Gitelman and Geoffrey Batchen, "Media History and the History of Photography in Parallel Lines," in *Photography and Other Media*, 205.

6 Nicoletta Leonardi and Simone Natale, introduction to *Photography and Other Media*, 4.

7 Gil Pasternak, "Photographic Histories, Actualities, Potentialities: Amateur Photography as Photographic History," Either/And, 2013, eitherand.org.

8 Gitelman and Batchen, "Media History," 212.

9 See James Mussell, *Science, Time and Space in the Late Nineteenth-Century Periodical Press: Movable Types* (Aldershot, UK: Ashgate, 2007); Kate Jackson, *George Newnes*; and a recent special issue of the *Victorian Periodicals Review* devoted to the *Strand Magazine* (52, no. 2, 2019).

10 Marc Olivier, "George Eastman's Modern Stone Age Family: Snapshot Photography and the Brownie," *Technology and Culture* 48, no. 1 (January 2007): 2–3, www.jstor.org.

11 Leonardi and Natale, introduction, 2.

12 Flichy, *Understanding Technological Innovation*.

13 Unlike George Newnes's first publication, *Tit-Bits*, which catered to the lower-middle classes, the *Strand* chiefly targeted a higher middle-class demographic that included intellectuals and professionals. See *Waterloo Directory of English Newspapers and Periodicals, 1800–1900*, ed. John S. North, series 2, s.v. "*Strand Magazine*, The," www.victorianperiodicals.com/series2; Kate Jackson, *George Newnes*, 88. While most of its audience was middle-class, the *Strand* boasted a relatively diverse readership that included even royalty. Queen Victoria was known to read the *Strand*, even contributing to articles about aspects of her life (Kate Jackson, *George Newnes*, 98).

14 John Sutherland, "*Pearson's Magazine*," in *The Stanford Companion to Victorian Fiction* (Stanford, CA: Stanford University Press, 1989), 495.

15 Kate Jackson, *George Newnes*, 1.

16 Elizabeth Tilley, "*Strand Magazine* (1891–1950)," in *Dictionary of Nineteenth-Century Journalism*, ed. Brake and Demoor (2009).

17 Kate Jackson, *George Newnes*, 88–90. Although the distribution of advertisements before and after the editorial contents varied, Kate Jackson

states that the *Strand* had over 250 advertisers per month (*George Newnes*, 94).

18 *Waterloo Directory*, s.v. "*Strand Magazine*, The."

19 Winnie Chan, *The Economy of Short Story in British Periodicals of the 1890s* (London: Routledge, 2007), 13.

20 "The Topsy-Turvy House at the Paris Exhibition," *Strand Magazine* 20 (August 1900): 211–14; "Wonders of the West," *Strand Magazine* 24 (December 1902): 776–85.

21 Reginald Pound, *Mirror of the Century: "The Strand Magazine," 1891–1950* (New York: A.S. Barnes, 1966), 30.

22 Prior to the *Strand*, artwork was typically the responsibility of a magazine's general editor. See Beare, *Index to the "Strand Magazine,"* 8.

23 Mussell, *Nineteenth-Century Press*, 81.

24 Ibid., 82.

25 Jon Klancher, *The Making of English Reading Audiences, 1790–1832* (Madison: University of Wisconsin Press, 1987), 21–3.

26 Margaret Beetham, "In Search of the Historical Reader: The Woman Reader, the Magazine and the Correspondence Column," in *SPIEL* 19, no. 1 (2000): 96.

27 Kate Jackson, "*Tit-Bits* Phenomenon," 211–14.

28 Beegan, *Mass Image*, 171.

29 Kate Jackson, "The *Tit-Bits* Phenomenon: George Newnes, New Journalism and the Periodical Texts," *Victorian Periodicals Review* 30, no. 3 (1997): 211, www.jstor.org.

30 Kate Jackson, *George Newnes*, 89.

31 "The Queer Side of Things: Vegetable Oddities," *Strand Magazine* 4 (August 1892): 215.

32 Kate Jackson, *George Newnes*, 98.

33 Mussell, *Science, Time and Space*, 74.

34 Shannon Smith and Ann Hale, "'You See, But You Do Not Observe': Hidden Infrastructure and Labour in the *Strand Magazine* and Its Twenty-First-Century Digital Iterations," *Victorian Periodicals Review* 49, no. 4 (2016): 670. Other articles on journalism and the production of the *Strand* included illustrated interviews with the magazine's popular authors and an article about writing periodical fiction. See, for example, Philip Trevor, "A British Commando: An Interview with Conan Doyle," *Strand Magazine* 21 (June 1901): 633–40; "Illustrated Interviews: No. VII – Mr. H. Rider Haggard," *Strand Magazine* 3 (January 1892): 2–17; "How Novelists Write for the Press," *Strand Magazine* 1 (January 1891): 295–8.

35 Reginald Pound points to its consistent publication at the end of the *Strand*'s editorial contents as evidence that the subject matter of "Curiosities" was perceived, at least by some, as less than

"compliment[ary] to the general intelligence of readers." See Pound, *Mirror of the Century*, 54–5.

36 This cockatoo-shaped potato was not the first vegetable oddity to appear in the *Strand* – the article "The Queer Side of Things" documented a series of strangely formed root vegetables in 1892 – and it would not be the last to appear in "Curiosities." This subject seems to be a preoccupation of the *Strand* community, or perhaps the Victorians generally.

37 "Dyak Darks and Quivers," Curiosities, *Strand Magazine* 12, August 1896, 239. *The Sign of Four* was not among the many Sherlock Holmes stories serialized in the *Strand*, but readers were likely familiar with this work, given Conan Doyle's popular association with the magazine and *The Sign of Four*'s frequent republication in the 1890s, including in a single-volume edition by Newnes in 1896. See Shafquat Towheed, "A Note on the Text," in *The Sign of Four*, by Arthur Conan Doyle (Peterborough, ON: Broadview Press, 2010), 43.

38 Gabrielle Moser, *Projecting Citizenship: Photography and Belonging in the British Empire* (University Park: Penn State University Press, 2019), 3.

39 Ibid., 19.

40 "Curiosities," *Strand Magazine* 12 (September 1896): 357.

41 "Curiosities," *Strand Magazine* 13 (January 1897): 115.

42 It is difficult to ascertain the degree to which editors continued to curate items in "Curiosities," but the participatory culture of the *Strand*, and Newnes's publication empire broadly, suggest that submissions to this feature were, at least in large part, genuine. Presumably, loyal readers would have protested if none of their contributions were finding their way into the article. Given that the feature ran for over twenty years, the regular publication of reader-contributed items likely supported its ongoing popularity. The reputation of the Newnes empire was too valuable to stake on an empty ruse. Publishing contributions to "Curiosities" was also consistent with Newnes's unusual approach to encouraging reader loyalty. Both *Tit-Bits* and the *Strand* sponsored audacious schemes, such as a months-long treasure-hunt in which clues were printed in each number, to foster a sense of community among readers and to boost sales. The prizes of such schemes were real, bestowed on individuals whom other readers would identify with as fellow *Strand* community members. This sense of authenticity, though transparently bound up with consumer marketing, was essential to the Newnes brand.

43 Reese V. Jenkins, "Technology and the Market: George Eastman and the Origins of Mass Amateur Photography," *Technology and Culture* 16, no. 1 (1975): 1, https://jstor.org.

44 As applied to photography, the term *snapshot* was coined in a periodical titled *Photographic News* in the 1860s. See Zuromskis, *Snapshot Photography*, 21.

45 Douglas Collins, *The Story of Kodak* (New York: N.H. Abrams, 1990), 55.
46 These innovations included roll film, which was easier to use than single-use glass-plate negatives; factory-based film development, which gave photographers the option to let professionals take care of this complex chemical process; and the hand camera, which simplified image capture itself. See Jenkins, "Technology and the Market," 8–14.
47 Collins, *Story of Kodak*, 76.
48 Throughout the late nineteenth and early twentieth centuries Eastman Kodak improved upon many other photographic supplies and developed new equipment, such as portable film-development tanks and bicycle carrying cases. These accessories catered to a broad spectrum of professional and non-professional photographers.
49 Jenkins, "Technology and the Market," 16.
50 Unfortunately, I have found no information regarding the method or the amount of the *Strand*'s payments to "Curiosities" contributors.
51 Joseph Horner, "Boiler Explosions," *Strand Magazine* 20 (July 1900): 80.
52 Jenkins, "Technology and the Market," 2.
53 Collins, *Story of Kodak*, 57.
54 From 1888 onward Eastman used advertising in popular American and British periodicals such as the *Strand*, *Lippincott's Magazine*, and *Harper's Bazaar* to target upper and middle-class consumers (Collins, *Story of Kodak*, 57). Copies of the *Strand* that retain their original advertisements are scarce, but an existing original monthly issue published in London in August 1911 includes one full-page Kodak advertisement, and a quarterly edition of the magazine published in New York in 1901 (May through July) includes three Kodak advertisements ranging from half- to full-pages.
55 Photography historians such as Marc Olivier have demonstrated the importance of acknowledging differences between the various Kodak cameras, which afforded different snapshot processes and produced different results. See Olivier, "Modern Stone Age Family," 3.
56 Ernest F. Phillips, "Taken from Above," Curiosities, *Strand Magazine* 16 (September 1898): 357.
57 "A New Style in Photography," Curiosities, *Strand Magazine* 18 (August 1899): 240.
58 Flichy, *Understanding Technological Innovation*, 82–5.
59 "Curiosities," *Strand Magazine* 21 (May 1901): 600.
60 Ibid., 595–600.
61 Geo. C. Embody, "A Literary Bird," Curiosities, *Strand Magazine* 21 (May 1901): 597. Self-conscious puffing of Newnes's publications (including the *Strand*, *Tit-Bits*, and the *Million*) was not unusual in "Curiosities." It was perhaps the result of contributors' canny recognition that such product

placement would improve their chance of getting an item published in the feature, although it is also possible that some of these items were editor contributions, inserted as advertisements in disguise.

62 Aubrey Colquhoun, "A Tree Tied in a Knot," Curiosities, *Strand Magazine* 15 (February 1898): 237.
63 Flichy, *Understanding Technological Innovation*, 81.
64 Ibid., 83.
65 For a discussion of de Certeau's theory of strategy and tactic and how I apply it throughout this book, see the introduction and chapter 2.
66 Flichy, *Understanding Technological Innovation*, 90.
67 Ibid., 87.
68 Collins, *Story of Kodak*, 98. According to Collins, the Brownie "averaged out the difficulties of photography," embodying "the sum of those figures" in its design (98).
69 Ibid., 56.
70 Ibid., 60.
71 Kodaks and Kodak Supplies: Being a Catalogue of Materials for the Amateur Photographer (Rochester, NY: Eastman Kodak: 1902), 5–8, Ryerson University Special Collections.
72 Alison Skyrme, "Kodak History," Ryerson Special Collections, in discussion with the author, 14 February 2017.
73 *Book of the Kodak Exhibition* (Rochester: Eastman Kodak, 1912), 2, HathiTrust, http://www.hathitrust.org.
74 Nancy Martha West, *Kodak and the Lens of Nostalgia* (Charlottesville: University of Virginia Press, 2000), xxiii. Eastman was highly conscious of brand reputation. One of Kodak's early slogans declared, "If it isn't an Eastman, it isn't a Kodak." This pronouncement, though oddly tautological, underscores the emphasis on product integrity in Eastman's marketing.
75 Flichy, *Understanding Technological Innovation*, 83.
76 *Book of the Kodak Exhibition*, 3.
77 Collins, *Story of Kodak*, 59.
78 West, *Kodak and the Lens*, 7.
79 Ibid., 53.
80 Flichy, *Understanding Technological Innovation*, 119.
81 A.S. Faulkner, "Capturing an Octopus," Curiosities, *Strand Magazine* 24 (October 1902): 480.
82 B. Priest, "A Fortunate Little Lady," Curiosities, *Strand Magazine* 24 (October 1902): 478.
83 West, *Kodak and the Lens*, 4.
84 Lilian Noble, "A Good Jump," Curiosities, *Strand Magazine* 17 (January 1899): 117.

85 C.L. Taylor, "A Novelty in Cameras," Curiosities, *Strand Magazine* 17 (January 1899): 120.

86 R.B. Robinson, "An Amateur Telephotographer," Curiosities, *Strand Magazine* 20 (October 1900): 480.

87 Winnifred Hayles, "A Top-Hat Camera," Curiosities, *Strand Magazine* 25 (February 1903): 238.

88 Herbert J. Mason, "Where Sherlock Holmes Died," Curiosities, *Strand Magazine* 22 (December 1901): 796.

89 Collins, *Story of Kodak*, 54.

90 Fred Common, "Conclusive Evidence," Curiosities, *Strand Magazine* 16 (October 1898): 480.

91 "The Post Office and Ourselves," Curiosities, *Strand Magazine* 22 (December 1901): 799.

92 Alfred Priest, "Dead and Alive," Curiosities, *Strand Magazine* 18 (November 1899): 599.

93 Frank H. Williams, "Helping Atlas," Curiosities, *Strand Magazine* 17 (May 1899): 612.

94 Geoffrey Batchen, "Snapshots: Art History and the Ethnographic Turn," *Photographies* 1, no. 2 (2008): 121.

95 Zuromskis, *Snapshot Photography*, 9.

96 Beetham, "In Search of the Historical Reader"; Hilary Fraser, Stephanie Green, and Judith Johnston, *Gender and the Victorian Periodical* (Cambridge: Cambridge University Press), 200.

97 Kodak advertisements first used the Kodak Girl in 1893. In her appearance and demeanour the Kodak Girl was inspired by the New Woman, a complex cultural figure of the era who embodied discourses about women's rights and roles. Fashionable, independent, and adventurous in her activities, she was often depicted travelling and engaged in outdoor leisure pursuits alone (West, *Kodak and the Lens*, 53–7. As West observes, she appealed to women as "an idealized image of youthful femininity and exuberance" (53).

98 Walter Benjamin, "The Work of Art in the Age of Mechanical Reproduction," in *Illuminations: Essays and Reflections*, ed. Hannah Arendt (New York: Schocken, 2007), 19.

99 Green, Spencer and Sons, "Two Curious Balloon Photos," Curiosities, *Strand Magazine* 15 (March 1897): 358.

100 E.F. Fox, "A Photographic Curiosity," Curiosities, *Strand Magazine* 14 (September 1897): 359.

101 At the turn of the twentieth century most amateur cameras worked best in bright daylight (Collins, *Story of Kodak*, 122). Kodak worked this into the implicit messaging of its advertisements and the explicit prescriptions of its manuals, encouraging people to take photographs of outdoor activities.

102 E.H. Horton. "A Photographic Freak," Curiosities, *Strand Magazine* 14 (November 1897): 600.
103 George E. Neeves, "Astonishing Photographic Freak," Curiosities, *Strand Magazine* 14 (December 1897): 799.
104 Miles Orvell, *The Real Thing: Imitation and Authenticity in American Culture, 1880–1940*, anniversary ed. (Chapel Hill: University of North Carolina Press, 2014), 77.
105 Roland Barthes, *Camera Lucida: Reflections on Photography*, trans. Richard Howard (New York: Hill & Wang, 1981), 87.
106 Zuromskis, *Snapshot Photography*, 11.
107 Ibid., 42.
108 Phillips, "Taken from Above."
109 Horace C. Knapp, "Taken by a Child," Curiosities, *Strand Magazine* 21 (January 1901): 116.
110 H. Sutcliffe Smith, "Looking Down from Blackpool Tower," Curiosities, *Strand Magazine* 15 (June 1898): 800.
111 "Studying Virgil," Curiosities, *Strand Magazine* 30 (September 1905): 360.
112 "A New Style in Photography," Curiosities, *Strand Magazine* 18 (August 1899): 240.
113 Lynn Berger, "Peer Production in the Age of Collodion: The Bromide Patent and the Photographic Press, 1854–1868," in *Photography and Other Media*, ed. Leonardi and Natale, 92.
114 Berger, "Peer Production," 100.
115 C. Harrington, "An All-Night Photograph," Curiosities, *Strand Magazine* 20 (September 1900): 355.
116 Cranfield, *Twentieth-Century Victorian*, 99–100, 105.
117 *The Amateur Photographer: An Illustrated Popular Journal, Devoted to the Interests of Photography, and Kindred Arts and Sciences* 14 (July–December 1891): 18–19.
118 Paul Spencer Sternberger, *Between Amateur and Aesthete: The Legitimization of Photography as Art in America, 1880–1900* (Albuquerque: University of New Mexico Press, 2001), xi.
119 "The Amateur Photographers' Prize Competition," *Pall Mall Magazine*, December 1909, 1051, ProQuest British Periodicals, https://proquest.com/britishperiodicals.
120 "Hand-Camera Notes," *Amateur Photographer* 64 (July–December 1916): 18, Ryerson University Special Collections.
121 John Taylor, "Kodak and the 'English' Market between the Wars," *Journal of Design History* 7, no. 1 (1994): 29–42, www.jstor.org.
122 Kate Flint, *The Victorians and Visual Imagination* (Cambridge: Cambridge University Press, 2000), 595–6.

Conclusion

1 Clement Shorter, "Illustrated Journalism: Its Past and Future," *Contemporary Review* 75 (1899): 492, ProQuest British Periodicals, https://proquest.com/britishperiodicals.
2 Ibid., 487.
3 Ibid., 494.
4 Jussi Parikka, *What Is Media Archaeology?* (Cambridge: Polity, 2012), 3.
5 William Wordsworth, "Illustrated Books and Newspapers," in *Victorian Literature: An Anthology*, ed. Victor Shea and William Whitla (Hoboken, NJ: Wiley Blackwell, 2014), 40; Guy Debord, "The Commodity as Spectacle," in *The Society of the Spectacle* (New York: Zone Books, 1994); Adriaan Van der Weel, *Changing Our Textual Minds: Toward a Digital Order of Knowledge* (Manchester, UK: Manchester University Press, 2011), 194.
6 W.J.T. Michell, "Image," in *Critical Terms for Media Studies*, ed. W.J.T. Mitchell and Mark B.N. Hansen (Chicago: University of Chicago Press, 2010), 38.
7 Ibid., 44.
8 Shorter, "Illustrated Journalism," 487.
9 Ibid., 492.
10 Wordsworth, "Illustrated Books and Newspapers," 40.
11 John Ruskin, *Ariadne Florentina: Six Lectures on Wood and Metal Engraving*, Brantwood edition (London: George Allen, 1904), 259, 267, archive.org.
12 Ibid., 255.
13 Ibid., 262.
14 Ibid., 267.
15 Wilkie Collins, "The Unknown Public," *Household Words* 18 (August 1858): 217–22.
16 Raymond Williams, *Culture and Society, 1780–1950* (New York: Columbia University Press, 1982), 289, quoted in Susan Zieger, *The Mediated Mind: Affect, Ephemera, and Consumerism in the Nineteenth Century* (New York: Fordham University Press, 2018), 13.
17 After André Gaudreault and Philippe Marion, I have described this late-Victorian phase of development as the second birth of the popular illustrated magazine as a medium. See chapter 1 and Gaudreault and Marion, "A Medium Is Always Born Twice …," *Early Popular Visual Culture* 3, no. 1 (2005): 3, https://www.tandfonline.com.
18 John Guillory, "Genesis of the Media Concept," *Critical Inquiry* 36, no. 2 (2010): 360.
19 This topic has received some attention, though not in-depth examination. For example, Robert Scholes and Clifford Wulfman gesture to this history

in *Modernism in the Magazines: An Introduction* (New Haven, CT: Yale University Press, 2010).

20 See Max Horkheimer and Theodor Adorno, "The Culture Industry: Enlightenment as Mass Deception," in *Dialectics of Enlightenment*, ed. Gunzelin Schmid Nuerr, trans. Edmund Jephcott (Stanford, CA: Stanford University Press, 2002), 100. Walter Benjamin is a telling exception in this media narrative. Unlike most of his peers, he recognized the complex interpretive dynamics at work in mass culture precisely because he studied the unique affordances of mechanical media on their own terms and theorized the range of user engagements made possible by these features. See, for example, Benjamin, "The Work of Art in the Age of Mechanical Reproduction," in *Illuminations: Essays and Reflections*, ed. Hannah Arendt (New York: Schocken, 2007).

21 United States Department of Commerce, *Circular of the Bureau of Standards No. 120: Construction and Operation of a Simple Homemade Radio Receiving Outfit* (Washington, DC: Washington Government Printing Office, 1922), Hathitrust, https:// hathitrust.org.

22 J. David Bolter and Richard Grusin, *Remediation: Understanding New Media* (Cambridge, MA: MIT, 2000), 8–11.

23 Liz Losh, "Home Inspection: Mina Rees and National Computing Structure," *First Monday* 23, no. 3 (2018), https://firstmonday.org.

24 Zieger, *Mediated Mind.*

25 Losh, "Home Inspection."

26 Cecilia Kang, "Bridging a Digital Divide That Leaves Schoolchildren Behind," *New York Times*, 22 February 2016, www.nytimes.com.

27 Nellie Bowles, "The Digital Gap between Rich and Poor Kids Is Not What We Expected," *New York Times*, 26 October 2018, www.nytimes.com.

28 See chapter 3 for a discussion of Michel Foucault's biopolitical theory and the role of biopolitics in Victorian society.

29 Richard Jean So, "All Models Are Wrong," *PMLA* 132, no. 3 (2017): 668–73, doi:10.1632/pmla.2017.132.3.668.

30 See Katy Börner, Andreas Bueckle, and Michael Ginda, "Data Visualization Literacy: Definitions, Conceptual Frameworks, Exercises, and Assessments," *PNAS* 116, no. 6 (5 February 2019): 1857–64, doi:10.1073/pnas.1807180116.

31 For journalism on this trend, see, for example, Harry McCracken, "Yes, Smartphones Are Plateauing – And That's Ok," *Time Magazine*, 8 April 2014, time.com; Geoffrey Fowler, "Samsung Galaxy S5 Review: Watertight Yet Still Not Quite Right," *Wall Street Journal*, 8 April 2014, www.wsj.com; Vlad Savov, "Apple and Samsung Feel the Sting of Plateauing Smartphones," *Verge*, 3 January 2019, www.theverge.com; Lauren Goode, "Have Phones Become Boring? Well, They're about to Get Weirder," *Wired*, 23 January 2019, www.wired.com.

32 Wikipedia, s.v. "Timeline of Instagram," https://en.wikipedia.org.

33 In 2016, Instagram switched from a chronological news feed, in which the posts of accounts followed by a user were simply displayed from most recent to oldest, to a curated feed that displays posts that are algorithmically determined to be of most interest to the user. See Wikipedia, s.v. "Instagram," https://en.wikipedia.org.

34 This phenomenon is not unique to Instagram but is pervasive across social media. See, for example, Kyle Chayka, "Welcome to Airspace: How Silicon Valley Helps Spread the Same Sterile Aesthetic across the World," *Verge*, 3 August 2019), www.theverge.com; Cher Tan, "So Much This," *Kill Your Darlings*, 12 August 2019, www.killyourdarlings.com.au.

35 See "How Does Instagram Decide Which Ads to Show Me?," in the Instagram Help Centre, https://help.instagram.com.

36 Arun Jacob, direct message conversation with the author, Twitter, 23 August 2019.

Index

STUDIES IN BOOK AND PRINT CULTURE

General Editor: Leslie Howsam

Hazel Bell, *Indexers and Indexes in Fact and Fiction*
Heather Murray, *Come, Bright Improvement! The Literary Societies of Nineteenth-Century Ontario*
Joseph A. Dane, *The Myth of Print Culture: Essays on Evidence, Textuality, and Bibliographical Method*
Christopher J. Knight, *Uncommon Readers: Denis Donoghue, Frank Kermode, George Steiner, and the Tradition of the Common Reader*
Eva Hemmungs Wirtén, *No Trespassing: Authorship, Intellectual Property Rights, and the Boundaries of Globalization*
William A. Johnson, *Bookrolls and Scribes in Oxyrhynchus*
Siân Echard and Stephen Partridge, eds., *The Book Unbound: Editing and Reading Medieval Manuscripts and Texts*
Bronwen Wilson, *The World in Venice: Print, the City, and Early Modern Identity*
Peter Stoicheff and Andrew Taylor, eds., *The Future of the Page*
Jennifer Phegley and Janet Badia, eds., *Reading Women: Literary Figures and Cultural Icons from the Victorian Age to the Present*
Elizabeth Sauer, *"Paper-contestations" and Textual Communities in England, 1640–1675*
Nick Mount, *When Canadian Literature Moved to New York*
Jonathan Earl Carlyon, *Andrés González de Barcia and the Creation of the Colonial Spanish American Library*
Leslie Howsam, *Old Books and New Histories: An Orientation to Studies in Book and Print Culture*
Deborah McGrady, *Controlling Readers: Guillaume de Machaut and His Late Medieval Audience*
David Finkelstein, ed., *Print Culture and the Blackwood Tradition*

Bart Beaty, *Unpopular Culture: Transforming the European Comic Book in the 1990s*
Elizabeth Driver, *Culinary Landmarks: A Bibliography of Canadian Cookbooks, 1825–1949*
Benjamin C. Withers, *The Illustrated Old English Hexateuch, Cotton Ms. Claudius B.iv: The Frontier of Seeing and Reading in Anglo-Saxon England*
Mary Ann Gillies, *The Professional Literary Agent in Britain, 1880–1920*
Willa Z. Silverman, *The New Bibliopolis: French Book-Collectors and the Culture of Print, 1880–1914*
Lisa Surwillo, *The Stages of Property: Copyrighting Theatre in Spain*
Dean Irvine, *Editing Modernity: Women and Little-Magazine Cultures in Canada, 1916–1956*
Janet Friskney, *New Canadian Library: The Ross-McClelland Years, 1952–1978*
Janice Cavell, *Tracing the Connected Narrative: Arctic Exploration in British Print Culture, 1818–1860*
Elspeth Jajdelska, *Silent Reading and the Birth of the Narrator*
Martyn Lyons, *Reading Culture and Writing Practices in Nineteenth-Century France*
Robert A. Davidson, *Jazz Age Barcelona*
Gail Edwards and Judith Saltman, *Picturing Canada: A History of Canadian Children's Illustrated Books and Publishing*
Miranda Remnek, ed., *The Space of the Book: Print Culture in the Russian Social Imagination*
Adam Reed, *Literature and Agency in English Fiction Reading: A Study of the Henry Williamson Society*
Bonnie Mak, *How the Page Matters*
Eli MacLaren, *Dominion and Agency: Copyright and the Structuring of the Canadian Book Trade, 1867–1918*
Ruth Panofsky, *The Literary Legacy of the Macmillan Company of Canada: Making Books and Mapping Culture*
Archie L. Dick, *The Hidden History of South Africa's Book and Reading Cultures*
Darcy Cullen, ed., *Editors, Scholars, and the Social Text*
James J. Connolly, Patrick Collier, Frank Felsenstein, Kenneth R. Hall, and Robert Hall, eds., *Print Culture Histories beyond the Metropolis*
Kristine Kowalchuk, *Preserving on Paper: Seventeenth-Century Englishwomen's Receipt Books*
Ian Hesketh, *Victorian Jesus: J.R. Seeley, Religion, and the Cultural Significance of Anonymity*
Kirsten MacLeod, *American Little Magazines of the Fin de Siècle: Art, Protest, and Cultural Transformation*
Emily Francomano, *The Prison of Love: Romance, Translation and the Book in the Sixteenth Century*
Kirk Melnikoff, *Elizabethan Publishing and the Makings of Literary Culture*

Amy Bliss Marshall, *Magazines and the Making of Mass Culture in Japan*
Scott McLaren, *Pulpit, Press, and Politics: Methodists and the Market for Books in Upper Canada*
Ruth Panofsky, *Toronto Trailblazers: Women in Canadian Publishing*
Martyn Lyons, *The Typewriter Century: A Cultural History of Writing Practices*
Marina Balina and Serguei Alex. Oushakine, eds., *The Pedagogy of Images: Depicting Communism for Children*
Alison Hedley, *Making Pictorial Print: Media Literacy and Mass Culture in British Magazines, 1885–1918*

www.ingramcontent.com/pod-product-compliance
Lightning Source LLC
LaVergne TN
LVHW090157080826
844660LV00013B/845/J

9781487506735